MATTHEW: HIS MIND

AND HIS MESSAGE

M A T

THE LITURGICAL PRESS

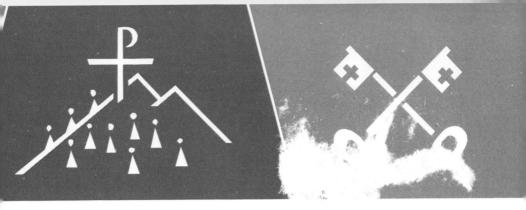

T H E W

his mind and his message

by **Peter F. Ellis,** C.SS.R.

Fordham University

COLLEGEVILLE, MINNESOTA

By the same author

THE MEN AND THE MESSAGE OF THE OLD TESTAMENT
FIRST BOOK OF KINGS — SECOND BOOK OF KINGS

Cover design: sixth century mosaic of the evangelist St. Matthew reproduced from: *The Monastery of St. Catherine at Mount Sinai — The Church and Fortress of Justinian* edited by George H. Forsyth and Kurt Weitzmann (University of Michigan Press, Ann Arbor, Michigan).

Rear cover top left: mosaic of the Transfiguration in the apse of the church on Mount Tabor; *right*: Church of the Beatitudes on the traditional site of the Sermon on the Mount; *bottom left*: view over the Sea of Galilee past the Chapel of Peter's Primacy with Church of the Beatitudes in upper right; *right*: final two verses of St. Matthew's Gospel from the Codex Sinaiticus.

Nihil obstat: William G. Heidt, O.S.B., S.T.D., *Censor deputatus. Imprimatur*: † George H. Speltz, D.D., Bishop of St. Cloud.

PREFACE

This book aims to reach the mind of Matthew and ascertain the theological message he sought to communicate to his Jewish-Christian readers at the end of the first century A.D.

Reaching the mind of a first century author, culturally conditioned by a semitic background, has required a careful study of Matthew's communications skills. Our part I "Rabbinic Matthew," as a consequence, deals with Matthew's background, audience, sources, and methodology. Our part II, "Meticulous Matthew," is a study of how Matthew structured, arranged, and interpreted his source materials in order to make his gospel as a whole reflect his mind and communicate his message. Our part III, "Theological Matthew," deals with the essentials of his message: namely, his Christology and his ecclesiology.

Our approach to Matthew's gospel is the approach to the interpretation of any properly literary work: that is, by way of composition criticism. It has been called the vertical, in contrast to the horizontal, approach. It consists in the analysis of a work as a whole in order to ascertain thereby the author's over-all purpose and viewpoint. The horizontal approach, which is rarely used outside the study of the synoptic gospels, presupposes that the synoptic gospels for the most part represent nothing more than the editing of pre-existing documents or oral traditions by different authors and consists in a comparison of the differences in editing the materials in order to ascertain the purposes and viewpoints of the authors.

It has been for the most part because the synoptic gospels were not in the past considered to be the proper literary work of individual authors that the horizontal approach to their interpretation was utilized. In the horizontal approach, as a consequence, the pre-existing sources have been considered of vastly greater importance than the minds of the men who edited them. We believe the horizontal approach would be the proper and adequate approach *only* if the evangelists were nothing more than editors or compilers or redactors in the strictest sense of the word.

Recent gospel research, however, has been almost unanimous in recognizing that the synoptic evangelists were individual theologian-authors who produced properly literary works. As a result, it has come to be recognized in recent years that the only adequate approach to an understanding of their works is the same approach as that used for the interpretation of any properly literary work, namely, the vertical or composition criticism approach. In passing, we might mention that the unintelligibility of many gospel commentaries due in large part to a carry-over from the time when the evangelists were considered hardly more than inspired editors.

In as much as the synoptic evanglists evince a much greater respect for and fidelity to the sources they use than modern authors, the horizontal approach retains validity and provides help in interpreting their gospels. In interpreting the mind and message of Matthew, therefore, we have not ignored the value of the horizontal approach. But we have consistently considered it secondary and subsidiary to the value of the vertical approach. Our understanding is that the true key to the interpretation of a gospel is the purpose of the author and that the author's purpose is revealed primarily by an analysis of his work *as a whole* rather than by comparison with other gospels utilizing the same or similar source material. This book, as a result, is properly a study in composition criticism.

Because most readers are already well acquainted with the introductory questions involved in a study of the synoptic gospels, we have not dealt with this material at the beginning of the book. For those who are not acquainted with such introductory matters, we have provided in the appendices brief treatments of the following introductory questions: the historicity of the gospels; the formation of the gospels and the meaning of such terms as gospel, kerygma, and didache; and the synoptic question.

The reader is asked to forgive the frequent repetitions in parts II and III. The repetitions are for the sake of clarity, and while the reader might draw the same conclusions as the writer from the material in part II, it has seemed best to summarize in part III much that had already been mentioned in part II.

With regard to bibliography, only author and title have been given in the footnotes. Full data has been included in a separate section on bibliography at the end of the book.

It remains to thank those who have helped me with this book. First, my students in the Graduate Institute of Religious Education at Fordham University, whose enthusiastic response and searching inquiries went a long way toward making this book the kind of book it is. Second, Miss Janet Grimm who typed the manuscript with care and devotion. Third, Miss Judith Monahan who has kindly taken in charge all matters dealing with bibliography. And finally, my professors and confreres, Rev. Louis Hartman (deceased August 21, 1970) and Rev. William Barry, whose love for the word of God has inspired in me a similar love and have made the labor of searching out the mind and message of Matthew not only a labor of love but a joyful and rewarding venture.

December 8, 1973

CONTENTS

Part Three

THEOLOGICAL MATTHEW

MATTHEW: HIS MIND

AND HIS MESSAGE

Part One

RABBINIC MATTHEW

It is a fact of literary life that we moderns read Sophocles' plays, Plato's Dialogues, and Plutarch's Lives with infinitely greater ease and comprehension than we read Matthew's gospel. The reason is not hard to discover. It is not antiquity. Matthew's gospel was written four centuries after Sophocles and Plato and almost a century after Plutarch. It is cultural background. Our cultural background is the same as that of Sophocles, Plato, and Plutarch. The cultural background of Matthew and his audience was Semitic. The reader who remembers this will have gone a long way toward understanding Matthew's gospel. We will begin, therefore, by saying something about the man, his audience, the date the gospel was written, the sources the author used and the author's methodology.

A CONVERTED RABBI

Modern scholars are inclined to believe that Matthew like Paul before him was a converted rabbi or, if not a converted rabbi, at least a highly educated Jewish Christian who had at his command a considerable knowledge of rabbinic lore and teaching expertise. His gospel shows his great respect for Moses, his passionate interest in the interpretation and fulfillment of the law and the prophets, and his extensive knowledge of the Old Testament. He knows how to formulate questions in a rabbinic manner.[1] He exhibits a considerable understanding of the haggadic and apocalyptic literature.[2] And he understands the Pharisees as perhaps only a former Pharisee like Paul or himself could understand them.

What is most revealing about Matthew's background is his concern throughout the gospel to demonstrate his conviction that Christianity represents the true Israel, that Jesus brings the true and final interpretation of the law, and that Christians are those chosen by God to manifest in their lives the true righteousness of the Kingdom of heaven. This teaching concern is

---

[1] See Mt 19:1-12.　　　　　　　　　　[2] See Mt 1-2; 24; 27:51-54.

3

one that would have continually occupied a converted rabbi. Nowhere is it so succinctly expressed as in the words: "Do not imagine that I have come to abolish the law or the Prophets. I have come not to abolish but to complete them" (5:17).

Jesus' statement that "every scribe who becomes a disciple of the Kingdom of heaven is like a householder who brings out from his storeroom things both new and old" (13:52) may well be, as many have observed, "a self-portrait of Matthew." Matthew's "storeroom" of Old Testament teaching and New Testament revelation is evident on every page of his gospel.[3] That he was a "disciple of the Kingdom of heaven" who theologized in depth about the relationship between the "new" (the gospel) and the "old" (the law, the prophets, and the Israel of old) is more than evident in his continual opposition to the Pharisees and their teaching.

A JEWISH CHRISTIAN AUDIENCE

Matthew's readers, as the tone and content of the gospel indicate, were as Semitic as himself. He takes for granted their acquaintance with the text of the Old Testament, with the haggadic and apocalyptic literature, with Jewish customs and expressions, with the oral tradition of the Jews, and with the teaching authority of the Pharisees.

What is most revealing about the audience is their strained relationship with the Pharisees. Matthew has to warn them against the Pharisees' bad example, wrong interpretation of the law, and intolerant opposition to Christianity.[4] As K. Stendahl says: "It is clear that the most obvious polemic in this gospel is directed against the 'scribes and the Pharisees'. In Matthew these are neither the actual opponents of Jesus, nor are they general examples of haughty behavior, as in Luke. They are the representatives of the synagogue 'across the street' in Matthew's community. The line between Church and synagogue is drawn definitely."[5]

Matthew's persistent polemic against the Pharisees indicates the Pharisees were an enemy to be fought, countered, and refuted. The same polemic is found in John's gospel and probably for the same reason.[6] Mark and Luke oppose the Pharisees but without the personal "animus" of Matthew and John. In the areas where Mark and Luke wrote, the Pharisees were not the "on the scene" enemy. Matthew's situation was different.

Despite some scholarly doubts,[7] the over-all Jewish tone of the gospel, the continuous polemic against the Pharisees as a class, the counter-propaganda

---

[3] Cf. K. Stendahl, *The School of St. Matthew*, p. xiii: "That he once was a Jew cannot be doubted. That he had had Jewish training in Palestine before the war is probable."
[4] Cf. Mt 10:17, 21-23; 23:29-35; 5:11-12; 7:29; 9:35.

[5] Cf. K. Stendahl, *op. cit.*, (2nd edition), xi.
[6] Cf. R. Brown, *The Gospel according to John*, Vol. I, lxx-lxxii.
[7] See Feine-Behm-Kummel, *Introduction to the New Testament*, 81f; K. Stendahl, *op cit.*, xi.

against Judaism,[8] and the gospel's dominant interest in establishing Christians as the true Israel in contrast to the pseudo-Israel led by the Pharisees indicate that Matthew's audience was made up primarily of Jewish Christians.

THE DATE OF THE GOSPEL

The date of the gospel is not easy to establish. There are indications, however, that it was written in the period after the fall of Jerusalem when Christians were being forced to dissociate themselves from Judaism and become completely independent of the synagogue. The author writes after the destruction of Jerusalem (cf. 22:7), uses Mark's gospel as a source, and gives no indication of having been an eyewitness of the events in his gospel. Allowing some ten or fifteen years for the spread of Mark's gospel (written between 65 and 75 A.D.) and approximately the same amount of time for the influence of the Jamnian synod to make itself felt by Christian Jews, the most likely date for the gospel is c. 85 A.D.

It was about this time that the Pharisees of the Jamnian synod took overt action against Jewish Christians. Prior to 85 A.D., the Pharisees, led by Rabbi Johannan ben Zakkai, had spent their time trying to preserve Jewish life in Palestine against the disruption caused by the Roman invasion and conquest of 66-71 A.D. The work had begun even before the fall of Jerusalem when Johannan ben Zakkai founded his school at Jamnia and began to take measures for the survival of Judaism. It is known that Jamnia sought to heal the differences between the rival schools of Hillel and Shammai. It is reputed to have worked at fixing the canon of the Old Testament, to have produced a common calendar for all the Jews, and to have established itself as the authoritative voice of Judaism. However little is known about it, its work was successful. Though other Jewish sects died, Pharisaic Judaism closed ranks, survived the dissolution of the Jewish state, and became the normative institutional group in Judaism. Judaism down the centuries has been substantially the Judaism of Jamnia.

But Jamnia did more than insure the survival of Judaism. Besides setting its own house in order, Jamnia set up its defenses against the burgeoning influence of its offshoot— Christianity. One of its defenses was the introduction into the synagogue worship of the *Birkath ha Minim* — a prayer (*birkath*) against heretics (*minim* was a catch-all expression for heretics) which went as follows, according to the translation of W. D. Davies:

> For persecutors let there be no hope, and the dominion of arrogance do thou speedily root out in our days; and let Christians and *minim* perish in a moment, let them be blotted out of the book of the living and let them not be written with the righteous.[9]

[8] Note the counter-content in Matthew's infancy narrative, in the missionary charge in ch 10, and in the resurrection account (28:11-15).

[9] *The Setting of the Sermon on the Mount,* 275ff.

One cannot give an exact date for the institution of the *Birkath ha Minim* as part of the liturgy, but scholars believe it to have come into force c. 85 A.D.[10] If the references in Matthew's gospel to Pharisaic persecution are a reflection of the effect of the *Birkath ha Minim*, then one may reasonably date the gospel sometime after the year 85 A.D.[11] Whatever the date, Matthew's gospel has all the characteristics of a Jewish-Christian reaction to the Judaism of Jamnia that Jews followed after the Roman destruction of Jerusalem.[12]

It is impossible to say precisely where Matthew and his community lived. G. D. Kilpatrick's conclusion that "the church of Matthew is to be found in Syria, probably in Phoenicia, at the end of the first century" may be correct.[13] Phoenicia was outside Palestine and not far from Jamnia. Matthew's Church, however, could have been any place in Syria or along the borders of Palestine. What was important was not the geographical but the religious proximity of Jamnia. How extensive Jamnia's influence was in the last quarter of the first century is difficult to say. But it was sufficient to provoke Matthew's heated reaction, giving us his gospel as a result. We cannot help but be grateful to Jamnia for that.

The points made here about the Jewishness of Matthew and his audience and the late date for the composition of the gospel are important for the interpretation of the gospel because they establish the gospel as a Jewish, as opposed to a "Greek" theological work. We shall have more to say about the differences between "Jewish" and "Greek" when we treat Matthew's literary techniques. For the present we shall have to advert to the significance of the "lateness" of Matthew's gospel.

MATTHEW'S SOURCES

The "lateness" of the gospel, any place from fifty to sixty years after the resurrection, obliges us to ask about Matthew's sources. Since the gospel is not an eyewitness account, the author must have had access to source materials for his narratives and discourses. The sources could have been oral, i.e., the remembered and retold account of what Jesus had said and done back in the years 27-30, or written, i.e., documents composed in the years between the resurrection and the time when Matthew wrote his gospel. Scholars have found it impossible to come to an absolute conclusion on

[10] See W. D. Davies, *The Setting of the Sermon on the Mount,* 276.

[11] J. L. Martyn, *History and Theology in the Fourth Gospel,* 22-41, adopts this dating and suggests the references in John's gospel to excommunication from the synagogue (Jn 9:22; 12:42; 16:2) can be explained in the light of the *Birkath ha Minim.*

[12] What W. D. Davies says about the Sermon on the Mount is true for the gospel as a whole: "The Sermon on the Mount is seen in true perspective only against the Judaism of Jamnia: other factors enter the picture but Jamnia is the chief formative influence" (*The Sermon on the Mount,* 90).

[13] Cf. G. D. Kilpatrick, *The Origins of the Gospel according to Saint Matthew,* 124.

the question, but the majority favors the opinion that Matthew used at least two written sources: Mark's gospel and the Q source, i.e., the material Matthew has in common with Luke, but not with Mark, and which scholars usually attribute to a collection of sayings known as the Q or *quelle* source.[14]

A third source, which may have existed in written form, is the "M" or special Matthew material, i.e., the material peculiar to Matthew which is not found either in Mark or Luke.[15] The "M" material is usually restricted to the infancy narrative, a number of parables, and some pericopes in Matthew's passion and resurrection narrative.

The apparent dependence of Matthew upon Mark and Q accounts for what scholars call the "Synoptic Question." The question quite simply is: who depends on whom? Do Matthew and Luke depend on Mark or is Mark an abbreviated version of either Matthew or Luke? Do Matthew and Luke both depend on the same Q document or does one copy Q from the other? The question, it seems, will be argued forever.[16] We will deal with it in Appendix C.

Whatever the solution to the synoptic question, the Markan material is important as a source of comparison, showing how Matthew used Mark's gospel (if he had a copy of it for his use) or at least how Matthew and Mark used the same common oral tradition. How Matthew changed Mark's text, or how each adapted the common tradition tells us much about each evangelist's particular viewpoint. Comparison is important also because Matthew regularly uses the text of Mark's gospel (or the same tradition as Mark if one does not accept Matthew's dependence on a written Markan source) as a departure point for his narratives and discourses. In this particular case, however, Matthew's dependence on the Markan gospel seems so self-evident that a number of scholars speak of Matthew's gospel as a new version of or as a commentary on Mark.

The Q material serves a similar purpose. It serves as a source of comparison with Luke, enabling the composition critic, by a judicious analysis of the differences, to discover the varying theological interpretations the two evangelists gave to the same material.

The "M" or special Matthew material is important because if it derives from Matthew himself, it serves in a special way as a key to his theological thinking. If it is not Matthew's composition but derives from a source peculiar

---

[14] *Quelle* is the German for "source", hence the abbreviation "Q". On the Q source, cf. H. C. Kee, *Jesus in History*, 62-103; A. Farrer, "On Dispensing with 'Q'" in D. E. Nineham, *Studies in the Gospels*, 55-108.

[15] Cf. C. T. Davis, "Tradition and Redaction in Mt 1:18–2:23," *JBL* 90 (Dec. 1971) 404–421.

[16] See J. A. Fitzmyer, "The Priority of Mark and the 'Q' Source in Luke," in G. D. Buttrick (ed.), *Jesus and Man's Hope*, vol. I, 51-98; B. Gerhardsson, *Memory and Manuscript*; H. Riesenfeld, *The Gospel Tradition*; J. M. Robinson and H. Koester, *Trajectories through Early Christianity*; F. W. Beare, *Earliest Records of Jesus*; Feine-Behm-Kummel, *Introduction to the New Testament*, 42-46; *JBC* 40:1-25; J. L. McKenzie, *DB*; L. Hartman, *EDB*; J. Jeremias, *New Testament Theology*, 37-41.

to him, the material still tells us much about Matthew's mind and interpretation.

Concerning the author, the audience, the date and the sources of Matthew's gospel, we have come to the following conclusions: (1) the author was a Jewish Christian; (2) the audience was largely Jewish Christian; (3) the gospel was written late in the first century; (4) the author depended for the material content of his gospel either on Mark and Q or on a well and widely known oral tradition.

MATTHEW'S METHODOLOGY

To speak about Matthew's methodology is to presuppose what modern scholars now take for granted, namely, that Matthew is an author in his own right and that his gospel is not the product of a faceless community but the opus of a formidable theological mind. The discovery that the gospel is not just a haphazard collection of sayings and deeds of Jesus but a well structured, highly articulated, and deeply theological opus came about as a result of the work of the redaction or composition critics.[17] To a large degree, therefore, our understanding of Matthew's gospel will depend on our ability to analyze the author's methodology according to the accepted principles of redaction criticism. We shall speak first about redaction or composition criticism. When we have seen what redaction criticism calls for, we shall be able to speak with more assurance about Matthew's methodology.

Redaction critics take for granted that the material content of the gospels passed through three stages: a primary stage in the life of the historical Jesus; a secondary stage in the life of the early Christian Church when the deeds and words of the historical Jesus were proclaimed, preached, and taught; and a third, final stage when the preached and taught materials of the secondary stage were utilized by the evangelists in the composition of the gospels.

The three-stage process is usually spoken of as "the formation of the gospels" and involves an understanding of such concepts as "the gospel as event", the kerygma, the didache, and "the gospel as a literary form."[18] Since these concepts are generally well known, we leave them to the appendices and proceed to a consideration of redaction criticism which deals properly with the composition of the gospels and with the methodology of the individual evangelists.

Redaction critics take for granted that the author's influence in the composition of a gospel is decisive and that as a consequence the work must be studied as a whole in order to discover the particular theological view-

---

[17] Cf. N. Perrin, *What is Redaction Criticism?*;   *Evangelists.*
J. Rohde, *Rediscovering the Teaching of the*   [18] See appendix B.

point of the individual evangelist. Redaction criticism, therefore, implies a meticulous study of the structure, arrangement, and over-all composition of the material utilized by the evangelist. It presupposes that all of these in one way or another testify to the intention of the evangelist to so deal with his source material that the arrangement of the material as a whole will testify to his central theological concerns.[19]

Redaction criticism, in brief, deals with the evangelist's selecting, adapting, revising, expanding, interpreting, arranging, and structuring of his material, and asks such questions as: why this particular selection, adaptation, revision, expansion, interpretation, arrangement, and structure?[20]

The answers to these questions, along with a greater attention to the vertical as opposed to the horizontal approach, have led authors in recent years to prefer the term "composition criticism" over the term "redaction criticism." The vertical approach consists in interpreting the individual parts of a work in the light of the over-all theological purpose of the author.[21] The horizontal approach, which is based upon the synoptic interrelationships of the gospels, consists in interpreting a gospel on the basis of differences between one gospel and another in the utilization of a common written or oral source.

Early redaction critics concentrated excessively on the horizontal approach and on the evangelists' dependence on their sources. More recently redaction critics have come to realize that the primary key to analyzing an evangelist's editing of his material is found in his over-all theological purpose. The tendency now is to study the evangelists in the same way as any other author, i.e., by way of composition criticism and the vertical approach.

The critical question asked by the vertical approach is more properly: what particular message did the evangelist wish to communicate and how did he compose his gospel in order to communicate that particular message? When a gospel is interpreted according to the vertical approach, it becomes evident that the evangelists took much greater liberties with their source materials than had hitherto been suspected, and with greater justification.[22]

The justification for the liberties and the effect such liberties have on the question of the historicity of the gospels will be treated in an appendix.[23] For the present we will deal with Matthew's techniques. His major literary techniques will indicate the over-all purpose of his gospel and pave the way for a vertical interpretation of each part of it. We shall concentrate on seven

[19] By source material is meant the units discovered by the form critics, e.g., miracle stories, parables, pronouncement stories, wisdom sayings, haggadic and biographical narratives.

[20] For a nuanced description of the redaction critical method, cf. Q. Quesnell, *The Mind of Mark*, 46-57.

[21] Cf. W. G. Thompson, *Matthew's Advice to a Divided Community*, 7ff.

[22] R. M. Frye, "A Literary Perspective for the Criticism of the Gospels" in *Jesus and Man's Hope*, Vol. II, 193-221, likens the liberties taken by the evangelists to the liberties taken by Shakespeare in the composition of his historical plays and by modern playwrights in the composition of plays about Joan of Arc (see especially, *op. cit.*, 206-216).

[23] See Appendix A.

major literary techniques: (1) the structure of the gospel; (2) the function of the discourses; (3) the function of the narratives; (4) the function of the ending pericopes; (5) concentric-circle presentation; (6) Mt 28:18-20 as the key to the gospel; (7) the movement of the gospel. In passing we shall deal briefly with some of the minor literary techniques used by Matthew, e.g., inclusion-conclusion, foreshadowing, chiasmus, summaries and recapitulations, the use of keywords to focus attention on themes, "take-off" points from Mark's text, stylized numbers, theological constructs, and Old Testament quotations to be understood against their Old Testament background. The need for such techniques has been admirably expressed by C. H. Lohr:

> As the collections of sayings and stories which are the product of the second stage of the history of the Gospel tradition increase in size, the problem for the Evangelist of bringing some unity out of the multiplicity becomes more and more acute. He has a long series of episodes and autonomous groups of sayings which must be put together in a suitable form. The *disjecta membra* of the narrative must somehow be bound together, gaps in the continuity must be overcome, transitions effected between the parts, unity achieved in the over-all development. For this purpose there are available to him devices similar to those used by the early classical authors, of equally great antiquity among the Semites, with which the early Jewish Christian community is familiar and which they expect him to use in his presentation of the life of Jesus.[24]

The structure of the gospel

Scholars generally agree Matthew structures his gospel by alternating narratives with sermons. Early opinion was that Matthew structured his gospel according to the five-fold division of the Torah. A Greek fragment from the second century shows advertance to the five great sermons in the book and speaks of the gospel in the following terms:

> Matthew curbs the audacity of the Jews
> Checking them in five books as it were with bridles.

The opinion is no longer in favor, but Matthew's rabbinic bent, his Moses' typology in the infancy narrative and the "mountain" location of the great sermon in ch 5–7, with his continual emphasis on Christ's authority over against Moses' throughout the gospel, make it inherently probable that the basic analogy with the Pentateuch was at least part of Matthew's structural plan.[25]

The precise structure, however, goes far beyond a simple five-fold parallel with the Pentateuch. C. H. Lohr has convincingly shown Matthew's mastery

[24] Cf. C. H. Lohr, "Oral Techniques in the Gospel of Matthew" *CBQ* 23 (Oct. 1961) 404.
[25] See W. D. Davies' criticism of this opinion in *The Setting of the Sermon on the Mount*, 14-108 with summaries of results on pp. 25,61, 82-83,92-93,108.

of structural techniques, emphasizing in particular the symmetry of the gospel: "The Gospel taken as a whole can be regarded as one great symmetrical structure. . . . Seen thus, the balancing of the discourses is especially clear. The first and last discourses pair off: the blessings and the woes; entering the Kingdom and the coming of the Kingdom (5–7 and 23–25). The second and fourth can also be compared: the sending out of the apostles, and the receiving of the little ones (10 and 18). The great central discourse (13) on the nature of the Kingdom forms the high point of the Gospel."[26]

J. D. Kingsbury, in a redaction study of Mt 13, substantiates Lohr's contention that "the great central discourse (13) on the nature of the Kingdom forms the high point of the Gospel."[27]

A structural analysis is not complete, however, just by showing that Matthew has made ch 13 the turning point of his gospel, that he has hinted at some kind of analogy with the Pentateuch, and that he has alternated his narrative material with his sermon material. The structure is far more intricate, and many more subtle techniques undergird and interconnect the parts of the whole within the over-all delicately balanced structure.[28] W. D. Davies indicates the depth of the intricacy and subtlety of the structure:

> Certain documents are so loosely constructed that it is possible to treat their separate parts in isolation from the whole. Various sections in the early chapters of Mark, for example, have sometimes been so treated. But there are other documents which are so closely knit that their parts can only be adequately understood in the light of the whole. Such is the Fourth Gospel, and such also is Matthew. It reveals not only a meticulous concern, numerically and otherwise, in the arrangements of its details, but also an architectonic grandeur in its totality. Its different parts are inseparable, like those of a well-planned and well-built house.[29]

It is this "architectonic grandeur" that makes the structure a major literary technique — a technique that not only holds together and interconnects the different parts of the gospel but contributes by itself to the understanding of the message of the gospel as a whole. It will be necessary, therefore, to take into account not only the alternation of narrative and discourse material and the chiastic[30] structure of the gospel as a whole, but the relationship of the narratives to the discourse material, the number and balancing of the discourses, and the relationship of both narratives and discourses to the central chapter of the gospel (ch 13) and the theme of that chapter — the Kingdom of God.

[26] Cf. C. H. Lohr, *art, cit.*, 427.
[27] Cf. J. D. Kingsbury, *The Parables of Jesus in Matthew 13*, pp. 12-16; 130-132.
[28] See W. G. Thompson, *op cit.*, 13-25; W. D. Davies, *Invitation to the New Testament*, 212f.

[29] W. D. Davies, *The Setting of the Sermon on the Mount*, p. 14.
[30] On the meaning and importance of "chiasmus", cf. W. W. Lund, *Chiasmus in the New Testament: a Study in Formgeschichte*; also J. Bligh, *Galatians*.

The chiastic form of the structure

Sermon	(f) ch 13 (f')	
Narratives	ch 11–12 (e)	(e') ch 14–17
Sermons	ch 10 (d)	(d') ch 18
Narratives	ch 8–9 (c)	(c') ch 19–22
Sermons	ch 5–7 (b)	(b') ch 23–25
Narratives	ch 1–4 (a)	(a') ch 26–28

Balance and thematic in the structure

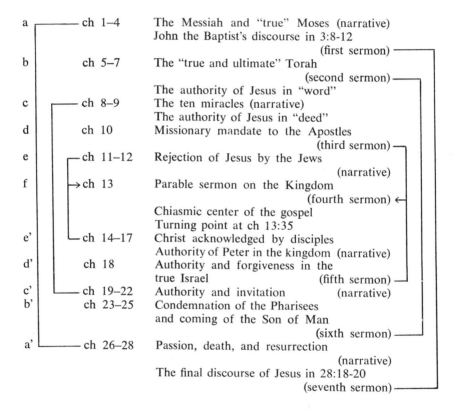

a	ch 1–4	The Messiah and "true" Moses (narrative)
		John the Baptist's discourse in 3:8-12
		(first sermon)
b	ch 5–7	The "true and ultimate" Torah
		(second sermon)
		The authority of Jesus in "word"
c	ch 8–9	The ten miracles (narrative)
		The authority of Jesus in "deed"
d	ch 10	Missionary mandate to the Apostles
		(third sermon)
e	ch 11–12	Rejection of Jesus by the Jews
		(narrative)
f	ch 13	Parable sermon on the Kingdom
		(fourth sermon)
		Chiasmic center of the gospel
		Turning point at ch 13:35
e'	ch 14–17	Christ acknowledged by disciples
		Authority of Peter in the kingdom (narrative)
d'	ch 18	Authority and forgiveness in the
		true Israel (fifth sermon)
c'	ch 19–22	Authority and invitation (narrative)
b'	ch 23–25	Condemnation of the Pharisees
		and coming of the Son of Man
		(sixth sermon)
a'	ch 26–28	Passion, death, and resurrection
		(narrative)
		The final discourse of Jesus in 28:18-20
		(seventh sermon)

A number of typical Matthaean characteristics suggest the above outline may correspond closely to the outline of the structure envisioned by the evangelist. As many scholars have indicated, a balance in the length of the discourses which flank the central discourse in ch 13 is observable. The discourse in ch 5–7 is approximately the same length as the discourse in ch 23–25; ch 10 is about the same length as ch 18; and, significantly, the minor discourses in ch 3:8-12 (the Baptist's only discourse) and ch 28:18-20 (Jesus' final discourse) are of equal length.

In addition to balance in length is balance in thematic presentation. Ch 5–7 emphasize the blessings of true discipleship in counterbalance to ch 23–25 which emphasize the curses in store for false disciples. Ch 10, dealing with the mission of the Apostles, is counterbalanced by ch 18, dealing with the Apostles' exercise of authority in the new community. Again, significantly, there is a balance in thematic presentation in relation to baptism in the Baptist's discourse (3:8-12) and in Jesus' final discourse (28:18-20). In addition both little discourses emphasize the "doing" of the commands of God (Christ).

Accepting with J. D. Kingsbury the thesis that chapter 13 and ch 13:35 represent the highpoint and turning point of the gospel, one readily notices a balance between the first half of the gospel and the second. Up to ch 13:35, Jesus speaks to all the Jews. After 13:35, as in Mk 8:27–10:46, Jesus bestows the major part of his attention upon his disciples, who, in contrast to the Jews, listen and understand him. Thus, in ch 13, Jesus turns from the pseudo-Israel which will not accept him (cf. ch 11–12) to the Church, the true Israel, which believes in him.

A final aspect of the structure that is significant is Matthew's use of seven discourses: the five great discourses and the two minor discourses in 3:8-12 and 28:18-20. Many have noted Matthew's liking for the number seven.[31] His genealogy (1:1-17) is made up of multiples of seven. He has seven petitions in the Lord's prayer (6:5-13), seven evil spirits (12:45), seven vices (15:19), seven loaves (15:34), seven brothers (22:25), seven "woes" (23:13ff), seven references to the "thirty pieces of silver" (27:3-10), and when Peter asks if he should forgive seven times he is told to forgive seven times seventy times (18:22). To these "sevens," we must add the seven discourses in the gospel, suggesting the possibility that Matthew has structured the whole gospel according to the number seven by adding the two minor discourses of 3:8-12 and 28:18-20, indicating in this way the fullness or perfection of the teaching of Jesus in contrast to the incomplete and imperfect Torah of Moses (cf. the antitheses in 5:20-48 and the divorce discussion in 19:1-12).

The function of the discourses

The composition of Matthew's five major discourses (5–7; 10; 13; 18; 23–25) as well as his two minor discourses (3:8-12 and 28:18-20) has come

[31] According to the *IDB*, 295: "It is hard to say what the numerous symbolic uses of seven in the Bible have in common. Perhaps the simplest and most comprehensive generalization that can be made is that seven denotes completeness, perfection, consummation." None of the uses of the number seven in Matthew's gospel taken by themselves would appear to have great significance. But if Matthew's contention against the Pharisees is that Christ brings the fulfilment of the expectations of Israel, the completion of the law, and the consummation of the divine plan of salvation, then it is not by accident that he emphasizes the number seven and has seven clearly defined discourses chiasmically balanced with each other in the structure of his gospel.

under critical scrutiny in recent years.[32] Authors have noticed that though Matthew's material is not particularly original, since three-fourths of it is found in either Mark or Luke, his use of the material is. A closer study of the discourses has shown them to be, like the structure of the gospel, the creation of Matthew, composed by him to expound his depth didache. As such, they constitute a major redactional technique. A convergence of literary evidence points to this conclusion.

First, the discourses, *in their present form*, are manifestly Matthew's compositions. They contain material found in Mark and Luke, but in different contexts of time, situation, and purpose. What is scattered in Mark and Luke is gathered by Matthew into five discourses purportedly delivered by Jesus. Matthew, in short, represents Jesus as saying in the discourses what he actually said in different places and at different times over the course of his preaching ministry in Galilee and Judea. From the compositional viewpoint, therefore, the discourses as they now stand are more properly Matthew's than Jesus' discourses; ultimately, of course, the teaching in the discourses goes back to the preaching of Jesus.

Secondly, as we already noted in discussing the structure of Matthew's gospel, the discourses are artfully balanced both in length and subject matter, with the first (ch 5–7) and the last (ch 23–25) concerned principally with the theme of "discipleship"; the second (ch 10) and the fourth (ch 18) with the mission of the Apostles and the use of apostolic authority in the community, and the central discourse (ch 13) with the Church as Kingdom of heaven on earth. Such an arrangement and symmetry can hardly be a matter of chance.

Thirdly, the five major discourses all terminate with the same formula: "Jesus had now finished what he wanted to say . . ." (cf. 7:28; 11:1; 13:53; 19:1; 26:1). The formulaic transition is manifestly editorial.

Fourthly, another characteristic of Matthew in introducing his major discourses is to choose a departure point from some saying or event in Mark's gospel, either a particular text or a particular incident.[33] This characteristic of Matthew's discourses could derive from reliance on the same oral tradition rather than from Mark, but it has all the earmarks of an author who wishes to expound further what is already familiar to his audience from a well known earlier gospel.

Fifthly, Matthew constructs the narrative sections of his gospel so that they lead up to the material treated in the discourses, either by stressing the same themes and keywords or by preparing and conditioning the minds

---

[32] Cf. Bornkamm, Barth, Held, *Tradition and Interpretation in Matthew*, 15-51; W. D. Davies, *The Setting of the Sermon on the Mount*; C. H. Lohr, *art. cit.*, 403ff.

[33] E.g., compare: Mk 1:39 and Mt 4:23 leading up to the Sermon on the Mount; Mk 3:13-14 and Mt 10:1 introducing the missionary discourse; Mk 4:1 and Mt 13:1 setting the scene for the parable discourse; Mk 9:35-36 and Mt 18:1ff. setting the scene for the community discourse; and Mk 12:38-40 and Mt 23:1-6 setting the scene for the "Woes" against the Pharisees and the sermon that follows.

of the readers to accept what Jesus will say in the ensuing discourses.[34] The artistic composition of the narratives suggests similar artistry in the composition of the discourses.

Sixthly, some or all of the basic themes constituting the central message of Matthew's gospel recur in all five discourses and in the minor discourses of ch 3:8-12 and 28:18-20. The recurrence of these themes suggests not only that Matthew has constructed the discourses to expound these themes, but that he has constructed them in such a way that his depth didache is presented in concentric-circle form.[35]

Lastly, in addition to the common themes appearing in concentric circles, a particular and consistent attitude toward the Pharisees, the disciples, the law, eschatology, and ecclesiology characterize Matthew's discourses.

Matthew's consistent attitude toward the Pharisees is one of reprobation. They talk, but they do not "do". They extol the law but they do not keep it. They exalt the Mosaic law, but they do not realize that the radical law of God goes beyond the Mosaic law. They revere tradition, but their traditions are the traditions "of men" and they betray their "man-madeness" by attempting to override the law of God. They interpret the law for their followers, but fail to understand that all laws are to be interpreted in the light of the law of love which is the central principle of interpretation for all laws.

Matthew's consistent attitude toward discipleship is one of discernment. The true disciple, unlike the Pharisees, not only teaches the law but "does" the law. He not only "does" the law, he does "all" the law; i.e., the true disciple governs his life by the "radical," "paradise" will of God. The true disciple recognizes that the law of love is the principle of interpretation for all laws. Finally, the true disciple is one who has faith, i.e., utter, childlike trust in God.

Matthew's consistent attitude toward the law is one of perception. He respects the law and reveres Moses. But he has learned from Jesus that the law of Moses is incomplete. He perceives in addition that man-made laws (by which he means what the Pharisees would call "the oral tradition") are frequently evasions of the true will of God — that will of God which the disciple prays he may "do on earth as it is done in heaven." Matthew perceives — central to his whole theology of the law — that the law of laws is the law of love of God and love of neighbor. Love for Matthew is the principle according to which all laws are to be interpreted.

Matthew's consistent attitude toward eschatology is one of seriousness. One must do God's will and make effective God's reign over the hearts and wills of men. In the end God will judge every disciple on the basis of his observance of the law of love.

Matthew's consistent attitude toward ecclesiology is one of continuity.

[34] See below, pp. 16-17.   [35] See below, pp. 19-22.

The true Israel is the Israel which has accepted Jesus and his law of love. The true Israel is the Israel which sees that Jesus is "a greater than" Moses; that Jesus is the fullness of Israel in himself; that the gospel is for all men; and that its mission in the world befQre the end-time is to teach all men to observe all that Jesus had commanded. Since the Israel of the Pharisees has failed to see the continuity and completion brought by Jesus to the law, the Kingdom, and the world, it is condemned. The old Israel which was "first" has become "last" and the true Israel, the Church, which has appeared "last" on the scene has become "first." It is for this reason that the Son of Man, who has received "all authority in heaven and on earth" (Mt 28:18), gives his authority to the true Israel, the Christian Church.

For all the above reasons, one may safely conclude that the discourses are Matthew's compositions, that he constructed them to serve his theological purposes; and that, as Matthaean constructions, they constitute a major literary technique. The technique consists in recasting the message of Jesus in such a way that Jesus speaks again — and now through Matthew — as Matthew expounds his depth didache.

Although the technique of reconstructing discourses which one puts into the mouth of another is in bad taste today, it should be remembered the technique was not in bad taste in ancient times and is not peculiar to Matthew. It was widely used in the Bible itself.[36] It was commonplace in extrabiblical literature.[37]

Undoubtedly, Matthew felt no literary compunction about constructing the discourses nor about putting them into the mouth of Jesus. The technique allowed him the great liberty of representing Jesus as speaking to his community in the eighties as if he were present in person. Christ had, after all, been named "Emmanuel," i.e., "God-with-us" (1:23) and had promised to be with his Church "until the end of the ages" (28:20).

The function of the narratives

Since Matthew took great liberties with Jesus' words in composing his five discourses, one might suspect he took similar liberties with the narrative materials from the tradition. That he has done so is now generally acknowledged. It follows that the redaction of the narratives constitutes another major literary technique. That he has composed his narratives to serve a definite function is a proposition which one can adequately test only by a study of the gospel as a whole and by a careful study of the function of each separate block of narrative material.

We will test the proposition as a "working hypothesis" in Part II by examining the validity of the three presuppositions upon which it is based. The first

[36] Cf. the "Mosaic" discourses in Deuteronomy, the discourses in Tobias and 2 Maccabees, and the "Johannine" discourses of Jesus in the fourth gospel.
[37] Cf. the speeches in Xenophon's *Anabasis* and in Plato's *Symposium*.

presupposition which literary criticism supports is that the narratives *as we have them now* are as much Matthew's redaction work as the discourses.[38]

This presupposition is supported by the structure of the gospel according to blocks of narrative followed by discourse recurring throughout the gospel and by the recurrence in the narratives of the same literary characteristics, the same concentric themes, and the same attitudes toward people and institutions as those found in the discourses.

The second presupposition is that the themes Matthew developed in the discourses have influenced both his selection and his redaction of this material in the narrative sections of his gospel. This presupposition will be abundantly borne out.

The third presupposition is that Matthew's narratives and discourses are not only intimately related, but that the narratives are subservient to the discourses, in the sense that they prepare us for the discourses; i.e., the narrative block in ch 1–4 prepares us for the Sermon on the Mount in ch 5–7; ch 8–9 prepare the way for the discourse in ch 10; ch 11–12 for ch 13; ch 14–17 for ch 18; ch 19–22 for the final long discourse in ch 23–25.[39] This too will be abundantly borne out.

The function of the ending pericopes

The strategic value of the final position in narrative or discourse has long been known. It is the place for a climax, a summary of conclusions, the solution to problems, the interconnection of hitherto disconnected themes. It is the logical place for a farewell address or for memorable words and ideas. In a chapter or section of a literary work, it can serve the above functions in addition to serving as the normal place for a transition from one part of a work to another.

Matthew's brilliant exploitation of the strategic value of the final position in his narratives and discourses and in the ending of his gospel as a whole supplies the reader with another key to his methodology and to the message his methodology serves.

When one studies Matthew's narratives, one becomes aware not only that each narrative prepares the way for the subsequent discourse but also that each narrative concludes with a pericope, either a narrated event or

---

[38] Cf., for a dissenting opinion, K. Stendahl, *The School of Matthew*, 26ff.

[39] The functional value of the narrative in preparing the way for the discourse that follows is not usually considered. As C. H. Lohr says: ". . . modern readers accustomed to suspense and surprise, must attend to and examine every detail, even those seemingly insignificant, because almost every detail introduced in the course of the narrative is used later on, and its reappearance may give the key to the meaning of the whole. This unobtrusive preparation of the mind of the audience for what is to come is of the utmost importance for our study, because in it we see how the evangelist coordinates his materials, that is, how, while leaving the elements of the tradition unchanged in themselves, he is able to stamp them with a single significance by preparing in the mind of his listeners through simple repetitions and rearrangements a whole net of expectations and conjectures, so that each new scene and each new collection of sayings is approached with a definite predisposition" (*art. cit.*, 413f).

a saying of Jesus, which provides a well-planned transition to the discourse that follows.

At the conclusion of his first narrative (ch 1–4), Matthew sets the stage for Jesus' proclamation of the Messianic Torah in the Sermon on the Mount (ch 5–7) by describing the large crowds that come to Jesus from Galilee, the Decapolis, Jerusalem, Judaea and Transjordan (4:23-25).

At the end of his second narrative (ch 8–9), Matthew sets the stage for the commissioning of the Apostles as the leaders of the true Israel by recounting Jesus' compassion for the multitude because they are "like sheep without a shepherd" and by quoting Jesus' remark to the Apostles: "The harvest is rich but the laborers are few, so ask the Lord of the harvest to send laborers to his harvest" (9:36-37).

The third narrative section (ch 11–12) concludes with two pericopes. The first categorizes the Jews, who do not accept Jesus, as a house inhabited by seven evil spirits (12:43-45). The second categorizes Jesus' disciples as those who do the will of the Father (12:46-50). In the subsequent discourse (ch 13), Jesus turns away from the Jews and directs himself to his Apostles who accept him.

The fourth narrative section (ch 14–17) ends with the pericope about Peter paying the tax for Jesus and himself (17:24-27) and serves as transition to the discourse in ch 18 which opens with the question: "Who is the greatest in the Kingdom of heaven?"

The conclusion of the fifth narrative section (ch 19–22) deals with the question of Jesus' identity (22:41-46) which is largely answered in the following discourse (ch 23–25) through an emphasis on Jesus as the Son of Man.

Very significantly, even the passion narrative (ch 26–28) is made to conclude with a resurrection account which serves as a transition by emphasizing Jesus' intention to meet his Apostles in Galilee (28:1-10) where he will deliver the final discourse of the gospel (28:18-20).

Matthew exploits the strategic value of the end position not only in his narratives but in his discourses as well. In the discourses, the ending pericope is used either to emphasize or to recapitulate a central teaching of the finished discourse. The Sermon on the Mount (ch 5–7) ends with the parable of the man who built on sand (those who do not do God's will) and the man who built on rock (those who do God's will). Doing as opposed to talking is a central theme of the Sermon on the Mount.

The missionary discourse (ch 10) in which Jesus gives his authority to the Apostles concludes and recapitulates with the statement: "Anyone who welcomes you, welcomes me; and those who welcome me, welcome the one who sent me" (10:40).

The community discourse (ch 18) ends with the parable of the unforgiving servant (18:23-35) and thus recapitulates the central teaching of the discourse.

The final discourse (ch 23–25) terminates with a scene of the last judgment (25:31-46) in which love of neighbor (Christ in the person of his messengers or men in general) determines each man's judgment. The scene sums up the eschatological implications of the whole discourse and makes Jesus' final teaching before the passion a revelation on the finality of a loving "yes" or a selfish "no" to his whole messianic work.

Matthew's proclivity for exploiting the strategic value of the end position is nowhere so brilliantly evident as in the final discourse of Jesus on the mountain in Galilee (28:18-20). The little discourse is made to serve as a recapitulation of the central themes of the whole gospel: the authority of Jesus, the authority of the Apostles, the mission of the Apostles to disciplize all nations by teaching them to observe all that Jesus has commanded, and the promise of Jesus to be with his Church till the end of time. In the final discourse, as D. W. Trilling says, "the main themes ring out and are focused like the rays of light through a lens."[40] The discourse not only recapitulates the whole gospel; it serves also, as many have observed, as a key to the interpretation of the gospel and as a key to its movement. We shall treat it at greater length below.[41]

Concentric-circle presentation

A fourth major literary technique used by Matthew is his concentric-circle form of presentation. The technique, which is typically Semitic, consists in an author's returning at regular intervals to the same fundamental themes under different forms, from different aspects, and with additional light on matters of detail.

The Old Testament provides two classic examples of concentric-circle presentation: Is 40–55, dealing with the New Exodus and the New Creation; and Dan 2; 7–12, dealing with the certain coming and triumph of the messianic Kingdom of God. The New Testament provides three examples in addition to Matthew: John's gospel,[42] Romans 1–11; and John's Apocalypse.

Concentric-circle presentation is difficult to understand because it is foreign to our western way of developing subject matter. It has been likened to the ripples caused by dropping an object into water. The ever widening ripples, although different individually, all go back to the impact of the one object. In a similar way, concentric-circle presentation provides different individual presentations of the same subject.

[40] Cf. D. W. Trilling, *Das Wahre Israel*, 4.
[41] See pp. 22-25.
[42] On concentric-circle presentation in John's gospel, cf. A. Plummer, *St. John*, 71; F. Clark, "Tension and Tide in St. John's Gospel," *Irish Theological Quarterly* 24 (1957) 154-167; J. Bligh, "The Origin and Meaning of *Logos* in the Prologue of St. John," *Clergy Review* 40 (1955) 405.

The pyramid presentation of material in newspaper accounts is somewhat similar to concentric-circle presentation. The substance of the story
is given in the headline and repeated in a subheadline. The story is then given
in summary detail and finally in longer detail.

While not congenial to western minds, concentric-circle presentation has
the decided advantage of keeping the central message continually before
the reader's eyes so that he always sees it as a whole and as a living rather
than a fragmented message. The repetition is sometimes boring, but the
variety of ways in which the author presents the message lessens the mon-
otony.

In Matthew, the presentation is so varied that one hardly notices the concentric circles. Matthew distills the concentrically-presented message into
a number of basic themes, all associated with the central theme of the Kingdom and all recurring regularly throughout the gospel. One may pinpoint
the themes in the narratives as well as in the discourses but, since the narratives, as we have seen,[43] function as preparation for the discourses, it will
suffice to indicate the basic themes in the discourses.

The themes have been recapitulated by Matthew in the final discourse
of Jesus (28:18-20). The discourse is important as a recapitulation of
Matthew's concentric-circle themes and as the key to the gospel as a whole.
Its importance can be assessed by its climactic position (it is the seventh
and farewell discourse of Jesus), its lapidary terms (each word or phrase
serves to summarize a rich and variegated theme), and its relationship to
the other discourses by way of themes and emphasis. The italicized words
and phrases indicate the basic themes. The outline which follows indicates
how often Matthew returns to the themes recapitulated in 28:18-20.

> *All authority* in heaven and on earth *has been given*
> *to me. Going,* therefore, *disciplize all the nations,*
> baptizing them in the name of the Father and of the
> Son and of the Holy Spirit, *teaching them to ob-*
> *serve all I have commanded you.* And behold, *I*
> *am with you* all the days *until the end of time.*

First theme:	The authority of Jesus.	
Lapidary form:	"All authority in heaven and on earth has been given to me."	
Discourses:	Ch 5–7	5:17-48; 7:28-29
	Ch 10	10:27,31-33,34-40
	Ch 13	13:41
	Ch 18	18:3,10,18
	Ch 23–25	23:1-10,30-31,34-36; 24:30,45-51; 25:31-33

[43] See p. 17.

Second theme:	The authority of the Apostles.
Lapidary form:	"Go . . . ." Jesus' transfer of authority to the Apostles is implicit in the sequence: "All authority . . . has been given to me. (I say to you) Go . . . ." To appreciate the full import of the commission, one should compare it with Yah-weh's commission of the prophets in the Old Testament.
Discourses:	

Ch 5–7	5:13-19
Ch 10	10:1,5,16,40
Ch 13	13:17,52 (only implicit)
Ch 18	18:18 (implicit throughout the chapter)
Ch 23–25	23:8-12,34

Third theme:	The ecclesial mission of the Apostles.
Lapidary form:	"Disciplize." The making of disciples calls for bringing men to do God's will. Where men become disciples, there God reigns.
Discourses:	

Ch 5–7	5:19-20; 6:9-10
Ch 10	10:5-6
Ch 13	13:52
Ch 18	18:12-14
Ch 23–25	24:45-51; 25:14-30

Fourth theme:	Scope of the apostolic mission.
Lapidary form:	"disciplize *all nations*."
Discourses:	

Ch 5–7	5:13-14
Ch 10	10:17-18,27
Ch 13	13:32,38
Ch 18	18:18
Ch 23–25	24:14,30; 25:32

Fifth theme:	Baptism — first means for accomplishing the mission.
Lapidary form:	"baptizing them."
Discourses:	Explict only in 3:8-12 and 28:19; implicit in 20:17-23 and in the passion narrative.

Sixth theme:	Teaching — second means for accomplishing the mission.
Lapidary form:	"Teaching them . . . ."
Discourses:	Only here in 28:19, perhaps because Matthew considers "teaching" to be the highest apostolic function (cf. 5:19). It is perhaps implicit in 5:13-16; 10:1,6,13; 13:52; 23:10.

Seventh theme:	To observe, i.e., do what Jesus commands — first characteristic of discipleship.
Lapidary form:	"to observe."
Discourses:	

Ch 5–7	5:19-20; 6:1-34; 7:15-27; especially 6:10
Ch 10	10:8,42
Ch 13	13:8,23 (implicit in 13:17,52)
Ch 18	18:33
Ch 23–25	23:3; passim; especially 25:31-46

Eighth theme: Observing all the commandments — second characteristic
                         of discipleship.
Lapidary form: "Teaching them to observe *all* I have commanded you."
Discourses: Ch 5–7   5:17-48
                         Ch 23–25   23:23; 25:31-46

Ninth theme: Assurance of Jesus' assistance in the in-between time.
Lapidary form: "I will be with you."
Discourses: Ch 10   10:22,40
                         Ch 18   18:20

Tenth theme: The end-time judgment.
Lapidary form: "till the end of time."
Discourses: Ch 5–7   6:13; 7:21-27
                         Ch 10   10:22
                         Ch 13   13:30,40-43,49-50
                         Ch 18   18:35
                         Ch 23–25   24:14,31,44,50,51; 25:13,14-30,31-46

Mt 28:18-20   *The key to the gospel*

By recapitulating his major themes in Jesus' final discourse, Matthew has
anticipated the French penchant for putting a book's table of contents at the
end instead of at the beginning. Wherever it is, a table of contents is a key
to a book's message and movement. We shall anticipate our redaction criticism of Jesus' final discourse, therefore, and omit it at the end of Part II. If
we can understand 28:18-20 as Matthew's original readers understood it,
we shall have a considerable headstart in understanding the message and
movement of the gospel as a whole.[44]

The full interpretation of 28:18-20 is dependent on the discovery of recent
authors that Matthew not only uses his quotations from the Old Testament
with consummate skill but also means them to be understood in their Old
Testament context.[45] Mt 28:18-20, of course, contains no explicit quotations.
It is filled, however, with an implicit quotation of Dn 7:13-14 and an over-all
formal allusion to Yahweh's commissioning of the prophets in the Old Testament,[46] which, for Matthew's Jewish Christian readers at the end of the first
century, would have been immediately recognizable.[47]

[44] Cf. G. Bornkamm, "The Risen Lord and
the Earthly Jesus" in *The Future of Our Religious Past: Essays in Honor of R. Bultmann*
(ed. by J. M. Robinson; N.Y.: Harper & Row,
1971); B. J. Malina, "The Literary Structure
and Form of Mt xxviii.16-20," *NTS* 17 (1970)
87-103; Bornkamm, Barth, Held, *op. cit.*, 131-137
142-143, 148; G. Rohde, *op. cit.*, 62-64; 75-78;
88-90.
[45] Cf. R. H. Gundry, *The Uses of the Old
Testament in Matthew's Gospel*; W. F. Albright,
Matthew, LXI; C. H. Dodd, *According to the
Scriptures*.

[46] See Is 6; Jer 1; Ez 1–3 for the commissioning of the prophets and cf. C. Westermann, *Basic
Forms of Prophetic Speech*, 90ff.
[47] Just as a speaker addressing an audience
well acquainted with Shakespeare's *Hamlet* expects them to understand the words "To be
or not to be" in the context of Hamlet's solilo-
quy, so Matthew addressing an audience well
acquainted with the Old Testament expects them
to understand his implicit quotations and allusions in their original Old Testament context.
When we remember it was not uncommon for
Jews to know the Scriptures by heart, it is all

"The real clue to Matthew's tradition," as W. F. Albright says, "is to be found in Dn 7:13."[48] What Albright means is that Matthew sees the risen Jesus as the Son of Man who has received power, authority, and dominion over all nations. Endowed with all authority, Jesus commissions his Apostles, as Yahweh had commissioned his prophets, and sends them out with his authority to teach the nations all he had commanded and taught them during his ministry.

The text of Daniel, therefore, is pivotal for the interpretation of the whole gospel. As H. Conzellmann says: "The passion is a stage on the way that runs like a straight line to the enthronement — (Mt 28:16-20)."[49] The enthronement he speaks of is Jesus' enthronement as Daniel's Son of Man.[50] What Conzellmann says about the passion being "a stage on the way that runs like a straight line to the enthronement" can equally well be said about the gospel as a whole, as we shall see when we consider the movement of thought in the gospel. But first we shall try to express the interpretation Matthew's original readers gave to Mt 28:18-20 in the light of Dn 7:13-14 and in the light of Yahweh's commissioning of the prophets. We shall begin by quoting the text of Dn 7:13-14.[51] We shall then paraphrase it.

> As the visions of the night continued,
> I saw one like a Son of Man
> coming on the clouds of heaven.
> When he reached the ancient of days
> and was presented before him,
> He received dominion, glory, and kingship;
> nations and peoples of every language serve him.
> His dominion is an everlasting dominion
> that shall not be taken away.
> His kingship shall not be destroyed.

Reading between the lines, with Dn 7:13-14, the commission of the Old Testament prophets, and the gospel as a whole as background, Mt 28:18-20 would have sounded as follows to his original Jewish Christian readers:

> Through my resurrection and exaltation,
> you see me, as Daniel foretold,
> "the Son of Man coming on the clouds of heaven.
> When I reached the Ancient of Days

the more understandable why Matthew might expect his readers to understand his quotations and allusions in their original context.
[48] Cf. W. F. Albright, *op. cit.*, XCVII.
[49] Cf. H. Conzellman, "History and Theology in the Passion Narratives of the Synoptic Gospels," *Interpretation* 24 (April 1970) 192.
[50] Matthew's references to Jesus as the Son of Man and as king of the Jews in his passion narrative (Mt 26:2,23-24,31-32,53,64; 27:30,37) indicate the narrative was composed in view of Jesus' exaltation and enthronement as described in Dn 7:13-14.
[51] As R. H. Fuller shows (*The Formation of the Resurrection Narratives*, 83), the Greek of Matthew and of Dn 7:14 is quite similar. He says: "The source of the delivery of all authority to the Son by the Father is Daniel 7:14, where it is stated of the "one like a son of man" that to him "was given (LXX *edothe*) dominion (LXX, B text: *exousia*) . . . that all peoples (B text: *panta ta ethne tes ges*) . . . should serve him."

and was presented before him,
I received dominion, glory, and kingship
so that nations and peoples of every language
should serve me. My dominion is an everlasting
dominion that shall not be taken away. My kingship
shall not be destroyed."[52]
By reason of the authority I have just now received,[53]
I commission you, my Apostles, as the Father, Yahweh,
commissioned his prophets: Go, disciplize all nations
"so that nations and peoples of every language
should serve me." Teach them to observe all I have
commanded you.
As the Father, Yahweh, promised to be "with" his
prophets, so I say to you I will be with you even to
the end of time.

The movement of the gospel

The well ordered advance of action and ideas in a literary work is an
indication of clear thinking and literary sophistication. In Matthew's gospel,
the action and the ideas (theology) progress steadily to the climactic missionary mandate of Mt 28:18-20, which provides not only a summary of
the central themes of the gospel but a clue to its movement as well.

The movement flows from the Christology, and the Christology is based
upon Jesus' fulfillment of the Son of Man prophecy of Dn 7:13-14.[54] Recalling W. F. Albright's observation, "the real clue to the evangelist's tradition
is to be found in Dn 7:13,"[55] we might pinpoint the substance of that clue
as *the authority given to Jesus as the messianic Son of Man*. The question
of authority, Jesus' versus Moses', and the Christian community's versus
the Pharisees', dominates the gospel and by its progressive resolution provides the movement of the gospel. Seen through the Christological lens of
Dn 7:13-14, the movement advances as follows:

Ch 1–9   *The authority of Jesus is established:*
      a) ch 1–4   Jesus is the messianic Son of David and 'like'
                    Moses.
      b) ch 5–9   Jesus is "greater than Moses":
                   (1) ch 5–7   Jesus has supreme authority "in
                                 word."
                   (2) ch 8–9   Jesus has supreme authority "in
                                 deed."

[52] Jesus' promise to Peter: "Upon this rock I shall build my Church . . . and the gates of hell can never prevail against it" (16:18) should be read in the context of Daniel's "My Kingship shall not be destroyed."

[53] J. Jeremias, (*NTT*, 310) understands the verb (*edothe*) of 28:18 as an ingressive aorist in the sense "there has *just* been given to me" and concludes: "Thus Mt 28:18 means that the prophecy that the Son of Man would be en-throned as ruler of the world was fulfilled in the resurrection."

[54] It has been observed by many that each evangelist's Christology is the most important single factor determining the make-up and struc-ture of his gospel. This is singularly true of John's gospel, certainly true of Mark's gospel, and now clearly true of Matthew's gospel.

[55] W. F. Albright, *op. cit.*

Ch 10–28   *The authority of the Apostles is established*:
   a) ch 10   Jesus gives to his Apostles the authority to
                   "preach" and "heal."
   b) ch 11–13   Jesus designates as pseudo-Israel the Jews who
                   do not accept him ("this perverse generation") and
                   as true Israel his disciples who accept him.
   c) ch 14–25   Jesus promises the Apostles full authority (16:17-
                   19; 18:18) and instructs them privately in his
                   teaching about discipleship.
   d) ch 26–28   Through his passion, death, and resurrection,
                   Jesus is constituted Son of Man with authority
                   over all nations.
   e) ch 28:18f   Endowed with all authority, Jesus authorizes his
                   Apostles to teach to all nations what he has taught
                   them.

In short, the gospel gravitates around the authority of Jesus and the authority of the Apostles as the leaders of the true Israel of God. Essential to the true Israel is the authority of Jesus and the authoritative mission he has given to the Apostles to make his will known and "done on earth as it is in heaven." To ensure the success of this work in the world, Jesus instructs the Apostles concerning the contents of God's will (the messianic Torah) and promises, as Yahweh promised his prophets, to be with them "till the end."

The in-between time, lasting from the resurrection until the end of time, is the time of the missionary Church when the gospel is preached and taught and men are called to decision. The decision hinges on doing all that Jesus commanded and taught the Apostles. It can be reduced to the decision to live or not to live according to the love commandment in Mt 22:37-40 and 25:31-46. The judgment at the end-time will bring about the definitive demarcation between those who belong to the Kingdom and those who do not.

Part Two

METICULOUS MATTHEW

Reading Matthew, one gets the feeling the author put together his gospel with the precision of a Swiss watch. The feeling comes slowly. There is a difficult stage of learning to recognize Matthew's rabbinic methods, an easier stage of familiarity with his methods, a rewarding stage of empathy with his rabbinic mind and increasing insight into his depth didache.

UNDERSTANDING MATTHEW

To facilitate the process of understanding Matthew, it seems best to begin by pointing out in each narrative and connected discourse those literary and ideological characteristics which help to identify the methodical hand of Matthew in the composition of the material.

When the literary and ideological characteristics have been identified, the reader will begin to perceive the intimate connection between each narrative and the discourse which follows it. The buildup of Matthew's concentric-circle presentation will then become apparent, and the movement of the gospel from the authoritative Son of David to the climactic missionary mandate of the authoritative Son of Man in 28:18-20 will force itself on the reader's consciousness.

When the reader has become familiar with the method of Matthew and aware of the movement of the gospel, he will be ready to appreciate the message of Matthew the theologian. In Part Two we will be concerned primarily with a redaction or composition study of each narrative and connected discourse. In Part Three we will deal with Matthew's message.

A redaction or composition study of Matthew depends, as we have seen,[1] upon a recognition of the evangelist's characteristic literary techniques and upon the presuppositions already discussed,[2] namely: (1) that Matthew reveals his mind and his major theological theses most clearly in his discourses; (2) that the themes elucidated in the discourses influence his selection and composition of the material in the preceding narrative blocks; and

[1] See pp. 8-10.   [2] See pp. 13-17.

(3) that consequently, the reader may expect a close connection between each narrative and the discourse that follows; e.g., ch 1–4 prepare the way for the Sermon on the Mount in ch 5–7; ch 8–9 for the missionary discourse in ch 10; ch 11–12 for the discourse on the Kingdom in ch 13; ch 14–17 for the discourse on the use of authority in the Church in ch 18; ch 19–22 for the discourse on discipleship and the end-time in ch 23–25; and ch 26:1–28:17 for the final authoritative mandate of ch 28:18-20.

PREPARATION FOR THE SERMON ON THE MOUNT
MT 1:1–4:25

The narrative has two parts: the infancy narrative in ch 1–2 and the narrative about John the Baptist and Jesus in ch 3–4. Each shows evidence of Matthew's redactional techniques.

Characteristics of Matthaean redaction in ch 1–2 are the following: (1) the fourteens in the genealogy (1:1-17) which are multiples of seven, Matthew's favorite number;[3] (2) the quotation of Old Testament texts with the formula "to fulfill what the Lord had spoken";[4] (3) the use of inclusion-conclusion in 1:23 and 28:20;[5] (4) the theme of opposition between the Jerusalem authorities of pseudo-Israel and Jesus (cf. 2:3, 16-21).[6]

Characteristics of Matthaean redaction in ch 3–4 are the following: (1) the quotation of messianic texts "to fulfill what the Lord had spoken"; (2) the opposition of John to the leaders of pseudo-Israel (3:8ff) and the epithet "brood of vipers" repeated by Jesus in 12:34 and 23:33; (3) the chiasmic balance of the discourse of John in 3:8-12 with the final short discourse of Jesus in 28:18-20; (4) the concentric-circle themes of John's discourse: a) necessity of producing fruit, i.e., "doing" the law (3:8,10); b) baptism with the "Holy Spirit" (cf. 28:19); c) the emphasis on the end-time judgment (3:8,12); (5) the use of inclusion-conclusion (cf. 3:2 and 4:17 and the larger inclusion-conclusion created by the quotation from Isaiah in 4:12-16 and the later implicit reference to the fulfillment of this prophecy in 11:2-6); (6) the use of Mark's gospel as departure point for his narrative (cf. Mk 1:1-8 and Mt 3:1-6).

The characteristic techniques and motifs testify to the redactional hand of Matthew. The purpose of the narrative, however, becomes evident only

[3] See p. 13.
[4] Cf. 1:23; 2:5,15,17,23; 3:3; 4:14; 8:17; 12:18-21; 13:14-15,35; 15:7; 21:4-5; 26:56; 27:9-10. Whether the quotations from Deuteronomy in the temptation account (Mt 4:1-11) are Matthaean redaction or from the Q source, Matthew's use of the quotations conforms with his manifest intention in ch 1–4 to parallel Christ and Moses. Thus, the temptation quotations probably provide another index of Matthaean redaction.
[5] Numerous authors have adverted to the inclusion-conclusion provided by Matthew's trans-

lation of the name Emmanuel, a name which means 'God-is-with-us' and the concluding words of Jesus: "I will be with you all days."
[6] The apparent incongruity of Herod and "the whole of Jerusalem" being perturbed at news of the arrival of the long-awaited Messiah has been explained, not as an historical fact, but as a Matthaean foreshadowing of Jesus' hostile welcome from his own people. Compare Mt 2:3 with an analogous statement in Mt 21:10, "And when he entered Jerusalem, the whole city was in turmoil."

in the light of the Sermon on the Mount for which the narative in ch 1–4 serves as preparation.

In the Sermon on the Mount, Matthew will present Jesus as one like, but "greater than," Moses. Like Moses, Christ goes up the mountain but, unlike Moses, he proclaims with full and lordly authority not the Old Law but the New Law — the messianic Torah which true disciples of the Kingdom must observe.[7] Christ speaks in the Sermon on the Mount with the same full authority he claims for himself in Mt 28:18, "All authority in heaven and earth has been given to me . . . ."

Matthew presents Jesus on the Mount as one "greater than" Moses, not as opposing Moses but as transcending Moses.[8] His thought is in the vein of Hebr 1:1-2, "In various times in the past and in various different ways, God spoke to our ancestors through the prophets; but in our own time, the last days, he has spoken to us through his Son, the Son whom he has appointed to inherit everything . . . ."

The primary function of the narrative in ch 1–4, therefore, is to establish Jesus as one like but "greater than" Moses.[9] The secondary function of the narrative is to prepare the way for the theme of true discipleship, which will be expounded in the Sermon on the Mount as "doing" and doing "all" that Christ, the promulgator of the messianic Torah, commands. These two themes, the messianic authority of Jesus and the essence of true discipleship as "doing" "all" the will of God, influence and thereby help to explain Matthew's selection and composition of almost all the material in ch 1–4.

The theme of Jesus' messianic authority explains (1) Matthew's use of the genealogy of Jesus to prove that Christ was truly the Son of David — a prerequisite for anyone claiming to be the authoritative Messiah;[10] (2) Matthew's claim that Jesus has fulfilled the predictions of the prophets (1:23 = Is 7:14; 2:6 = Mi 5:1; 2:15 = Ho 11:1; 2:18 = Jer 31:15; 2:23 = Is 11:1 [?]; 4:14-16 = Is 8:23–9:1); (3) the inclusion of John

[7] By messianic Torah is meant Jesus' concept of the will of God — a concept which fulfills and supersedes the Mosaic teaching about the will of God. See N. Perrin, *The Kingdom of God in the Teaching of Jesus*, 76-78.

[8] The expression "greater than" to explain how Matthew conceives Jesus as transcending but not being in opposition to Moses is borrowed from Mt 11–12 where Jesus speaks of himself as someone "greater than" John the Baptist (cf. Mt 11:11-15), the Temple (12:6), Jonah (12:41), Solomon (12:42). Authors categorize Matthew's Jesus in the Sermon on the Mount as another Moses, a perfect Moses. But Matthew's thought is more nuanced. The parallels with Moses' infancy (cf. Mt 2) and with Moses on the Mount (cf. Mt 4:2; 5:1) make the point that Christ is like Moses; but the gospel as a whole, especially in 5:17-48 (the antitheses) and 17:1-9 (the Transfiguration) make it clear that Matthew is out to establish Christ as one who is "greater than" Moses. If

the Pharisees argued, "We have Moses as our authority." Matthew's response would be: "We obey Christ whose authority is greater than and transcends completely the authority of Moses" (cf. also Jn 1:17; Hebr 3:3).

[9] See R. N. Longenecker, *The Christology of Early Jewish Christianity*, 32-38.

[10] Explanations of Matthew's division of Jesus' ancestors into three groups of fourteen generations each are legion. Most appealing is the suggestion that Matthew, following the Jewish custom of reckoning seven years as seven weeks of years (as in Dn 9:2,24), has divided salvation history prior to Christ into six weeks of years (two weeks for each set of fourteen generations), with the six weeks corresponding to the first six days of creation as in Gn 1 and with the eschatological seventh week or seventh day beginning with the birth of Christ (See J. C. Fenton, *Saint Matthew*, 35ff; H. Riesenfeld, *The Gospel Tradition*, 114ff).

the Baptist's testimony to Jesus as Messiah (4:11-14); (4) the inclusion of the testimony of the "voice from heaven" (4:16-17).

As Messiah and as the one who fulfills the prophecies, Jesus is certainly "greater than" Moses. But Matthew wants to show as well that Jesus, as the messianic teacher and promulgator of the perfect, radical, paradise will of God, is "like" Moses. To prepare his audience to look upon Jesus as he will present him in the Sermon on the Mount — as the teacher par excellence — Matthew composes his narrative in such a way and with such parallels with the life of Moses that his audience will see Jesus as "like" Moses.

Jesus is "like" Moses in that (1) as Pharaoh persecuted Moses (Ex 1:15-22), Herod persecutes the infant Jesus (Mt 2:16-18); (2) as Pharaoh massacred the infants in Egypt (Ex 1:1ff), Herod massacres the infants in Bethlehem (Mt 2:16-18); (3) as Pharaoh forced Moses to flee into exile in Midian (Ex 1:11-15), Herod forces Jesus to flee into exile in Egypt (Mt 2:13-14); (4) as Moses returned to Egypt after the death of Pharaoh, Jesus returns to Palestine after the death of Herod (2:21);[11] (5) as Moses spent forty days and forty nights fasting in the desert (Ex 24:18 and 34:28), Jesus spends forty days and forty nights fasting in the desert (Mt 4:2); (6) as Moses promulgated the Old Law from Mount Sinai (Ex 19 and 24), Jesus promulgates the New Law from the Mount of the Beatitudes (Mt 5:2ff). To further emphasize the authority of Jesus, Matthew concludes the Sermon on the Mount with the comment: "Jesus had now finished what he wanted to say, and his teaching made a deep impression on the people *because he taught them with authority* and not like their own scribes" (Mt 7:28).

In ch 1–4 Matthew not only emphasizes the foundations for the theme of Christ's authority, he also prepares his audience for the Sermon on the Mount theme that flows from the theme of Christ's authority — the theme of discipleship, i.e., doing all the radical, paradise will of God that Christ teaches and commands. He does this in several ways.

In 3:8-12 Matthew constructs a discourse for John the Baptist which balances chiasmically with Jesus' short discourse in 28:18-20[12] and emphasizes concentric themes developed in the Sermon on the Mount: the theme of "producing fruit", i.e., doing the will of God, and the theme of the end-time judgment. In addition, John attacks the Pharisees for the first time as those who do not "produce fruit" and thus prepares for the contrast in the Sermon on the Mount between those who do the will of God and

---

[11] To further emphasize his parallel, Matthew has purposely imitated the wording of Ex 4:19. Compare Ex 4:19, "Yahweh said to Moses in Midian, 'Go, return to Egypt, for all those who wanted to kill you are dead' ", with Mt 2:19-21 where Matthew has the angel say to Joseph in Egypt: "Get up, take the child and his mother and go back to the land of Israel, for those who wanted to kill the child are dead."

[12] It should be noted that the Baptist is not relegated to a pre-Christian era of salvation as in Lk 16:16. Matthew presents John preaching the same message as Jesus with some of the same themes and with a summary of his message identical to the summary of Christ's message (cf. 3:2 and 4:17). Thus, Matthew for all practical purposes makes John a preacher to the congregation of his own time.

those who do not — a class categorized in the rest of the gospel as "hypocrites."[13]

In 3:13-15 Matthew adds an explanation of Jesus' allowing John to baptize him. The explanation conforms with Matthew's insistence in the Sermon on the Mount on the "full observance" of the law: "It is fitting," Jesus says, "that we should, in this way, do *all* that righteousness demands."[14]

In 4:1-11 Matthew expands Mk 1:12-13 concerning Jesus' temptation in the desert so that Jesus is made to represent the "true Israel" — the Israel that conquers all temptations against covenant fidelity. The theme of perfectly doing God's will is implicit in the whole temptation story. It is verbalized by Matthew in Jesus' first reply to the devil: "Man does not live on bread alone, but on *every* word that comes from the mouth of God." It is noteworthy that in Luke's version the "every word" is not mentioned: "Scripture says: Man does not live on bread alone" (Lk 4:4).[15]

If it is true that Matthew is using here (3:16–4:11) a literary form or device, known from the Targums, according to which a great man at the beginning of his career is shown in a vision the significance of his whole life, then the narratives of the baptism and the temptation are meant by Matthew to present Jesus' whole life as an example of the perfect doing of the will of God. Since this is what constitutes perfect discipleship in relationship to Jesus and the Father (cf. 28:19) and since the theme of perfect discipleship is so central to the Sermon on the Mount which follows, it is not unlikely that Matthew has ordered these two narratives in this way so as to prepare his audience for his fuller teaching on perfect discipleship in ch 5–7. Luke's accounts of Paul's vision on the road to Damascus (Acts 9; 22; 26), especially the account in Acts 26:12-18, would seem to belong to the same literary form and to serve the same purpose.[16]

THE SERMON ON THE MOUNT—THE AUTHORITY OF JESUS 'IN WORD'
Mt 5:1–7:29

The Sermon on the Mount is the jewel of Matthew's gospel.[17] It grasps and portrays the "essential" Jesus. It is to Matthew's gospel what 1 Cor 13 is to the Pauline writings and Jn 13–17 to the Johannine writings.

[13] Cf. 6:2,5,16; 7:5; 15:7; 22:18; 23:13ff.
[14] The explanation is peculiarly Matthaean. It is absent from the other gospels. As G. Barth says: "In the context of Matthew's Gospel a special emphasis lies upon *pasan* [all]; it has to do with the whole will of God, with the whole righteousness" (Bornkamm, Barth, Held, *Tradition and Interpretation in Matthew*, 141).
[15] It may be argued that the Matthaean version is dependent on the Q source and is not therefore a redactional expansion. The Lukan version of Q would indicate the opposite. But in either event, whether the "every word" clause is from Q or represents a Matthaean expansion of Q,

the result is the same — an emphasis on doing "*all*" that God wills.
[16] Cf. E. Haenchen, *The Acts of the Apostles*, 328.
[17] Cf. W. D. Davies, *The Sermon on the Mount*; *The Setting of the Sermon on the Mount*; J. Jeremias, *The Sermon on the Mount*; Bornkamm, Barth & Held, *op. cit.*, (passim); H. Windisch, *The Meaning of the Sermon on the Mount*; J. Dupont, *Les Beatitudes* (new ed. 1958), J. M. Boice, *The Sermon on the Mount: an Exposition*; L. S. Keck, "The Sermon on the Mount" in *Jesus and Man's Hope*, Vol. II, 311-322.

Like any jewel, however, the Sermon on the Mount must be seen in its setting which composition criticism shows is the gospel as a whole. Only composition criticism can answer such questions as (1) who structured the sermon as we have it in Matthew's gospel? (2) for what particular audience was the sermon intended? (3) why was the sermon cast in its present format? (4) what part does the sermon play in Matthew's gospel as a whole?

In view of what has been said about methodical Matthew and on the basis of composition criticism, there is good reason to believe: (1) that Matthew, not Jesus, structured the Sermon on the Mount as we have it now;[18] (2) that Matthew directed it to his Jewish-Christian community of the eighties; (3) that he cast it in its present format as a polemic against and contrast with the teaching of the Pharisees of his time;[19] (4) that it plays the part in Matthew's gospel of presenting for Matthew's Jewish-Christian audience and for the public at large the authoritative teaching of Jesus which the Pharisees and Judaism in general have rejected.[20]

The following Matthaean characteristics indicate Matthew, rather than Jesus, is responsible for the structure of the Sermon on the Mount in its present form: (1) in typical Matthaean manner, the sermon takes its departure point from the text of Mark (cp. Mt 4:23 with Mk 1:39); (2) it terminates with the stereotyped Matthaean closing formula (cf. Mt 7:28); (3) it contains *seven* petitions in the Lord's Prayer (versus five in Luke's version); (4) it exhibits the typical Matthaean polemic against the Pharisees (cf. Mt 5:11,12,20; 6:1-2,5,16); (5) it balances chiasmically in several ways with its counterpart in the chiasmic structure of the gospel — ch 23–25: a) in length; b) in its beginning, i.e., ch 5–7 begins with blessings (the beatitudes) whereas ch 23–25 begins with curses (the woes against the Pharisees); c) in its ending, i.e., ch 5–7 ends with the warning: "It is not those who say to me, 'Lord, Lord', who will enter the kingdom of heaven" and ch 23–25 ends with the words of the cursed: "*Lord,* when did we see you hungry or thirsty" (25:44-46); (6) it continues the parallels with Moses introduced into ch 1–4 by situating Christ on a mountain like Moses on Mount Sinai and by having Christ promulgate from the Mount the New Law; (7) it develops Matthew's characteristic concentric-circle themes: a) the authority of Jesus; b) the mission of the Apostles; c) doing the law; d) doing "all" the law; e) the end-time.

Matthaean restructuring is further supported by the conclusions of source and form criticism, which take for granted: (1) that Jesus originally gave a great sermon in Galilee; (2) that the oral traditions transmitted this ser-

18 See pp. 13-16.
19 See pp. 36-37.
20 As Mt 11:2-27 will make clear, the Pharisees, by rejecting the testimony of Jesus' word (Mt 5-7) and the testimony of Jesus' deeds (Mt 8-9), have by that very fact constituted themselves the pseudo-Israel in contradistinction to Matthew's Church which constitutes the true Israel (cf. Mt 13:1ff; 23:1ff; 28:18-20).

mon for some twenty or thirty years; (3) that the sermon was preserved
in the Q document (c. 50 A.D.); (4) that Matthew and Luke, sometime in
the eighties, used the Q sermon as a source, with Luke preserving and
Matthew expanding the original form found in Q.

The original sermon

It is impossible to outline perfectly the original sermon of Jesus. However, a comparison of the Matthaean with the Lukan version (Lk 6:20-49)
suggests the original had three parts:

I Perfect justice: a) General statement (5:17-20).
                  b) Five examples (5:21-24; 27-28; 33-37; 38-42; 43-48).

II Good works: a) General statement (6:1).
                  b) Three examples (6:2-4; 5-6; 16-18).

III Three warnings: a) Do not judge (7:1-2) followed by one example: the parable of the speck and the beam (7:3-5).
                  b) Beware of false prophets (7:15) followed by one example: the parable of the tree and its fruit (7:16-20).
                  c) Necessity of practicing justice (7:21) followed by one example: the parable of the two houses (7:24-27).

The following outline, containing Matthew's material in the left column,
the Lukan parallels in the center column, and some notes in the right
column, shows how both Matthew and Luke have the same basic sermon
and how Matthew has expanded his version by inserting material into the
framework of the original sermon:

	MATTHEW	LUKE	NOTES
Introduction	5:1-2	6:17-20	Matthew: on mount / Luke: in plain
Beatitudes	5:3-10	6:20-23	Matthew: eight / Luke: four and four
Salt	5:13	14:34-35	Not in Luke's sermon
Light	5:14-16	11:33	Not in Luke's sermon
Law's fulfillment	5:17-20		Peculiar to Matthew
Antitheses	5:21-48		Peculiar to Matthew
Retaliation	5:34-42	6:29-30	Common to both sermons
Love of enemies	5:43-48	6:27-28, 32-36	Common to both sermons
Almsgiving & prayer	6:1-8		Peculiar to Matthew
Lord's Prayer	6:9-15	11:2-5	Not in Luke's sermon
Fasting	6:16-18		Peculiar to Matthew
Treasures in heaven	6:19-21	12:33-34	Not in Luke's sermon
Single eye	6:22-23	11:34-36	Not in Luke's sermon
Serving two masters	6:24	16:13	Not in Luke's sermon
On cares	6:25-34	12:22-31	Not in Luke's sermon
On judging	7:1-5	6:37-38, 41-42	Common to both sermons

Continued	MATTHEW	LUKE	NOTES
Pearls before swine	7:6		Peculiar to Matthew
Answer to prayer	7:7-11	11:9-13	Not in Luke's sermon
Golden rule	7:12	6:31	Common to both sermons
Narrow gate	7:13-14	13:23-24	Not in Luke's sermon
Fruits	7:15-20	6:43-45	Common to both sermons
"Lord, Lord . . ."	7:21-23	6:46; 13:26-87	Common to both sermons
Hearers and doers	7:24-27	6:47-49	Common to both sermons

The material common to Matthew and Luke would appear to derive from a common source, probably the Q source.[21] The material peculiar to Matthew is more difficult to trace. It could be material from the Q source omitted by Luke but included by Matthew. It could be from the floating oral tradition. It is more likely, however, Matthew's own unique expression of judgments originally voiced by Jesus.[22]

The material included by Matthew in his sermon and found in Luke, but not in Luke's sermon on the plain, would seem to indicate Matthew included much material not used by Jesus in the original great sermon. The additional material, which just about doubles the length of the original discourse of Jesus, is taken by Matthew from sayings of Jesus uttered at different times and in different places and more than anything else points up the freedom of Matthew in his composition of the Sermon on the Mount.

Matthew, in short, has expanded the account of the original sermon given by Q by inserting extraneous material into the original framework of the sermon. The clearest indication of method is the expansion of the original by dilating on keywords and themes (e.g., 5:13-16, 18-19, 25-26, 29-32, 36; 6:7-17, 19-34; 7:6-14, 22-23).

His section on prayer exemplifies the method. Originally, Mt 6:2-18 probably consisted of three examples: a) 6:2-4 on almsgiving; b) 6:5-6 on prayer; c) 6:16-18 on fasting. Matthew expands the brief section on prayer by taking the Our Father from its more natural context in Lk 11:1-4 and placing it after 6:5-6 as an example of how the perfect disciple is to pray. In 6:14-15 he develops the theme of forgiveness from 6:12.[23]

Matthew's audience

Matthew's audience for the Sermon on the Mount is a problem. As a general rule, Matthew has Jesus address himself to the disciples. This is certain for the discourses in ch 10, ch 23–25, and 28:18-20, which are clearly directed to the twelve apostles, and probably for the discourse in ch 18, which is directed either to the twelve apostles or to the community

[21] On the Q source in Matthew, cf. W. D. Davies, *The Setting of the Sermon on the Mount*, 366-386; H. C. Kee, *Jesus in History*, 86-90; V. Taylor, *New Testament Essays*, 90-118.

[22] Matthew's general principle concerning the fulfillment rather than the abolition of the law (5:17-20) and the formulation of the antitheses

(5:21-48) give every indication of being typically Matthaean.

[23] The theme of forgiveness, first expressed in the Our Father in 6:12, and then developed in 6:14-15, not only helps constitute a summary of Jesus' teaching on prayer, but also prepares the way for Matthew's lengthy discourse on forgiveness in ch 18.

in general. The first part of the discourse on the Kingdom (13:1-35), however, is directed to the crowd in general. And the discourse fashioned by
Matthew for John the Baptist (3:8-12) is directed to the Pharisees.

At first sight, the audience for the Sermon on the Mount is ambiguous.
Matthew prefaces the sermon with the words: "Seeing the *crowds*, he went
up the hill. There he sat down and was joined by his *disciples*. Then he
began to speak. This is what he taught *them*" (5:1-2). The antecedent of
"them" in 5:2 is unclear. Is it the crowds or the disciples? When Jesus goes
up the hill, is he leaving the crowds to be with his disciples, or is he looking
for a place from which to address the crowds? The ambiguity is further
compounded by Matthew's use of the third person in phrasing the beatitudes
(Luke uses the second person), by his arranging to have the crowds on the
scene in 4:25–5:1, and by his reference to the crowds' reaction to the sermon
in 7:28-29.

The ambiguity, as we shall see, is not entirely unintentional. In 11:2-19,
Matthew will have Jesus accuse the Jews of rejecting the preaching and
witness of both John the Baptist and himself. In the case of John, the
reference is to John's discourse in 3:8-12. In the case of Jesus, the reference
can only be to the Sermon on the Mount. For his audience in the eighties,
Matthew is preparing an indictment of the Pharisees. Part of the bill of
particulars is the charge that the Pharisees and Jews in general have heard
the messianic Torah of Jesus, the Sermon on the Mount, and have rejected
it (cf. Mt 11:16-20). Similarly, in 11:2-20, Matthew will accuse the Jews
of having witnessed the "works," i.e., the messianic miracles of Jesus (Mt
8–9) and of having rejected not only the "words" but the "works" of Jesus.
The condemnation of the Jews in Mt 11:2-24 is the key to the intentional
ambiguity of Mt 5:1-2 and 7:28-29.[24]

In anticipation of ch 11, therefore, Matthew has Jesus speak in the
presence of the crowds but address himself to the disciples, who are carefully distinguished from the crowds.

The distinction of the disciples from the crowds is introduced subtly in
4:23-25 by Matthew's reference to Jesus teaching in "their" synagogues
(4:23). The "their" is intentional and is used elsewhere in the gospel (cf.
9·35; 10:17; 23:34) to distinguish between the disciples and the Pharisees
or recalcitrant Jews in general.[25]

In 5:1-2, one may infer that Jesus went up the hill, leaving the crowds
in order to be with his disciples. If the inference is valid, the "them" of
"This is what he taught them" refers to the disciples.

---

[24] M. Jack Suggs, *Wisdom, Christology, and Law*, 122, says: "The well-known problem of the shift from the third person in the beatitudes of 5:3-10 to the second person in that of 5:11-12 is to be explained as due to the fact that Matthew here moves from the beatitudes proper (which announce in a general way the conditions of entrance into the Kingdom) to a commission-ing of the disciples (who are the primary audi-ence, although the subject matter of the sermon is of universal validity)."

[25] In ch 13, Matthew uses a similar tactic, referring consistently to the Pharisees and Jews in general as "them" in contradistinction to the disciples.

The ambiguity, continued in the third person (indefinite) of the beatitudes (5:3-10),[26] is resolved in the rest of the sermon and particularly in 5:11-20 where Jesus not only addresses the disciples in the second person but speaks of them being "persecuted as the prophets before you" (5:11-12 and compare with 23:37-39). The contrast with the Pharisees and Jews in general is further emphasized in 5:13-16 where the disciples are designated the "salt of the earth" and the "light of the world" and then told "if your virtue goes no deeper than that of the scribes and Pharisees, you will never get into the kingdom of heaven." In the remainder of the sermon, the disciples are several times warned against doing what the "hypocrites do" (cf. 6:2,5,16 and compare with 23:13-32). A similar ambiguity in relation to Matthew's audience is evident in the last great discourse, ch 23–25, where Jesus begins by addressing himself to the crowds and the disciples but then quickly turns to the disciples alone.

Matthew's purpose in the Sermon on the Mount

The identification of the disciples as Matthew's immediate audience in the Sermon on the Mount and the Jews as his "off-stage" audience contributes greatly to the understanding of Matthew's purpose. By having the Jews hear the sermon and marvel at the authority with which Jesus spoke (cf. 7:28-29), Matthew has prepared the way for Jesus' later condemnation of the Jews in ch 11–12 — a condemnation which, in reality, is directed toward the Jews of Matthew's time who have continued to reject Jesus and persecute his followers.

At the same time, by promulgating in the Sermon on the Mount the quintessence of Christianity in such a way that it is contrasted with the teaching of the Old Law by the Pharisees and their school, Matthew has emphasized for his Jewish Christian community of the eighties (1) the superiority of the New Law over against the Old Law championed by the Pharisees;[27] (2) the superiority of Jesus over against Moses; (3) the superiority of Christian discipleship over against the discipleship of the Old Law as expounded by the Pharisees; (4) the necessity for Christians as true disciples of Jesus to *do* the law and to do *all* the law.

Matthew's delicacy in dealing with Moses should be noted. Matthew and his audience are Jews. They respect and love Moses. It is of some impor-

[26] W. D. Davies, *The Setting of the Sermon on the Mount*, 289, sees a contrast between the disciples and Jews even in the beatitudes: "The Matthaean emphasis falls on those who are blessed, as constituting a peculiar people. The repeated *autoi* [they] in the second clause in each part of the beatitudes in v. 3,4,5,6,7,8,10 has an antithetical effect. It is not reading too much into these verses to find that it is 'these' people rather than 'those' who are blessed. In 5:11ff these two groups emerge as Christians and Jews."

[27] As W. D. Davies puts it: "The Sermon on the Mount is seen in true perspective only against the Judaism of Jamnia: other factors enter the picture but Jamnia is the chief formative influence. What chiefly led him (Matthew) to concentrate on using the words of Jesus himself, sectarian conventions, and rabbinic forms in the Sermon on the Mount was the desire and necessity to present the ethic of the New Israel, the Church, at a time when the rabbis were engaged in the same task for the Old Israel at Jamnia" (*The Sermon on the Mount*, 90).

tance then to note that Matthew's parallels between Moses and Jesus enhance the position of Jesus without negatively diminishing Moses; that Jesus explicitly states he has not come "to destroy" the Law and the Prophets but "to complete" them (5:17-29); that in the antitheses (5:21-48) where Jesus goes on to complete the Law of Moses by expounding the radical, paradise will of God, he does not deny the validity of the Law of Moses but simply goes beyond it to the perfection of God's will.[27b] The parallel of Christ on the mountain promulgating the New Law recalls Moses on Mount Sinai promulgating the Old Law and implies great respect for the old lawgiver. Similarly, in his description of the scene at the Transfiguration (Mt 17:1-7), Jesus' superiority in relation to Moses is made clear in the words: "This is my Son, the Beloved; *he* enjoys my favor. Listen to *him*." But *Moses* is *there*. Matthew and his community are not opposed to Moses. They are opposed to the Pharisees and their interpretation of the law of Moses.

The nature and structure of the Sermon on the Mount

More than anything else, Matthew's purpose in view of the situation of his Jewish Christian community in the eighties explains the nature and structure of the Sermon on the Mount. It is not a sermon at all in the strict sense of the word. It is a statement of principles which Matthew more or less systematically collected and arranged — principles whose ultimate historical source was Jesus.[28] It is Matthew's Christian Manifesto or declaration, in which Jesus expounds the quintessence of Christianity in such a way that it is seen as opposed to the teaching of Judaism expounded by the Pharisees and as constitutive of the true Israel, the Church, as opposed to the pseudo-Israel of the Pharisees.[29]

If there is any familiar pattern in the sermon, it is probably the pattern familiar to the rabbis, expressed in the words of Simon the Just: "By three things is the world sustained: by the law, by the Temple service or worship, and by deeds of loving-kindness." The first part of the sermon deals with the law (5:17-48); the second with the nature of true worship: almsgiving, prayer, fasting (6:1-18); and the third with deeds of loving-kindness (6:19–7:12).[30] The structure and division follow accordingly:

[27b] In Mt 19:1ff, it is notable that Matthew has the Pharisees, rather than Jesus, ask about Moses' legislation, and that Jesus is shown *defending* Moses. Mark (10:1ff) has Jesus ask the question about Moses' legislation.

[28] Cf. J. L. McKenzie, "Matthew" in the *JBC*, 76.

[29] G. Bornkamm, *Tradition and Interpretation in Matthew*, 17, maintains the Sermon on the Mount has the character of a catechism similar to the post-apostolic writing known as the Didache, which he claims it largely parallels

in that each follows a basic pattern: the law of admission, the directions for worship and behavior, and warnings about the end-time.

[30] As W. D. Davies says (*The Setting of the Sermon on the Mount*, 307): "On these three elements is the house of the new Israel to be built: they alone enable it to stand in the eschatological trial. Matthew's neat division of his material suggests that he is working under the influence of a traditional arrangement. He confronts the Synagogue with a triadic formulation which would not be alien to it."

Introduction (5:2-16)

a) 5:2-10   The beautitudes express the essential spiritual characteristic of a true disciple. He is to have the 'anawim's spirit of complete trust in and dependence on God alone.

b) 5:11-16   The mission of the apostles is to be the salt of the earth and the light of the world.[31]

Body of the Sermon (5:17–7:12)

a) 5:17-19   Programmatic declaration concerning the perfection of Jesus' messianic Torah in relation to the Torah of Moses. The perfection and the 'more' of Jesus' Torah is explained in 5:21-48.[32]

b) 5:20   Programmatic declaration concerning the greater response expected from Christians in contrast with the response of the Pharisees.[33] The greater response is elaborated in 6:1–7:12.

c) 5:21-48   The antitheses establish Jesus' authority as greater than the authority of Moses and Jesus' Torah as the perfection and completion of Moses' Torah.[34]

d) 6:1–7:12 The contrast between the way of true discipleship and the way of false (Pharisaic) discipleship with regard to (1) almsgiving (6:1-4); (2) praying (6:5-15); (3) fasting (6:16-18); (4) material things (6:19-34); (5) the neighbor (7:1-12).[35]

Conclusion (7:13-27)

a) 7:13–23   Three warnings contrasting the two ways and substantiating the seriousness of the demand in 5:20.

b) 7:24-27   Matthew's ending pericope likens the doer to one who builds on rock and the non-doer to one who builds on sand.

The sermon in relation to the gospel as a whole

The Sermon on the Mount is not a self-contained entity. It is intimately related to the gospel as a whole and especially to the first half of the gospel, i.e., ch 1:1–13:35. Its relation to the narrative in ch 1–4 has already been noted. But it is also related to the account of Jesus' miracles in ch 8–9, to the commission of the Apostles in ch 10, to the condemnation of pseudo-Israel in ch 11–12, and to the great sermon on the Kingdom in ch 13.

In the second half of the gospel, the overtones of the Sermon on the Mount will be heard in the commission of Peter as the "rock" (16:17-19), in the transfiguration scene on "a mountain" (17:1-8), in the final great discourse (ch 23–25), and in the missionary mandate given on "a mountain" in Galilee (28:18-20).

When Matthew follows his account of the Sermon on the Mount in ch 5–7 with an account of Jesus' messianic miracles in ch 8–9, his major theme, the authority of Jesus, is consistently pursued. He intends his readers

[31] See pp. 135-137.
[32] See pp. 137-141.
[33] See pp. 142-150.
[34] See pp. 143-144.
[35] It should be noted that in each section the love commandment takes the final climactic position: 5:21-48 ends with the love commandment in 5:43-48, and 6:1–7:12 ends with the love commandment expressed as the golden rule in 7:12.

to recognize his twofold demonstration of Jesus' authority "in word" (ch 5–7) and his authority "in deed" (ch 8–9).

When he begins ch 10 with Christ giving his authority to the Apostles (10:1), he takes for granted that his readers have been convinced by ch 5–7 and ch 8–9 that Christ has this authority; first, because he is the Messiah and "greater than Moses" (ch 1–4) and, second, because of his demonstration of authority in the Sermon on the Mount and the miracle narrative.

When Matthew opens ch 11 with a recapitulation of Jesus' miracles (11:2-6) and then goes on to condemn the Jews for not listening either to John the Baptist or to Jesus (11:7-20), he is referring back not only to the miracle narrative in ch 8–9 but to the discourse of John in ch 3:8-12 and to the sermon of Jesus in ch 5–7.

The Kingdom discourse in ch 13 with its distinction between "those outside the house" (13:1) who "listen without hearing or understanding" (13:13-15) and those "inside the house" (13:36) who "hear" (13:16) and "understand" (13:51) hearkens back not only to the condemnation of the Jews in ch 11–12 but to the preaching of Jesus in ch 5–7 which the Jews heard but without "understanding" or acceptance.

The concentration of Jesus on the 'education' of the disciples in the second half of the gospel (ch 13:36–28:20) presumes not only that they constitute the true Israel (cf. ch 13) and have received authority from Christ (ch 10:1) but also that they are those who have heard, understood, and accepted the teaching of Jesus in the Sermon on the Mount.

The missionary mandate of ch 28:18-20, by which the Apostles are given authority to teach, takes for granted that they have heard, understood, and accepted the teaching of Jesus in the Sermon on the Mount and are now to disciplize all nations . . . teaching them all I have commanded you" All that Jesus commanded is summarized in the Sermon on the Mount, particularly in 5:17-48.

Matthew's redaction of Mark's text

Whatever the solution to the synoptic problem and however one explains Matthew's penchant for utilizing either the Marken text or the same tradition as Mark for his "departure points" in composing his narratives and discourses, it is noteworthy that Matthew uses the material in Mk 1:1-45 almost in its entirety: (1) Mk 1:1-8 on the preaching of John the Baptist is found in Mt 3:1-12; (2) Mk 1:9-11 on the baptism of Jesus is found in Mt 3:13-17; (3) Mk 1:12-13 on the temptation of Jesus is found in Mt 4:1-11; (4) Mk 1:14-15 on the preaching of Jesus is found in Mt 4:12-17; (5) Mk 1:16-20 on the call of the disciples is found in Mt 4:18-22; (6) Mk 1:22 is found in Mt 7:28; (7) Mk 1:29-31 is found in Mt 8:14-15; (8) Mk 1:40-45 is found in Mt 8:2-4.

Matthew's redaction of the Markan material is significant in many ways but primarily in the confirmation it provides for the structure and movement of his gospel. His postponement of the miracle stories in Mk 1:29-45, in addition to other Markan miracle stories, to ch 8–9 of his gospel, where he has amassed a block of ten miracle stories, confirms his intention of using the Sermon on the Mount to establish Jesus' transcendent authority "in word" and the narrative block of ten miracles in ch 8–9 to establish Jesus' transcendent authority "in deed."

His revision and expansion of the Markan material in Mk 1:1-13 confirms his intention of using the narrative material in ch 3–4 to prepare his audience for the themes of the Sermon on the Mount. Thus, (1) in 3:8-12 Matthew constructs a discourse for John the Baptist, emphasizing the discipleship theme he will develop in the Sermon on the Mount; (2) in 3:13-15 he adds the significant explanation, not found in Mk 1:9-11, of Jesus' allowing John to baptize him because "it is fitting that we should, in this way, do *all* that righteousness demands"; (3) in 4:1-11, he expands Mk 1:12-13 concerning Jesus' temptation in the desert in such a way that he emphasizes Jesus' total obedience to the Father.[36] The expansions without exception point up the teaching on discipleship which will be so prominent in the Sermon on the Mount.

THE MESSIANIC MIRACLES—THE AUTHORITY OF
JESUS 'IN DEED'
Mt 8:1–9:38

Characteristics of Matthaean composition in ch 8–9 are the following: (1) the quotation of a messianic text from Isaiah (Is 53:4) with the usual fulfillment formula (cf. 8:17); (2) the appropriation of material from Mark's gospel (only 8:5-13; 8:18-22; 9:32-34 are not from Mark); (3) the inclusion of concentric-circle themes: a) Jesus' authority (passim); b) the mission of the apostles (cf. 8:19-27 and 9:9-17); c) the "I will be with you" theme (cf. 8:23-27); (4) the typical Matthaean high-lighting of the opposition between Jesus and the Pharisees (cf. 8:11; 9:3-4; 9:34b) and between the pseudo and the true Israel (cf. 9:10-17); (5) the use of inclusion-conclusion (cp. 9:35 and 4:23); (6) the use of a subtle transition to connect the narrative of ch 8–9 with the discourse in ch 10 (cf. 9:36-37).

The function of the narrative

Matthew's narrative in ch 8–9 serves to prepare his readers for Jesus' missionary discourse in ch 10 just as the narrative in ch 1–4 prepared his

---

[36] Matthew's quotations from Deuteronomy in his version of the temptation in the desert (4:1-11) serve, as so many have noticed, to point up Jesus as the "true Israel" incarnate in opposition to the Israel of old (and probably in opposition to the pseudo-Israel of the Pharisees) which, similarly tempted in the desert, was found unfaithful to God. Whether the quotations are Matthew's expansion or come from the Q source, they continue his proclivity for quoting scripture (as manifest in the infancy narrative) and serve the same purpose.

readers for the Sermon on the Mount in ch 5–7. To appreciate Matthew's procedure in preparing for ch 10, it will suffice to point out the basic themes of the missionary discourse and then note how these themes have influenced Matthew's selection of material and use of keywords in ch 8–9.

The central theme of the missionary discourse is stated in its introduction: "He summoned his twelve disciples, and gave them authority" (10:1). Jesus gives to his twelve Apostles the authority-power to do what he has done, namely, to "cure all kinds of diseases and sickness" and to "proclaim that the kingdom of heaven is near" (10:6). The mission of the Apostles to "proclaim the kingdom" had already been foreshadowed in the promise, "I will make you fishers of men" (cf. 4:17), and to some extent in the declarations, "You are the salt of the earth. You are the light of the world" (cf. 5:13-16).

Another theme of the discourse is the hardships of the apostolic calling (cf. 10:17-25). The theme is related to the theme of mission and had been anticipated at early as the introduction to the Sermon on the Mount in the words: "Happy are you when people abuse you and persecute you and speak all kinds of calumny against you on my account" (cf. 5:11-12; 11:19; 23:37-39). The theme is explicit in the stories about the hardship of discipleship or 'following' in 8:18-27; 9:14-17. It is alluded to in the warning: "If they have called the master of the house Beelzebul, what will they not say of *his household*" (cf. 10:25; 9:34; 12:24).

Another theme related to the theme of mission is the "lost sheep" theme (cf. 10:5). The theme is anticipated in the words: "I did not come to call the virtuous, but sinners" (9:13) and explicitly mentioned in the transition passage with which Matthew concludes his narrative and leads into the missionary discourse. Compare: "When he saw the crowds he felt sorry for them because they were harassed and dejected, *like sheep without a shepherd*" *(*9:36) with ". . . go rather to the *lost sheep* of the house of Israel" (10:5).

Two keywords recur in ch 8–9, the keyword 'authority-power' (always *exousia* in the Greek) and the keyword 'follow' (Greek: *akoleuthein*). The keyword 'authority' occurs five times in the strict sense (cf. 7:29; 8:9; 9:6; 9:8; 10:1) and three times equivalently, i.e., where the concept of 'authority' or 'power' is implicit in the verb 'to have the power' (Greek: *dynamai*) or to be able to do something (cf. 8:2; 8:27; 9:28).[37] The keyword 'follow' is used in the strict sense of discipleship in four places (8:19; 8:22; 8:23; 9:2 [bis]) and four times in the wide sense (cf. 8:1; 8:10; 9:19; 9:27).

In substance, Matthew prepares his readers for the missionary discourse by demonstrating that Christ himself has the authority-power over disease, death, devils, and nature which he will delegate to his Apostles in ch 10.

---

[37] The concept of 'authority-power' is implicit in all the accounts dealing with Jesus' power over disease, devils, and nature (e.g., the statement in 8:27, "Even the winds and the sea *obey* him").

He indicates this power-authority is given for the sake of sinners, i.e., "sheep without a shepherd." And he warns about the hardships involved in following him.

The demonstration is achieved by putting together a collection of ten miracle stories testifying to Christ's authority-power. But Matthew does not simply heap up miracle stories. He arranges the stories in a strategic manner and repeats his keywords 'authority-power' (*exousia*) and 'follow' (*akolouthein*). The arrangement of the material is typical of meticulous Matthew's love for chiasmic balance:[38]

a)   8:1-17 / *Three miracle stories*
       8:1-4   The leper
       8:5-13   The centurion's servant
       8:14-15   Peter's mother-in-law
       8:16-17   Summary and messianic quotation from Is 53:4
           b) 8:18-27 / *Three discipleship stories*
               8:18-20   The scribe who wants to "follow" Jesus
               8:21-22   The disciple who wants to bury his father first
               8:23-27   The storm at sea: Jesus enters the boat
                           "followed" by his disciples
a.1)   8:28–9:8 / *Two miracle stories*
       8:28-34   The two demoniacs
       9:1-8   The paralytic
           b.1) 9:9-18 / *Three discipleship stories*
               9:9   The call to Matthew to "follow me"
               9:10-13   Pharisees, disciples, and Jesus at table
               9:14-18   "But the time will come for the bridegroom to
                           be taken away from them, and then they (the
                           disciples) will fast."
a.2)   9:20-34 / *Four miracle stories*
       9:20-22   The woman with the hemorrhage
       9:23-26   The official's daughter
       9:27-31   Two blind men
       9:32-34   The dumb demoniac
9:35-37 / *Conclusion of the narrative*
9:35   Inclusion-conclusion with 4:23
9:36-37   Transition to the missionary discourse: "the crowds are like *sheep without a shepherd*" . . . "so ask the Lord of the harvest to send *laborers* to his harvest."

a) 8:1-17 / Three miracle stories

In analyzing Matthew's first grouping of three miracle stories (8:1-17), the following should be noted: (1) Matthew has already introduced the theme of 'authority' in the transition passage from the Sermon on the Mount: "He taught them with authority" (*exousia*) (7:29). (2) The cure of the leper highlights the question of Jesus' power-authority. The leper

[38] On the arrangement of the material, see Fenton, *op. cit.*, 119-121; Albright-Mann, *Matthew*, lvii-lviii.

says: "Sir, if you want to, you can (*dynamai*) cure me." Jesus then cures the leper, showing he not only wants to but has the *power* to cure him.[39] (3) The story about the cure of the centurion's servant contains a significant digression on what it means to have *authority* (8:8-9). (4) The section concludes with the story of the cure of Peter's mother-in-law (8:14-15) and with a summary concerning Jesus' power over evil spirits and over disease (8:16). The cures are then seen, in typical Matthaean fashion, to be the fulfillment of the prophecy of Isaiah: "He took our sicknesses away and carried our diseases for us" (Mt 8:17; Is 53:4). They are *messianic* miracles.

b) 8:18-27 / Three discipleship stories

The first grouping of discipleship stories (8:18-27) is simple except for the third story — the storm at sea (8:23-27).[40] G. Bornkamm, in his analysis of Matthew's version of the storm at sea, shows Matthew has taken the story from Mk 4:35-41 and applied it to make it a story dealing primarily with discipleship rather than, as in Mark's version, with a miracle simply. Bornkamm notes that Matthew, unlike Mark, has Jesus entering the boat first, with the Apostles *following*. He concludes that the word 'follow' in 8:23 should be taken in the same sense as in the two stories about discipleship in 8:18-22. The significance of the change is not lost on Bornkamm. He says:

> If this observation is correct it means: Matthew is not only a hander-on of the narrative, but also its oldest exegete, and in fact, the first to interpret the journey of the disciples with Jesus in the storm and the stilling of the storm with reference to discipleship, and that means with reference to the little ship of the Church.[41]

In short, all three stories center on the 'hardships of discipleship' and contain the keyword 'follow.' The first (8:19-20) warns against a decision which ignores the difficulties in following Jesus. The second (8:21-22) warns against procrastination in answering the call to discipleship. The third (8:23-27) deals with the dangers disciples will encounter and reminds them that Jesus will be 'with them' (cf. 1:23; 28:20) even when he seems to be asleep in the boat (of the Church?).[42]

a.1) 8:21—9:8 / Two miracle stories

The second grouping of miracle stories (8:28–9:8) emphasizes again Jesus' authority. The exorcism of the demoniacs demonstrates Jesus' power over the devils (8:28-34). The cure of the paralytic is a simple miracle story but with a significant digression on the theme of authority (9:5-8),

[39] The sending of the leper to the priest to make the offering prescribed by Moses is significant in as much as it is mentioned immediately after the Sermon on the Mount and thus shows Jesus' respect for Moses and the Law.

[40] Cf. Bornkamm, Barth, Held, *op. cit.*, 52-57.

[41] *Op. cit.*, 55.

[42] The stilling of the storm is a discipleship story but it serves as well to show Christ's authority-power over the forces of nature. This aspect of the story is reinforced by the reaction of the Apostles in 8:27, "Even the winds and the sea *obey* him."

similar to the discussion of authority in 8:5-13. The miracle is worked "to prove to you that the Son of Man has authority (*exousia*) to forgive sins." And the crowd, like a Greek chorus, is made to react with awe and praise God "for giving such power (*exousia*) to men" (9:8; cf. 8:27; 9:34). The emphasis on authority, of course, was already in Matthew's Markan source (cf. Mk 2:1-12). He did not have to add to the material in Mark as he did in other places (e.g., his redaction of the storm at sea account). What is significant is Matthew's use of the story in the context of the whole narrative to further bolster his demonstration of Jesus' messianic authority-power.

b.1) 9:9-18 / Three discipleship stories

The second grouping of discipleship stories (9:9-17) is taken almost word for word from Mk 2:13-22. It served Matthew's purpose particularly well because it brought together the three themes he wanted to develop in the missionary discourse. The call of Matthew (9:9) uses the keyword 'follow' (*akolouthein*). Jesus' answer to the objections of the Pharisees (9:10-13) demonstrates Jesus' authority and introduces the theme of the 'lost sheep': "I did not come to call the virtuous but sinners" (9:13). The question about fasting (9:14-17) contains the implicit claim that Jesus is the Messiah in the use of the messianic title Bridegroom and at the same time foreshadows the hardships of discipleship in the declaration: "But the time will come for the Bridegroom to be taken away from them, and then they will fast" (9:15).

a.2) 9:18-34 / Four miracle stories

The third grouping of miracle stories (9:18-34) contains four miracles and, if one includes the stilling of the storm, brings to ten the number of miracles and the number of people cured. The first two miracles, the cure of the woman with the hemorrhage and the raising of the official's daughter (9:18-26) are taken from Mk 5:21-43 and considerably shortened. Mark has twenty-three verses, Matthew only nine. The last two miracles are largely the composition of Matthew himself and may well reflect Matthew's desire, as J. C. Fenton suggests,[43] to conclude his account of the mighty works of Jesus with two miracles strongly reminiscent of the miracles predicted by Isaiah for messianic times: "Then the eyes of the blind shall be opened, and the ears of the deaf unstopped" (Is 34:6).

If the cure of the two blind men is Matthew's composition, as well it seems, then the discussion with the blind men about Jesus' 'power' to work the miracle is probably meant to balance off with the discussion of 'power' in 8:1-4. In 8:2, the leper testified to Jesus' power with the words, "Sir, if you want to, you *can* cure me." When Jesus questions the blind men in

[43] *Op. cit.*, p. 143.

9:28, "Do you believe that I *can* do this?", their reply testifies to Jesus' power: "They said, 'Sir, we do'."

The final miracle story, the cure of the deaf-mute (9:32-34), not only brings to ten the number of miracles in ch 8–9 but also gives Matthew the opportunity to close his narrative section on the power-authority of Christ 'in deed' in a manner similar to his conclusion to the Sermon on the Mount which demonstrated Christ's power 'in word.' Compare 7:29, "His *teaching* made a deep impression on the people because he taught them *with authority*" and the exclamations of the crowd in Greek chorus fashion in 9:34, "Nothing like this has ever been *seen* in Israel."

9:35-37 / Conclusion of the narrative

The conclusion of the narrative (9:35-37) is significant on two counts. The repetition in 9:35 of the words earlier used in 4:23, "He went round the whole of Galilee teaching in their synagogues, proclaiming the Good News of the kingdom and curing all kinds of diseases and sickness among the people," brings the miracle account to a close by providing an inclusion-conclusion. The inclusion-conclusion is important because it shows Matthew's intention of linking the two sections embraced by the inclusion-conclusion, namely, the Sermon on the Mount (ch 5–7) which emphasizes Christ's power 'in word' and the miracle narrative (ch 8–9) which emphasizes Christ's power 'in deed.' In ch 10 Matthew intends to make it clear to his readers that Christ has delegated this double power to his twelve Apostles.

Matthew's transition passage from the miracle narrative in ch 8–9 to the discourse in ch 10 is given in 9:36-37 and like his transition passage from the Sermon on the Mount (7:29) serves to prepare his readers for the discourse which follows. The observation of Jesus that the crowds are "like sheep without a shepherd" and that the laborers "are few" (9:37) leads directly to the central theme of the missionary discourse — Jesus' authoritative commission of the Apostles to "proclaim that the kingdom of heaven is close at hand" and to "cure the sick, raise the dead, cleanse the lepers, and cast out devils" (10:6-7).

In summary, the reader of Mt 8–9 (whether he realizes it or not) has been conditioned by Matthew to accept the major themes of ch 10.[44] He now knows that Jesus, who will give his authority to the Apostles, possesses 'in word' (ch 5–7) and 'in deed' (ch 8–9) this messianic authority. It has been more than intimated to the reader, by means of the 'follow' stories (8:19-27; 9:14-17) that 'following' Jesus will not be easy. As a result, the reader will not be surprised when Jesus tells the Apostles that preaching

---

[44] As H. J. Held says: "It follows therefore that Matthew presents Jesus at the beginning of his gospel not only as the 'Messiah of the word' and the 'Messiah of deed' but also as the one who commissions, who gives his disciples authority to do the same messianic work" (Bornkamm, Barth, Held, *op. cit.*, 252).

the gospel will involve suffering, hatred and contradiction (10:17-25). Finally, the reader has been told that Jesus came "to call not the virtuous but sinners" (9:13) and he has heard Jesus say that the crowds are "like sheep without a shepherd" (9:36). It will come as no surprise when Jesus sends his Apostles to the 'lost sheep of the house of Israel' (10:5).

THE MISSIONARY DISCOURSE
Mt 10:1-42

With the missionary discourse in ch 10, Matthew comes to the climax of the first half of his gospel.[45] In ch 1–9 he has established the authority of Jesus. In ch 10 he shows Jesus providing for the continuation of that authority in the true Israel by commissioning his twelve Apostles to preach and work with his authority.

The discourse looks backward to the promise in 4:19, "Follow me and I will make you fishers of men" and forward to the mandate in 28:18, "Going, therefore, disciplize all nations." It provides an historical precedent from the ministry of Jesus for the more universal mandate of 28:18-20. At the same time it provides a preliminary explanation of the lapidary terms of the mandate in 28:18-20, especially the words: "all authority," "Going, therefore," and "I will be with you."

The discourse has most of the characteristics of a typical Matthaean discourse: (1) it balances chiastically in the structure of the gospel with ch 18, which is a discourse, like ch 10, directed to the Apostles. (2) It is related to the preceding narrative section in ch 8–9. (3) It includes most of the concentric-circle themes of Mt 28:18-20, a) the theme of authority (cf. 10:1); b) the theme of mission (cf. 10:5-6); c) the theme of 'doing' (cf. 10:42); d) the encouragement theme 'I will be with you' (cf. 10:17-31); e) the theme of the end-time judgment (cf. 10:22,31b-33). (4) It reflects the on-going polemic of Matthew with the Jews of his own time (cf. 10:17-19,21-23,24-25,34-36). (5) It ends with Matthew's ending formula (cf. 11:1).

Matthew's procedure, as usual, is to build on Mark's text. Choosing as departure point Mark's account of the missionary mandate (Mk 6:7-13), Matthew expands Mark's brief account, conflating it with Luke's missionary mandate to the seventy-two disciples (Lk 10:1-16), working into it

[45] Cf. J. Jeremias, *New Testament Theology*, 232-240; *Jesus' Promise to the Nations*; H. Conzellmann, *An Outline of the Theology of the New Testament*, 45-46; B. Gerhardsson, *Memory and Manuscript*; H. Riesenfeld, *The Gospel Tradition*; W. Schmithals, *The Office of Apostle in the Early Church*; P. Meye, *Jesus and the Twelve*, 173-209; J. Rohde, *Rediscovering the Teaching of the Evangelists*, 80-82; H. K. McArthur, *In Search of the Historical Jesus*, 194-198 (a resume of V. Taylor's *The Life and Ministry of Jesus*, 113-119 from the *Interpreter's Bible*, Vol. VII); J. Coutts, "The Authority of Jesus and of the Twelve," *JTS* 8 (1957), 111-118; G. Bornkamm, *Jesus of Nazareth*, p. 150; D. L. Dungan, *The Sayings of Jesus in the Churches of Paul*, 41-74; F. W. Beare, "The Mission of the Disciples and the Missionary Charge: Mt 10 and Parallels", *JBL* 89 (March 1970) 1-13.

material from different contexts in Mark and Luke and, in addition, several sayings of Jesus not mentioned by either Mark or Luke. In short, he follows the same procedure he used in the composition of the Sermon on the Mount.

Two features of the discourse have much bearing on the interpretation: first, Matthew's retention of Jesus' original mandate to the Apostles (10:5-15); second, his expansion of the mandate to reflect the conditions of his own time (10:16-42). A study of Matthew's audience will show the significance of both features.

Matthew's audience

Read as an actual discourse of Jesus, Mt 10 has many puzzling features. Read as Matthew's discourse to Christian missionaries of the eighties, most of the puzzles find satisfying solutions.

Like the missionary mandate of 28:18-20, the missionary discourse envisions the conditions of the late first century. It is a time when Christian missionaries are still preaching to the Jews but with increasingly negative results. The Jews are not only not listening, they are persecuting the Christians, scourging them in their synagogues (10:17), delating them to pagan courts (10:18-20), accusing them of being in league with the devil (10:24-25), and reacting with such intolerance that they compel individual Jewish converts to Christianity to break with their own families (10:21; 34-39).[46]

If W. D. Davies is correct in his contention that "the Sermon on the Mount can be seen in its true perspective only against the Judaism of Jamnia,"[47] it would seem equally true, and for the same reasons, that the missionary discourse can be seen in its true perspective only against the background of the bitter struggle going on between the Christian Jews of Matthew's Church and their intolerant synagogue brethren.

Addressing himself both to Christian missionaries and their hearers, Matthew puts into the mouth of Jesus a discourse which (1) establishes the authority of the missionaries (10:1-5a,40);[48] (2) insists on their mandate to preach to Israel first (10:5b-16); (3) envisages the hostile reception they encounter at the hands of their recalcitrant Jewish brethren (10:17-25); (4) calls upon all, especially the Jews, to make the necessary decision for Christ, even though it brings about bitter dissension and the break-up

---

[46] For a similar situation in the Johannine Church, see J. L. Martyn, *History and Theology in the Fourth Gospel*. Martyn shows the importance the struggle with Judaism had in the shaping of the fourth gospel, a struggle equally important in the shaping of the first gospel.

[47] Cf. W. D. Davies, *The Sermon on the Mount*, p. 90.

[48] The impact of Matthew's discourse is largely lost on us because we have for so long taken for granted the authority of the Apostles in the Church. It was different for Matthew's readers. They were accustomed to look to Moses as the inspired and authoritative lawgiver and to the scribes and the Pharisees as the authoritative interpreters of the law. In this context, Matthew had to show them how the 'old' had passed and how it was that the Apostles had taken the place of the scribes and the Pharisees, just as Jesus had taken the place of Moses. The words of Jesus, "They are like sheep without shepherds" (9:36), foreshadow the commissioning of the Apostles, who will fill the vacuum of leadership in Israel (cf. 10:1-6; 16:17-19; 18:20; 23:1ff; 28:18-20).

of family ties (10:32-39). The discourse concludes with the significant reminder to all that "Anyone who welcomes you welcomes me; and those who welcome me, welcome the one who sent me" (10:40)[49] and with the encouraging promise that those will be rewarded who welcome the missionaries (10:41-42).

The movement of the discourse is from the traditional, and basically historical, mandate of Christ (10:5b-15) to the expanded mandate (10:16-25), and from the expanded mandate with its counterpoint theme, "Do not be afraid . . . I will be with you" (10:26-31), to a concluding section which deals with the attitudes of those to whom the message is preached (10:32-42). The discourse has five parts:

  a) 10:1-5a   Introduction with central theme of the discourse.
  b) 10:5b-15   The traditional mandate of the historical Jesus.
  c) 10:16-25   The hardships of apostleship. What has happened to the "Master" will happen to his "household."
  d) 10:26-31a   Encouragement: "Do not be afraid."
  e) 10:31b-42   Conclusion of the discourse: a warning to all who hear the gospel that it is imperative to make a decision in favor of Jesus and the Apostles whom he has sent as the Father sent him (10:40).

a) 10:1-5a / Introduction to the discourse

The discourse opens with a declaration of a central tenet of Matthew's gospel: the Apostles have received their authority directly from the teacher of the messianic Torah and the doer of the messianic deeds (10:1). In the context of the foregoing saying about the crowds being "like sheep without a shepherd" (9:36), the clear intimation of the missionary charge is that the Apostles have now become the shepherds of the sheep (cf. Jn 21:15-17).[50] In Mark's account (Mk 6:34), Jesus' compassion on the multitude because they are like sheep without a shepherd impels him to *teach* the multitudes. In Matthew's account, Jesus' compassion leads him to appoint new authoritative leaders to fill the vacuum of leadership left by the scribes and Pharisees.[51]

The declaration anticipates Jesus' similar declaration in 28:18 and like

---

[49] Of Matthew 10:40, J. Jeremias (*NTT*, 238) says: "The magnitude of the authority of the messengers becomes clear in the climactic parallelism:
ho dekomenos hymas eme deketai
kai ho eme dekomenos deketai ton aposteilanta me.
[50] The historicity of the twelve 'as a group' in the time of Jesus' ministry is disputed by some (cf. W. Schmithals, *The Office of Apostle in the Early Church*) and sustained by others (cf. E. Haenchen, *Acts*, 123-127). P. Meye (*Jesus and the Twelve*, 192-209) analyzes the problem and comes to the conclusion that ". . . the New Testament, and the Marcan picture of the Twelve as the company of Jesus is not at all

open to doubt. Careful examination of the critical view has the effect of demonstrating how firmly the Twelve are a part of Jesus' history. And this gives momentous support to the depiction of the first evangelist, who in narrating the gospel of Jesus Christ, in so many ways bears witness to his Lord as the Teacher who established a company of Twelve to be those about him" (p. 209).
[51] The expression "sheep without shepherds" is significant in the context of leadership because it was an old figure of speech used to describe the desperate situation of a nation without leadership (cf. Nm 27:17; 1 Kings 22:17; Ez 34:1ff; Jn 10:1ff).

28:18 entails the inevitable conclusion expressed at the end of the discourse: "He who welcomes you welcomes me; and those who welcome me, welcome the one who sent me" (10:40). At the same time, 10:1 neatly summarizes the narrative in ch 8–9 in words which describe the Apostles' authority as authority "over unclean spirits with power (*exousia*) to cast them out and to cure all kinds of diseases and sicknesses," an authority, therefore, similar to that exercised by Jesus himself in ch 8–9.

The abruptness with which Matthew introduces the twelve Apostles as a group in 10:2-4 seems unusual but probably only reflects the lateness of the gospel (c. 85 A.D.). At such a late date, Matthew can assume his readers' acquaintance with the oral tradition concerning the 'twelve' (cf. 1 Cor 15:5; Gal 1:18-19; Mk 1:16-20; 3:13-19; 6:7-13; Lk 5:1-11; 6:12-16: Jn 1:35-51) and perhaps even with the text of Mark's gospel.

b) 10:5b-15 / The mission of the Apostles

Our understanding of the precise way in which Jesus "sent" the twelve on a preaching mission in the course of his own ministry is a matter of dispute among scholars.[52] In any case, Matthew found it in his sources (Mk 6:7-13 and probably an account in the Q source) and used it for his own purposes. He incorporates the traditional missionary charge not simply out of reverence for the authentic words of Jesus but as testimony to an important fact of Salvation History theology.[53] The fact of the matter was that Jesus did indeed direct his own preaching primarily to the Jews. Matthew emphasizes the fact (cf. 10:5-6; 15:24) because Salvation History demanded that Jesus preach first to the Jews even though the prophets foretold the rejection of that preaching (cf. 13:10-15). Paul patterned himself on Jesus by preaching first to the Jews and then only to the Gentiles and in Rom 15:8 gives the explanation: "The reason Christ became the servant of circumcised Jews was . . . so that God could faithfully carry out the promises made to the patriarchs . . . ."

The saying of Jesus in 10:5b, "Do not turn your steps to pagan territory, and do not enter any Samaritan town; go rather to the lost sheep of the house of Israel," is probably the composition of Matthew, as expressive of the practice of the historical Jesus. The use of the saying has a theological purpose. The words emphasize Jesus' devotion to his own people and at the same time anticipate the Jews' rejection of Jesus, a rejection already anticipated in the infancy narrative account of Herod's persecution of the infant Jesus, foreshadowed in the sayings of 10:15, 34-36, confirmed in 11:16-24, and described at length in the passion account (cf. 27:20-26). It is because Jesus is rejected by his own that he is forced to provide new leaders for the shepherdless sheep of Israel.

Presupposing the substantial historicity of the Apostles' missionary tour during the ministry of Jesus, Matthew's instructions on the support of the missionaries (10:8b-15) make eminent sense and in all probability depend upon an authentic tradition of Jesus' actual words. As D. L. Dungan says: "In short, Matthew's version best attests an account of very early origin, probably based upon certain actual events in Jesus' public activity, describing how on a certain occasion he sent his disciples on a flying tour through the farms and towns of Galilee to proclaim the Kingdom's imminence."[54]

The limited scope of the mission precludes the necessity of provision for long range support. At the same time, however, Jesus lays down for the future a two-edged regulation concerning the support of missionaries. They are not to make money from preaching the gospel — "You received without charge, give without charge" (10:8b) — but at the same time they are to be supported by the voluntary contributions of the faithful — "for the workman deserves his keep" (10:10-11).[55]

Matthew's redactional purpose in this whole section (10:1-15) becomes evident when one considers the interplay of ideas in 9:37, 10:6,14-15,40, and 11:21-24. In 9:37 Jesus speaks of laborers for the harvest of souls in Israel. In 10:6 Jesus sends the Apostles to seek a harvest among the lost sheep of Israel. In 10:14-15, the "sheep" are warned that if they do not welcome Jesus' missionaries in their towns, "on the day of judgment, it will not go as hard with Sodom and Gomorrah as with that town" which does not welcome them. In 10:40 Jesus solemnly declares concerning his missionaries that "those who welcome you, welcome me, and those who welcome me, welcome him who sent me." The whole complex of ideas prepares the way for the condemnation of the Jews in 11:21-24 where Jesus declares they have not welcomed him and as a consequence bring down upon themselves the judgment: "I tell you that it will not go as hard with the land of Sodom on judgment day as with you" (11:24 and cp. 10:15).[56]

[52] The historicity of the mission of the twelve is supported by P. Meye, *Jesus and the Twelve*, 110-113; 198-199; by T. W. Manson, *The Sayings of Jesus*, p. 73; by V. Taylor, *The Gospel According to St. Mark*, p. 302. F. W. Beare, "The Mission of the Disciples and the Mission Charge: Matthew 10 and Parallels" *JBL* 89 (March 1970) 1-13, equivalently denies the historicity of the mission. He says: ". . . if there were indeed such a mission, we have so little information about it that it is not worth while to argue for or against its historicity" (p. 13).

[53] It is difficult to identify authentic words of Jesus, and the variations between Matthew, Mark, and Luke on the exact wording of the traditional missionary charge of Jesus make it impossible to identify the precise words.

[54] Cf. D. L. Dungan, *The Sayings of Jesus in the Churches of Paul*, 63. Dungan's form-critical study of Mt 10:1-16 takes into account in a particularly felicitous manner the originality of the material, the rabbinic attitude toward missionary support as contrasted with the Qumran

and later Jamnian attitude, and Matthew's attitude (*op. cit.*, 53-63).

[55] This regulation accounts for Matthew's incorporating the material in his discourse which is properly directed to missionaries of his own time.

[56] Although he does not advert to Matthew's theological and redactional use of the material in Mt 9:38 and 10:14b, D. L. Dungan understands perfectly the import of the ideas. He says: "The action Jesus here requires of his emissaries [in 10:14f] is nothing less than the eschatological curse. This is the meaning of wiping off the dust of the town's streets: 'we want no part of you, even the dust from your streets, *for you are to be utterly destroyed!*' What is being laid on the shoulders of the disciples is nothing less than the task of 'harvesting' (Mt 9:38) the crop of the elect. Along with their authorization to pronounce the eschatological curse they will bring eschatological blessing" (*op. cit.*, 56).

c) 10:16-25 / The hardships of apostleship

In composing 10:16-25, Matthew borrows from Mark almost word for word (cf. Mk 13:9-13) and directs himself to his contemporaries as Mark had to his in the apocalyptic discourse (Mk 13). The persecutions mentioned in 10:16-25 are applicable only to the period after the ministry of Jesus.[57]

Floggings in the synagogues, delations to pagan courts, and disruptions of family unity occurred only after the death of Jesus and only at a time when Judaism began to consider the new Christian sect heretical. That this happened relatively early, perhaps as early as the forties, can be gathered from Paul's references to the number of times the Jews had him scourged, stoned, and imprisoned (cf. 2 Cor 11:23-27). There is no indication, however, that such persecution took place during the ministry of Jesus.

Almost everything in 10:16-25, therefore, would be out of historical context in the time of the traditional missionary mandate. Nothing, however, would be out of context in the time of Matthew. It is in the context of the struggle between Judaism and Christianity in Matthew's time that Matthew's words should be interpreted.[57a]

In short, Matthew has Jesus speak to the Christian missionaries of the eighties to remind them that "the disciple is not superior to his teacher" and that "if they have called the master of the house Beelzebul, what will they not say of his household?" (10:24-26).

It is Matthew's Church that is the "household" of Jesus, and the missionaries may expect the same treatment from their Jewish contemporaries as Jesus received from his. It is against this background that the warnings and promises of the next two sections of the discourse (10:26-31a and 10:31b-42) can be seen to make sense.

d) 10:26-31a / Encouragement: "Do not be afraid!"

In his final missionary mandate in 28:18-20, Matthew will present Christ as the Son of Man who has received all authority from the Father and who, enjoying absolute authority, commissions his Apostles as Yahweh had commissioned the Old Testament prophets (cf. Jer 1; Ez 1–2).[58]

In the two places where Matthew is concerned with the mission of the

---

[57] Jesus' statement in 10:23, "You will not have gone the round of the towns of Israel before the Son of Man comes" has found no fully satisfactory explanation. If understood as Matthew's quotation of the actual words of Jesus, it becomes a sheer enigma, unless one holds with those who claim that Jesus was mistaken about the meaning and time of his coming. If understood as Matthew's statement in reference to the fall of Jerusalem, i.e., to the time when the Son of Man brought to a definite close the Old Testament era by his 'visitation' and destruction of Jerusalem and the Temple in 71 A.D., the statement not only makes sense but puts Matthew's remarks in the context of missionary work *after* 71 A.D. Matthew, like Paul before him (cf. 9–11), looks upon the Jewish rejection of Jesus as a fact of Salvation History which had come about prior to 71 A.D. and was considered definitive once Jerusalem and the Temple had been destroyed. For a dissenting opinion, see Albright-Mann, *Matthew*, p. xcvii and p. 125.

[57a] See the nuanced conclusions of D. R. A. Hare's *The Theme of Jewish Persecution of Christians in the Gospel according to St. Matthew* (167-171).

[58] See C. Westermann, *The Basic Forms of Prophetic Speech*.

Apostles (10:1ff; 28:18-20), the basic elements of the Old Testament prophetic commission can be found: a) the commission, i.e., the expression of an authoritative mandate (cf. 10:1,5-6,40); b) the mission, i.e., the message the Apostle is to preach or the work he is to perform (cf. 10:5-8); c) the encouraging assurance: "Fear not, I will be with you" or its equivalent. The most succinct formulation of this last element is found in the account of Jeremiah's inaugural vision:

> Say not, "I am too young."
> To whomever I send you, you shall go;
> whatever I command you, you shall speak.
> *Have no fear* before them,
> *because I am with you* to deliver you,
> says the Lord (Jer 1:7-8).

In 10:26-31a, it is the third element of the missionary mandate that Matthew emphasizes. Matthew has Jesus three times repeat the words "Do not be afraid" (10:26,28,31). The third time, Jesus says: "Do not be afraid" because "every hair on your head has been counted . . . you are worth more than hundreds of sparrows" (10:29-31a), equivalently saying: "Do not be afraid because I am with you to deliver you."

Earlier in the gospel, Matthew had recalled how Christ said to the Apostles: "Blest are you when they insult you and persecute you and utter every kind of slander against you because of me. Be glad and rejoice, for your reward is great in heaven; they persecuted the *prophets* before you *in the very same way*" (5:11-12).

Later in his gospel, Matthew will have Jesus say to the Pharisees: "For this reason I shall send you *prophets* and wise men and scribes. Some you will kill and crucify, others you will flog in your synagogues and hunt down from city to city" (23:34).

For Matthew, the Apostles are to the New Covenant era what the prophets, the wise men, and the scribes (cf. 13:52) were to the Old Covenant era. When he speaks about their mission, therefore, he does not hesitate to use the Old Testament literary format for establishing the authority of a prophet.

e) 10:31b-42 / Conclusion: a warning to Matthew's readers

In the conclusion to his discourse, Matthew has Jesus look beyond the Apostles, who are the immediate audience, to the circle of Christians and Jews who will read the gospel. To be consistent in his literary presentation, which is a discourse directed to the Apostles by Jesus, Matthew can only speak to his readers in an oblique way. He does so by his use of the indeterminate "anyone" (cf. 10:31b, 37, 40, 41, 42). The "anyone" is his readers and especially, it would seem, his Jewish readers who are "on the fence," hesitating or fearing to make a decision which would involve their leaving the synagogue to join the Christian Church.

It is almost as if Matthew said to them: "You have heard the Messiah authoritatively commission his Apostles as Yahweh authoritatively commissioned the prophets. You must now decide whether you will accept his messengers and their message." In short, whereas Jesus had said to his Apostles, "Do not be afraid" (10:26-31a), he now says to the readers of Matthew's gospel: "You must make a decision one way or another" (10:31a-33); "the decision will involve great sacrifice, but you must make it" (10:34-39); "you must welcome my Apostles as you would welcome me" (10:40-42).

THE REJECTION OF PSEUDO-ISRAEL
Mt 11:1—12:50

Characteristic of Matthaean composition in ch 11–12 are the following: (1) the use of inclusion-conclusion (cf. 11:2-6 in relation to 4:12-17); (2) the quotation of a messianic text from Isaiah (Is 42:1-4 = Mt 12:18-21) with the usual fulfillment formula (Mt 12:17); (3) the inclusion of some concentric-circle themes: a) the authority of Jesus (cf. 11:25-27); b) the messianic Torah (cf. 12:1-14); c) universality (cf. 12:18-21); (4) the typical Matthaean emphasis on the opposition between Jesus and the Pharisees (cf. 11:18-19; 12:9-14; 12:22-45) and between the pseudo and the true Israel[59] (cf. 11:20-27; 12:46-50); (5) the Matthaean propensity for the number seven (cf. 12:45); (6) the use of keywords to focus the themes (e.g., "someone greater than," "this perverse generation," "on judgment day"); (7) the use of a subtle transition passage to connect the narrative in ch 11–12 with the discourse in ch 13 (cf. 12:46-50).

The function of the narrative

Matthew's narrative in ch 11–12 prepares the way for the discourse in ch 13. Again, as in dealing with the narratives in ch 1–4 and ch 8–9, it will suffice to indicate the basic themes of ch 13 and then note how these themes have influenced Matthew's selection of material and use of keywords in ch 11–12.

In ch 13 the major themes for which Matthew prepares his audience in his narrative are (1) the turning of Jesus from the pseudo-Israel which has rejected him to the continuing, true Israel that accepts him, i.e., to the community of the Church which constitutes the true Israel; (2) the characteristics of the true Israel, which hears and understands Jesus and does

[59] Cf. M. Jack Suggs, *Wisdom, Christology, and Law in Matthew's Gospel.* Suggs provides a particularly penetrating study of Mt 11; also W. Wink, *John the Baptist in the Gospel Tradi-* tion, 18-41 but especially pp. 23-26; 29-30; 40-41; 112; Bornkamm, Barth, Held, *op. cit.,* 250ff; N. Perrin, *Rediscovering the Teaching of Jesus,* 74-77; 85f; 105f; 119f.

the will of the Father in contrast to the pseudo-Israel which neither accepts nor understands the "word" of Jesus.

Matthew emphasizes these themes not only by his choice of material but also by his use of keywords. The key words in ch 11–12 are: (1) "*someone greater than*" — Jesus is the "someone greater than" John the Baptist (11:11), the Temple (12:7), Jonah the prophet (12:41), Solomon (12:42); (2) "*this perverse generation*", i.e., the pseudo-Israel (cf. 11:16,20,25; 12:39,41,42,45); (3) "*on judgment day*" (cf. 11:22,24; 12:36,42,44).[60]

The implicit argument of the keywords summarizes the message of the narrative and points up its function. Its function is to highlight the failure of the pseudo-Israel and at the same time call attention to the disciples of Christ who constitute the true Israel. Its message is that Jesus, who is the "someone greater than" John the Baptist, the Temple, Jonah, and Solomon, has announced the Kingdom and has been rejected along with John the Baptist by "this perverse generation," the pseudo-Israel of the Pharisees. Since pseudo-Israel has refused to listen and repent, it will be condemned "on judgment day" and the Kingdom will be given to those "to whom the Son chooses to reveal him (the Father)" (11:27). This theme will be elaborated more forcefully in ch 21 in the parables of the "barren fig tree" (21:18-22), the "two sons" (21:28-32), and the "wicked husbandmen" (21:33-46).

The movement of Matthew's thought in ch 11–12 oscillates between belief and unbelief, with emphasis on unbelief implicit in the keynote statement: "Blessed is he who is not scandalized in me" (11:6).[61] The arrangement of the material, as in Mt 8–9, is chiasmic, i.e., a, b, a[1]:

a) 11:2-27   The condemnation of pseudo-Israel[62] which has rejected Jesus (11:7-24) and the designation of the true Israel which has accepted him (11:25-27).

b) 11:28–12:21 Jesus' interpretation of the Law which the Pharisees reject (11:28–12:14), forcing him to turn to the Gentiles (12:15-21).

a[1]) 12:22-50   The condemnation of pseudo-Israel (12:22-45) and the designation of the true Israel (12:46-50).

---

[60] It is unclear whether the "judgment day" referred to is (1) the final eschatological judgment (as in Mt 25:31-46); (2) the day of Jesus' passion and death (cf. 26:64); (3) the fall of Jerusalem in 70 A.D. (Mt 24:15-21). Least likely is (1). Equally possible are (2) and (3).

[61] "To be scandalized in me" means to sin, or to be caused to sin, in the sense that, faced with the messianic words and works of Jesus, the Pharisees and pseudo-Israel in general sin by not accepting Jesus as the one sent by God. Note that the Apostles are "blessed" in 5:11-12 and Peter in 16:17, and the gospel makes it clear that it is the disciples in general who are "not scandalized in Jesus" precisely because they accept him.

[62] The use of the expression "pseudo-Israel" is intentional. Authors speak of the "old Israel" and the "new Israel," but in Matthew's mind (and in Paul's as well, cf. Rom 9–11) there is only one Israel, the true Israel, which is made up of those who believe and do God's will whether in the Old Testament or the New Testament era. According to Matthew's concept of the Kingdom of heaven, Jesus did not found a "new Israel." Those who were not "scandalized" in Jesus but accepted him bridged the gap between the Old and New Testament eras and thus constituted the continuing "true Israel." That large part of the Jewish nation which did not accept Jesus broke with the true Irsael of the Old Testament and from the time of Jesus onwards constituted what we have termed the "pseudo-Israel."

a) 11:2-27 / Condemnation of pseudo-Israel and designation of true Israel

The change in tone between ch 1–10 and ch 11–28 warrants believing Matthew has entered into a new stage of development in his presentation of Jesus and the Kingdom of heaven.

Ch 1–10 concentrated on establishing the authority of Jesus as Messiah and one "greater than" Moses. It presented as testimony to Jesus' authority the witnesses of John the Baptist, the voice from heaven, Jesus' own preaching (ch 5–7) and acting (ch 8–9) with authority. In addition, ch 10 indicated Jesus would pass on this authority to his Apostles (cf. 5:11-16; 10:1ff).

Ch 11–28 concentrates on the condemnation of pseudo-Israel, on the designation and characteristics of the true Israel, and on the true Israel's authority and mission as the Apostolic community sent into the world to preach the gospel to all nations.

Matthew had already foreshadowed the themes of ch 11–28 in his opening thelogical construct (ch 1–2). Herod's persecution of Jesus foreshadowed the persecution of Jesus by the pseudo-Israel. The coming of the Magi foreshadowed the new community which, in contradistinction to the pseudo-Israel, would accept Jesus as Messiah and King.

It seems then that ch 11:2-27 serves as a theological construct for ch 11–28 just as ch 1–2 served as a theological construct for the gospel as a whole. It comes at the strategic position for a theological construct, i.e., at the beginning of part two of the gospel. It clarifies the more obscure foreshadowings of ch 1–2 dealing with pseudo-Israel's rejection and true Israel's acceptance of Jesus. In addition, it serves as a major transition from the first to the second part of the gospel.

The transition is clear in the recapitulation of ch 1–10 provided by ch 11:2-5 and in the new direction indicated for part two of the gospel by the vehement rejection of pseudo-Israel (11:6-24; 12:15-45) and the designation of the true Israel (11:25-27; 12:46-50). The teaching of the discourse on the Kingdom in ch 13 validates the thesis. In ch 13, Jesus turns away from the "Jews" who refuse to "hear" him and concentrates on his disciples who not only "hear" him but "understand" him.

With the theological construct in 11:2-27, then, Matthew begins the second part of his gospel. In ch 11–12, he will emphasize pseudo-Israel's rejection; in ch 13, the turning of Jesus from the pseudo to the true Israel; in ch 14–17, the authority of the Apostles in the true Israel; in ch 18, the use and abuse of authority in the true Israel; in ch 19–25, true as opposed to false discipleship; in ch 26–28, the passion, death, and resurrection of the Son of Man; and in ch 28:18-20, the authoritative mission of the true Israel to disciplize all nations. The theological construct in 11:2-27 has three parts: (1) 11:2-5, (2) 11:6-24, (3) 11:25-27.

1) 11:2-5 / *Recapitulation of ch 1–10*

The Baptist's question, "Are you the one 'who is to come?'" poses the question Matthew has already answered in ch 1–10. In ch 1–2, he established the messianic ancestry of Jesus. In ch 3, he adduced the witness of John to Jesus as Messiah. In ch 5–7, he established the authority of Jesus 'in word'. In ch 8–9, he established Jesus' authority 'in deed.'

John's question could not be more specific. It begins with the observation that John had heard of the "works of the Christ" (*ta erga tou Xristou*), i.e., of the Messiah. It continues by using the title "the one who is to come," which is a messianic title from either Dt 18:15 or Ps 118:26.

Jesus' answer, "Tell John what you *hear* and *see*," alludes respectively to what they have *heard* (the Sermon on the Mount, ch 5–7) and what they have *seen* (the ten miracles, ch 8–9). Matthew indicates the works they have *seen* are messianic works characteristically through his allusions to the prophecies of Isaiah. In his collection of miracles in ch 8–9, Matthew purposely gave examples of the miracles characteristic of the messianic age as predicted by Isaiah, e.g.:

Is 29:18f	In that day the *deaf shall hear*	(cf. Mt 9:32-34)
	the eyes of the *blind shall see*	(cf. Mt 9:27-31)
Is 35:5f	Then the eyes of the *blind* shall be opened, and the ears of the *deaf* unstopped; then shall the lame man leap like a hart	(cf. Mt 8:5-18)
	and the tongue of the *dumb* sing for joy	(cf. Mt 9:32-34)
Is 61:1f	The Spirit of the Lord God is upon me, ... to bring *good tidings to the poor*	(cf. Mt 5:1-10)

John's question, Jesus' answer, and the allusions to the messianic signs predicted by Isaiah testify to the messianic authority of Jesus and suitably summarize the argumentation of ch 1–10.[64]

While serving as a recapitulation of ch 1–10, 11:2-5 also functions as a sort of inclusion-conclusion, recalling the reader's attention to 4:12-17, and thus marking the end of a large section of the gospel. The reader should compare the two passages:

4:17	John is put in prison.	11:2	John is in prison.
4:14	Matthew says Isaiah's prophecy is fulfilled: Jesus will be "a light in Galilee," i.e., through his preaching (ch 5–7) and through his miracles (ch 8–9).	11:4-5	Jesus mentions his messianic works which prove he has indeed been the "light in Galilee" predicted by Isaiah.

In passing, it should be noted that recognition of John's question in 11:2-3 as part of a *literary construction* (at least in Matthew, though not

Cf. Bornkamm, Barth, Held, *op. cit.*, 250-253.

necessarily in Lk 7:18-20), aimed at a recapitulation of Mt 3–10, may well dispose of the problem, agonized over by commentators, whether John, who had testified to Jesus as the Messiah at an earlier stage of his career, might not have entertained doubts about Jesus later on (cf. the question: "Are you the one who is to come?"). The literary technique utilized by Matthew in 11:2-6 makes it possible that John's sending of messengers to calm his doubts about Jesus is more literary-fictional than historical. At least it leaves the question open.

2) 11:6-24 / *The condemnation of "this generation"*

The second part of Matthew's theological construct begins with the keynote statement: "Blest is the man who finds no stumbling block in me" (11:6). As Matthew will show in recounting Jesus' condemnation of the Jews (11:16-20), the Jews have found in Jesus a great stumbling block.

Jesus' questions about John (11:7-9) have as their purpose to establish John as a prophet whose testimony to Jesus the Jews should have accepted (cf. Mt 21:24-26). Jesus' assertion that John is more than a prophet is made on the assumption that since Jesus is the Messiah, John, as a consequence, must be the prophet par excellence of whom Malachy spoke when he said: "I send my messenger ahead of you to prepare your way before you" (Mal 3:1). Since Jesus is the Messiah, it follows that John is the Elijah who was to return in the days of the Messiah (11:10-14). It follows, therefore, that anyone who has "ears to listen," should listen to John as an authentic prophet (11:15).[65]

The Jews will listen neither to John nor to Jesus (11:16-19). It should be recalled in relation to Jesus' condemnation of the Jews for not listening either to him or to John the Baptist that Matthew had John preaching the same basic message as Jesus: "Reform your lives! The kingdom of heaven is at hand" (cf. 3:2; 4:17). Since the Jews do not have "ears to listen," they refuse to listen to John (11:18) and to Jesus (11:19). As a consequence, they are condemned (11:20-24).

3) 11:25-27 / *Jesus turns to the true Israel*

Matthew ends his theological construct by having Jesus turn to those who "know" him and the Father whom he has revealed to them.[66] This highly theological statement sets the tone and direction of the remainder of the gospel. From this point on, Matthew will have Jesus concentrate his attention on the instruction and strengthening of the true Israel. There will be little public and much private instruction, as a consequence, in the remainder of the gospel.

b) 11:28–12:21 / Jesus' interpretation of the law

In 11:2-27 Matthew dealt with unbelief and belief, the major difference between the pseudo-Israel and the true Israel. In 11:28–12:21 he deals with

---

[65] Cf. M. Jack Suggs, *op. cit.*, p. 55.

[66] For a discussion of the theological content of 11:25-27, see M. Jack Suggs, *op. cit.*, 83-97.

a major difference between Jesus and the Pharisees, namely, the difference between Jesus' and the Pharisees' interpretation of the law.[67]

To a certain extent there is a reprise in 11:28–12:21 of the first two sections of the Sermon on the Mount. Here as there Jesus speaks first about the characteristics of the true Israel (cp. the beatitudes in 5:2-10 and Jesus' characterization of himself as "gentle and humble of heart" in 11:28-30) and then about the interpretation of the law (cp. the antitheses in 5:21-48 and the two stories dealing with the interpretation of the Sabbath law in 12:1-14). Here as there, Jesus speaks as one "greater than" Moses. The "greater than" Moses is implicit in the statement, "The Son of Man is indeed Lord of the Sabbath" (12:8). It is implicit also in his statement, "take my yoke upon your shoulders and learn from me" (11:29). The "yoke" was a rabbinical term for the law. When Jesus speaks about "my yoke," he is speaking first about his law as expounded in the Sermon on the Mount (5:17-48), but secondly, and more properly, about his interpretation of the law as contrasted with that of the Pharisees.

The two miracle stories that follow (12:1-14) are recounted by Matthew not for the sake of the miracles but for the sake of the light they cast on Jesus' interpretation as opposed to the Pharisees' interpretation of the law seen as the expression of God's will.

In 22:34-40, as in the Sermon on the Mount though less clearly there, Jesus will declare that the law of love is not only the law of laws (a thesis the Pharisees would agree with) but the law against which or according to which all other laws must be interpreted. Here in 12:1-14, as in 22:34-40, it is Jesus' insistence on the law of love as the law in the light of which all other law are to be interpreted that separates him from the Pharisees.[67a]

In Mark's gospel (2:23–3:6), the same two stories formed part of a collection of stories (Mk 2:1–3:6) whose purpose was to emphasize the opposition between Jesus and the Pharisees. In Matthew, the opposition motif is still present (Mt 12:14-15), but what is emphasized is not simple opposition but opposition on the basis of differing interpretations of the law. The stories as they stand in Matthew are meant to serve as a commentary on Jesus' words, "my yoke is easy and my burden light" (11:30).

The section ends up in typical Matthaean fashion with a quotation from Isaiah (Is 42:1-4 = Mt 12:15-21) recalling how Isaiah had long before predicted the Messiah would "proclaim justice (Hebrew: *mishpat* in the sense of Torah or law) to the Gentiles" (Mt 12:18).[68]

c) 12:22-50 / Condemnation of pseudo-Israel and designation of true Israel

In the first part of his narrative in preparation for the discourse in ch 13,

---

[67] For the wisdom motif in this section, see M. Jack Suggs, *op. cit.*
[67a] See pp. 150-154.

[68] Cf. J. Grindel, "Matthew XII 18-21" *CBQ* 29 (Jan 1967) 110-115.

Matthew spoke in general terms about pseudo-Israel as "this generation" (11:16-24) and about true Israel as "mere children" (11:25-27). In 12:22-50, which balances chiasmically with 11:2-27, Matthew is more specific. Pseudo-Israel is "this generation" led by the scribes and Pharisees (12:22-45), and the true Israel is specifically identified with Jesus' disciples (12:46-50).

In the first part of the narrative (11:6-24), "this generation" was threatened with condemnation because it would heed neither John nor Jesus and because it ignored the witness of Jesus' messianic signs. In the last part of the narrative (12:22-45), "this generation" led by the scribes and the Pharisees is accused of far more heinous crimes. They are guilty of blaspheming against the Spirit of God (12:22-32) and of *willful* blindness to the testimony of the signs Jesus had already performed (12:38-42). Their situation, as a consequence, is described in the direst terms. They are on the way to becoming like a house infested with seven evil spirits, i.e., totally evil (12:43-45).

Matthew has made his case against the Pharisees. In 12:46-50 he terminates his narrative with a passage taken from Mark (Mk 3:31-35). In typical Matthaean fashion, the passage serves as an excellent transition to the discourse which follows in ch 13. Jesus identifies the true as opposed to the pseudo-Israel by "stretching out his hand toward his disciples" and by saying: "Here are my mother and my brothers" (12:49). In ch 13 he will make the same distinction between the true and the pseudo-Israel by pointing to the Jews as those who neither listen nor understand his words and to his disciples as those who both listen and understand (cf. 13:10-17, 51-52).

THE DISCOURSE ON THE KINGDOM
Mt 13:1-53

The parable discourse[69] has the typical characteristics of Matthaean composition: (1) it takes its point of departure from Mark 4:1ff; (2) it contains "seven" parables as opposed to five in Mark's discourse; (3) it deals with several of the concentric themes summarized in Mt 28:18-20, namely, a) universality (cf. 13:32-33; 13:38); b) discipleship (cf. 13:36-50); c) the "end-time" (cf. 13:30; 13:41-43; 13:49-50); (4) it makes use of an Isaian text with the fulfilment formula to make a point (cf. 13:14-15); (5) there is the customary ending formula (cf. 13:53).

What is noticeable about Matthew's composition is the way he has struc-

---

[69] See J. D. Kingsbury, *The Parables of Jesus in Matthew 13*; J. Jeremias, *The Parables of Jesus; New Testament Theology*, 96-121; C. H. Dodd, *The Parables of the Kingdom*; W. F. Albright, *Matthew*, cxxxii ff; G. D. Buttrick (ed.), *Jesus and Man's Hope*, Vol. II, 287-304; D. Crossan, "Parable as Religious and Poetic Experience" *JR* 53 (July 1973) 330-358; "The Seed Parables of Jesus" *JBL* 92 (June 1973) 244-266.

tured the discourse to emphasize the central themes of ch 11–12 — the rejection of pseudo-Israel and the continuity of the true Israel in the community of the disciples (cf. 12:43-50 where Matthew has made this theme the transition from his narrative to his discourse).

The discourse is so structured that in the first half (13:1-35) Matthew has Jesus *outside the house* (cf. 13:1) speaking to the *Jews who do not understand* him; and in the second half (13:36-52) has Jesus *inside the house speaking to the disciples* who do *understand* him. The distinction between unhearing and unrepentant Israel and the disciples who hear and obey, so central to ch 11–12, is thus built into the structure of the discourse on the Kingdom.

The function of Mt 13 within the overall plan of Matthew's gospel as a consequence is to indicate the *turning point* in Jesus' attitude toward the Jews. From ch 13 on, Matthew has Jesus concentrating on the instruction of the disciples and the messianic community.

The turning point is indicated not only by the structure of the chapter but by Matthew's choice of terms. He continually refers to the unrepentant Jews as "them" (cf. 13:3,10,13,24,31,33,34), indicating the distinction he makes between the Jews and the disciples. He introduces the term parable here for the first time, uses it twelve times, and so uses the term that by his definition the parables are enigmatic to the Jews but understood (with and sometimes without instruction) by the disciples (cf. 13:10-17, 51-53).

It has been pointed out in discussing the structure of the gospel[70] that Matthew designedly placed the discourse on the Kingdom at the chiasmic center of his gospel. The build-up to the Kingdom as the center of the gospel can now be seen more clearly.

In ch 3:2 Matthew introduced the Baptist with the words: "Repent, for the kingdom of heaven is close at hand." In 4:17 he introduced Christ's preaching with the same words. In ch 5–10 he showed Christ demonstrating by word and work that he was the "light" predicted by Isaiah and that in him the *Kingdom* "close at hand" had truly arrived.

In ch 11:6-19 Matthew has Jesus first authenticate John as a prophet and then proceed to show that the Jews have accepted neither the preaching of John nor his own. In substance, they have heard John and Jesus proclaim: "Repent, for the kingdom of heaven is close at hand"; and they have neither repented nor accepted the message of the Kingdom. For this they are condemned by Christ (11:20-24) who then turns to the true Israel (11:25-27).

The Kingdom preached by John and Jesus and rejected by the Jews becomes the subject of the parable discourse. The discourse begins with the parable of the sower (13:4-9) which is interpreted in 13:18 in relation

---

[70] See pp. 10-13.

to the preaching of the "word of the kingdom": "You, therefore, are to hear the parable of the sower. When anyone hears the *word of the kingdom without understanding* . . . ." The parable is made by Matthew to serve as a summary of Christ's preaching to the Jews and to illustrate graphically the negative reception accorded the message: "Repent, for the kingdom of heaven is close at hand."

The Word of the Kingdom has not fared well in the soil of Galilee except in the case of "the one who received the seed . . . hears the word and understands it." The theme of the one who "hears and understands" is important because it bears on the question of who is the pseudo- and who the true Israel and because it contributes to Matthew's delineation of the disciples as those who "understand" Jesus' teaching and are prepared thereby for their mission to teach all that Christ has commanded them (28:18-19).

A comparison with Mark's parable discourse (Mk 4:1-35) shows how radically Matthew's version differs and how he has changed it to make it serve his own purposes.

Where Mark has five parables, Matthew has seven. Two of Matthew's parables are found in Mark (the sower and the mustard seed); five are peculiar to him (the darnel, the leaven, the treasure in the field, the pearl, and the dragnet). Where Mark uses the parable sermon to show that the Kingdom will succeed despite the opposition of the forces of evil, Matthew uses the sermon to identify the true Israel and to describe the salient characteristics of the Kingdom. The discourse has two parts.

Part I / The Kingdom and the Jews who neither hear nor understand (13:1-35)

vv 1-3 The setting: a) outside the house;
b) addressed to all.

vv 4-9 The sower and the seed (the word of the Kingdom which the Jews have rejected).

vv 10-17 Matthew's parable theory. Matthew arbitrarily defines the parables as enigmatic to the Jews, in fulfilment of the prophecy of Is 6:9-10, but comprehensible to the disciples to whom "the mysteries of the Kingdom of heaven are revealed" (13:11 and cp. 11:25-27). The quotation (Mt 13:14-15) from Is 6:9-10 expresses perfectly the theme of rejection.

vv 18-23 Explanation of the parable of the sower against the background of the Jews' rejection of Christ's preaching in Galilee (cf. 4:17–11:24).

vv 24-30 The parable of the darnel which Jesus will explain in 13:36-43.

vv 31-32 The parable of the mustard seed explaining how the little community of the Christians will someday develop into a universal Kingdom as symbolized by the great tree of Dn 4:9,18, where the tree represents the Kingdom of the Son of Man (cf. Dn 7:13).

v 33   The parable of the leaven — a companion parable to the parable of the mustard seed. Note how Matthew balances the parables of the mustard seed and the leaven with the two brief parables of the treasure hidden in a field and the pearl of great value (13:44-46).[71]

vv 34-35   Addendum to the parable theory of 13:10-17 with a reference to the fulfilment of the words of Ps 78:2 — a psalm which deals with Israel's history leading up to the foundation of the messianic dynasty of David (cf. Ps 78:65-72). The allusion to the context of the psalm provides a transition to the second half of the discourse which deals with the messianic Kingdom of the Son of Man (cf. 13:41).

Part II / The Kingdom and discipleship (13:36-52)

vv 36-37   The setting: a) inside the house;
                            b) addressed only to the disciples.

vv 38-43   The explanation of the darnel reminds the disciples that there will be good and bad in the Kingdom (the messianic community) and the ultimate distinction will be made only at the end of time by the Son of Man (cf. 25:31-46). The allusion to Dn 12:3 in v 43 recalls the allusion to the imagery of the messianic Kingdom-tree of 13:32 and foreshadows the numerous allusions to Dn 7:13 and the Son of Man and his Kingdom in the remainder of the gospel (cf. especially 24:15,30,37,44; 25:31; 26:64; 28:18).

v 44   The parable of the treasure emphasizes the privilege and the price of discipleship, reminding the disciples that it is not enough to be a member of the messianic community in which, according to the explanation of the darnel, there will be good and bad. The good will be those who have paid the cost of discipleship by selling all to possess it (cf. 19:1-12,16-29; 20:20-28).

vv 45-46   The pearl of great value, a companion parable to the treasure hidden in the field, is added in order to provide chiasmic balance with the two short parables in the first half of the discourse (13:31-33).

vv 47-50   The parable of the dragnet balances off the parable of the darnel and contains the same message.

vv 51-52   The conclusion of the sermon emphasizes what had already been said concerning the disciples who see and hear in 13:16-17 and foreshadowed in 11:25-27. The "understanding" of the disciples looks forward to their further instruction in "the mysteries of the Kingdom of heaven" in ch 14–25 and to their eventual commission to "make disciples of all nations, baptizing . . . and *teaching* them to observe all I have commanded you" (28:18-20).

v 53   Matthew concludes the sermon with his customary ending formula.

[71] See R. W. Funk, "Beyond Criticism in Quest of Literacy: The Parable of the Leaven," *Interpretation* 25 (April 1971) 149-170; J. Jeremias, *op. cit.,* 149; C. H. Dodd, *op. cit.,* 155f.

THE COMMUNITY, PETER, AND DISCIPLESHIP
Mt 13:54–17:27

In Matthew's first three narrative complexes (ch 1–4; 8–9; 11–12), the functional relationship of the narratives to the subsequent discourses (ch 5–7; 10; 13) was easy to establish because of Matthew's extremely artificial selection and arrangement of material from Mark and the Q source.

In the second half of the gospel (ch 14–28), the relationship of the narratives (ch 14–17; 19–22; 26–28) to the discourses (ch 18; 23–25; 28:18-20) is not so readily recognizable because Matthew remains remarkably faithful to the traditional sequence of events given in Mark. Any synopsis will show that Matthew's narrative in ch 14–17 contains almost everything in Mk 6–9 and his narrative in ch 19–22 almost everything in Mk 10–12.

It would appear that Matthew has abandoned his wholesale rearrangement of Mark's material because the material in Mk 6–12 served his purposes almost as it stood. In Mt 1–10 wholesale redaction was necessary because Matthew wanted to emphasize the authority of Jesus as Messiah and as one "greater than" Moses. The same procedure was necessary in ch 11–13 in order to establish Matthew's thesis that pseudo-Israel had rejected Jesus and that as a consequence the true Israel was to be found henceforward in the community of Jesus' disciples.

In Mk 6–12 the major part of the material already dealt with the themes of discipleship and the messianic community. Since Matthew intended to focus his attention on these two themes in the rest of his gospel and particularly in ch 14–17; 19–22, it sufficed for him to take the material almost as it stood and re-orientate it to his discourses by means of minor changes and additions.

Whatever the reason,[72] the interpreter of ch 14–17 and ch 19–22 must make do with the available redactional evidence. The evidence consists of two sorts. First, the now demonstrated presupposition that Matthew structures and redacts his narratives in order to have them prepare the way for the subsequent discourses should lead us to expect that the themes of the subsequent discourse will be prepared for in some way in the preceding narrative. Second, Matthew's retention of the Markan material with almost perfect fidelity to the Markan sequence of events will make all the more significant any additions to the Markan narrative and any consistently different emphases not found in the Markan narrative.

Function of the narrative

As usual we may expect Matthew's narrative to prepare the way for his discourse in ch 18. This is true, however, only to a limited extent in ch 14–17. The discourse in ch 18 deals with the question of "who is the greatest in the

---

[72] See F. V. Filson, "Broken Patterns in the Gospel of Matthew, " *JBL* 75 (1956) 227ff.

kingdom of heaven," i.e., in the community, and also with the forgiveness of sinful members of the community. The forgiveness theme is prepared for in two places: first, in 14:28-33, where Peter, who will ask the question about forgiveness in 18:21, is implicitly forgiven his lack of faith on the waters; and, second, in 16:19, where Peter is given the power of the keys, a power which deals with the situation of sinners in the community. The preparation for the theme "who is the greatest" is for more complex.

The narrative has three parts, each of which terminates with a pericope about Peter. Part I (13:53–14:33) terminates with the episode about Peter on the waters (14:28-33); Part II (14:34–16:20), with the promise of the primacy (16:17-19); Part III (16:21–17:27), with the story about Peter paying the tax for Jesus and himself (17:24-27). By concluding each section in this way, Matthew lets the structure of the narrative as a whole point up the pre-eminence of Peter and thus prepare the way for the theme "who is the greatest?"

The preparation for this theme is most evident in Matthew's additions. The Apostle Peter already stood out in the Markan material as the spokesman of the Apostles (cf. Mk 8:29; 9:5). In the Matthaean redaction, however, Peter is made even more prominent.

Three new incidents dealing with Peter are introduced by Matthew: (1) Peter comes to Jesus on the water (14:28-31); (2) Peter is called the "rock" and given the power of the keys (16:13-20); (3) Peter is consulted by Jesus about the paying of the temple tax and is then instructed to take the shekel and "give it to them *for me and for you*" (17:24-27). In addition, Matthew changes Mk 7:1-23 by introducing Peter as the spokesman of the disciples (cp. Mk 7:17, "*his disciples* questioned him about the parable," with Mt 15:15, "At this, *Peter* said to him: 'Explain the parable for us' ").

In view of the question, "Who is the greatest in the kingdom of heaven?" which Matthew uses to introduce his discourse in ch 18, the additional references to Peter take on new significance. The question "Who is the greatest" also puts in a new light the episode of the payment of the temple tax with which Matthew concludes his narrative. The episode (17:24-27) concludes with Jesus having Peter pay the tax "for me and for you." The pericope is not found in Mark or in any other gospel and appears to have been purposely introduced by Matthew in order to provide a subtle transition from the narrative in ch 14–17 to the discourse in ch 18. Matthew's use of such strategic transitions has already been pointed out in the transition to the missionary discourse (9:36-37) and in the transition to the parable discourse (12:46-50).

In addition to inserting three Petrine episodes and utilizing a Petrine episode as his transition from narrative to discourse, Matthew made other subtle changes in the Markan material. Where Mark has the disciples consistently failing to understand Jesus,[73] Matthew represents them as understanding. In Mark's account of Jesus' second prediction of the passion, for example, the Apostles greet the prediction with incomprehension (Mk 9:33-34). In Matthew's account, the prediction is followed by a comment which implies full understanding of Jesus' words: "And a great sadness came over them" (17:23).

The change testifies to Matthew's abiding concern to show that the Apostles, who will later be sent to teach (28:19), truly understood the message they were to preach. The change, moreover, was necessitated by the stance Matthew had taken toward the Apostles in ch 13. One of the points Matthew emphasized in ch 13 was that while the Pharisees were unable to understand Jesus, the Apostles understood (cf. 13:52). As a consequence, Matthew was obliged to change his Markan material wherever it represented the Apostles as failing to understand. In place of representing the Apostles as obtuse — the Markan literary technique — Matthew introduces his own technique of "little faith" (cf. 14:32; 16:8; 17:20), which allows him to have the Apostles understanding but not trusting Jesus as they should.

Another redactional touch rarely noticed is Matthew's use of Mk 6:1-6 as introduction to his narrative. The Markan story recounted the rejection of Jesus by his fellow townsmen of Nazareth. Matthew uses the incident to recapitulate a major theme of the preceding narrative-discourse block in ch 11–13, namely, Jesus' rejection by the Jews. At the same time, the rejection story provides a smooth transition to the main theme of ch 14–18, which is concerned with the community of the true disciples. In ch 14–17 it is noticeable that Jesus turns his attention more and more to the community of disciples and to Peter the leader of the community.

The narrative has the usual Matthaean characteristics: (1) departure point from Mark's text (cp. Mt 13:53ff with Mk 6:1ff); (2) an Isaian prophecy with fulfillment formula (cf. 15:7-9); (3) polemic against pseudo-Israel (cf. 13:53-58; 15:1-20; 16:1-12); (4) concentric-circle themes: a) doing the law (cf. 15:1-20); b) universality (cf. 15:21-28); c) Jesus' authority (cf. 15:1-20; 17:1-8); d) Apostles' authority (cf. 16:17-19); e) discipleship (passim); (5) a liking for the number seven (cf. 14:17; 15:19,36; 16:10); (6) the use of a subtle transition from narrative to discourse (cf. 17:24-27).

The following synoptic outline of Mk 6–9 and Mt 13:53–17:27 shows how closely Matthew has followed Mark and at the same time indicates the more significant additions, omissions, and changes made by Matthew in his redaction of the source material. For a more detailed study, the reader should consult the commentaries.

[73] Cf. Mk 6:52; 8:14-21; 9:33-34; 10:35-38.

Part I / Lead-up to Peter "on the waters" (13:54–14:33)

Pericopes	Mark	Matthew	Matthew's changes
Rejection at Nazareth	6:1-6	13:54-58	Changes Mk 6:2[74]
Beheading of the Baptist	6:14-30	14:1-12	Abbreviates Mark
First miracle of the loaves	6:32-44	14:13-21	Omits Mk 6:34f[75]
Jesus walks on the water	6:45-52	14:22-27	Omits Mk 6:52[76]
Peter walks on the water	——	14:28-33	Adds pericope[77]

Part II / Lead-up to Petrine primacy (14:34–16:20)

Pericopes	Mark	Matthew	Matthew's changes
Summary	6:53-56	14:34-36	
A dispute about tradition	7:1-23	15:1-20	Adds 15:12-14[78] Omits Mk 7:19[79] Changes Mk 7:17[80] Changes Mk 7:21-22[81]
The Canaanite woman	7:24-30	15:21-28	Adds 15:23[82]
Summary	7:31,37	15:29-31	Omits Mk 7:32-36[83]
Second miracle of the loaves	8:1-10	15:32-39	
The Pharisees ask for a sign	8:11-13	16:1-4	Adds 16:4[84]
A warning against the teaching of the scribes and Pharisees	8:14-21	16:5-12	Changes Mk 8:21[85]

[74] In place of Mark's "in the synagogue," Matthew adds "in *their* synagogues," continuing the distinction introduced in ch 13 between "them" (the pseudo-Israel) and "us" (the true Israel).

[75] Matthew omits Mark's statement (Mk 6:34) about Jesus "teaching" the Jews because in ch 13 he had Jesus turn away from the Jews and concentrate on the disciples.

[76] Matthew omits Mk 6:52 because it represents the Apostles as obtuse whereas for Matthew (cf. ch 13) they, as opposed to the Jews, understand Jesus.

[77] One of the three pericopes about Peter introduced by Matthew to highlight Peter's position in the community and to conclude part I of his three-part narrative.

[78] By adding 15:12-14 Matthew continues his polemic against the Pharisees.

[79] Matthew omits Mark's comment about Jesus declaring "all foods clean" (Mk 7:19); did he perhaps consider the line of argumentation a bit unsuitable?

[80] In Mk 7:17 the disciples question Jesus. Matthew makes Peter the questioner (15:15).

[81] Where Mark has thirteen evils (Mk 7:21-22), Matthew abbreviates the number to seven.

[82] Unlike Mark, Matthew has the disciples intercede for the Canaanite woman. He does this to heighten the collaboration of the disciples with Jesus in the work of evangelization that had been committed to them in ch 10.

[83] Matthew omits Mark's story about the cure of the deaf mute (7:23-36) because he has already included a similar story in his collection of miracle stories in ch 8–9 (cf. Mt 9:32-33).

[84] Matthew adds: "An evil and faithless generation asks for a sign but no sign will be given it except the sign of Jonah." The statement is a reprise of the "evil and unfaithful generation" theme of ch 11–12 and of the "sign of Jonah" mentioned in 12:39.

[85] In Mk 8:21, the Apostles do not understand Jesus. Typically in Matthew it is said "Then they understood . . ." (16:12).

Part II / *Lead-up to Petrine primacy* (14:34–16:20) Continued

Peter's profession of faith in Jesus	8:27-30	16:13-16	Omission[86] Addition[87]
Jesus' promise to Peter	———	16:17-19	Addition[88]

Part III / *Lead-up to Peter paying the tax* (16:21–17:27)

Pericopes	Mark	Matthew	Matthew's changes
First prediction of the passion	8:31-33	16:21-23	Change[89]
Instruction on discipleship	8:34–9:1	16:24-28	
The transfiguration	9:2-8	17:1-8	Changes[90]
A question about Elijah	9:9-13	17:9-13	Addition[91]
The epileptic demoniac and the Apostles	9:14-29	17:14-20	
Second prediction of the passion	9:20-32	17:22-23	
The temple tax	———	17:24-27	Addition[92]

THE DISCOURSE TO THE COMMUNITY
Mt 18:1-35

The discourse exhibits the usual Matthaean characteristics:[93] (1) departure point from Mark (cf. Mk 9:33-36); (2) a predilection for the number seven (cf. 18:21-22); (3) a thematic relationship with the preceding narrative section, especially in its references to: a) the Church (cp. 18:18 with 16:18-20), to Peter (cp. 18:21 with the numerous references to Peter in ch 14–17); and to the question of authority in the Church (cp. 16:18-19

[86] Matthew omits Mark's cure of the blind man (Mk 8:22-26) probably because he had already included a similar story in his collection of ten miracles in ch 8–9 (cf. Mt 9:27-30).

[87] For Matthew's addition of the words "the Son of the living God," see the commentaries. Also, see 14:27 "It is I" allusion to Jesus' divinity.

[88] This additional Petrine story, like Peter walking on the water (14:28-32) and Peter paying the temple tax for Jesus and himself (17:24-27) points unmistakeably to Peter's position of eminence in the community. See below, pp. 125-134.

[89] Matthew changes Mark's harsh statement "he rebuked Peter" (Mk 8:33) to the softer "he said to Peter" (Mt 16:23).

[90] For the subtle changes introduced by Matthew, see the commentaries.

[91] Matthew's addition of the words, "The disciples understood then that he had been speaking of John the Baptist," is typical and recalls 11:16-19.

[92] Only in Matthew, the story further highlights Peter's position in the community and at the same time provides an excellent transition to the question with which ch 18 opens: "Who is the greatest in the kingdom of heaven? (18:1). For the third time Peter is associated with Jesus in a unique way (cf. 14:28-31; 16:17-19).

[93] See W. G. Thompson, *Matthew's Advice to a Divided Community*; P. Meye, *Jesus and the Twelve*; W. H. Wuellner, *The Meaning of "Fishers of Men,"* 183-185, 226-231; G. Gerhardsson, *Memory and Manuscript*, 324-335; H. Riesenfeld, *The Gospel Tradition and Its Beginning*; W. Schmithals, *The Office of Apostle in the Early Church*; G. Bornkamm, "The Authority to 'Bind' and 'Loose' in the Church in St. Matthew's Gospel" in *Jesus and Man's Hope* (ed. D. G. Buttrick) I, 37-50; J. H. Elliott, "Ministry and Church Order in the New Testament: A Tradition Historical Analysis (1 Peter 5:1-5 and Parallels)" *CBQ* 32 (July 1970) 367-391.

and 17:24-27 with 18:1); (4) concentric-circle themes: a) authority and discipleship; b) Christ present in the Church (cf. 18:20); c) the end-time (cf. 18:23,35); d) the centrality of the love command (implicit in the emphasis on forgiveness throughout but especially in 18:21-35); (5) chiastic balance with the discourse in ch 10; (6) the customary ending formula (cf. 19:1).

Matthew's audience

It is not clear whether Matthew directs the discourse to the community in general (Matthew's community in the eighties) or to the leaders of the community. If Matthew directs the discourse to the community as a whole, then it deals with the relationship of Christian to Christian within the community. If he directs it to the leaders, then the discourse deals with the relationship of superiors to inferiors and to the problem of the rightful use of authority. The difference is considerable and conditions the interpretation of the discourse as a whole as well as the relationship of the discourse to the preceding narrative section.

Since authors disagree and the ambiguity can be resolved only by determining the precise meaning of the word "disciples" in 18:1 (does it mean disciples in general or does it specify the "twelve"?), we shall deal with the discourse first as directed to the community as a whole and second, as directed to the "twelve," i.e., as directed to the apostolic authorities in Matthew's time.

The discourse interpreted as directed to the community

If understood as directed to the community at large,[94] the discourse should be interpreted as dealing with problems in the Matthaean community, problems reflected in 24:9-12 and 7:15-23.

In 18:1-4 Matthew deals with the essence of discipleship in answer to the question: "Who is the greatest?" The child is taken as an example, not of humility, but of dependence. The child has nothing, looks to God for everything, and is consequently an appropriate example of the Christian who is to be "poor in spirit" (cf. 5:3). Paradoxically, the "greatest in the kingdom of heaven" is the one who realizes how "least" he is in himself.

In 18:5-10 Matthew deals with the problem of scandal in the community. It is not clear what the scandal is. The seriousness of the scandal, however, is brought out by showing that what is done to the Christian brother is done to Christ (cf. 18:5-6). The transition to the members of the community is achieved by using the metaphorical term "little child" (18:3) as a catchword to refer to individual Christians as the "little ones who have faith in me" (18:6). The value of the individual Christian is brought out

94 Cf. W. G. Thompson, op cit., 265-267.

in 18:14, where the "little one" is the "lost sheep," and in 18:10, where it is said "their angels in heaven are continually in the presence of my Father in heaven" (cf. also 10:42 and 25:40,45 where the "little ones" are clearly the disciples irrespective of age or condition).

In 18:11-14 Matthew is dependent on Ez 34. He gives the example of the Father's care for the little ones in the parable adapted from Ez 34:11-16 (cf. Lk 15:3-7 and Jn 10 for another use of Ez 34). And in 18:34 he is probably alluding to Ez 18:32, "I have no pleasure in the death of anyone who dies, says the Lord God. Return and live!"

In 18:15-17 Matthew gives norms for dealing with a sinful brother. From this point on, the word brother becomes a catchword for an *errant* brother (cf. 18:21, 35).

It should be noted that by sandwiching the rules in 18:15-17 between two illustrations testifying to the fundamental principal of love and forgiveness — the illustrations provided by the story of the lost sheep in 18:12-14 and the story about forgiving seventy times seven in 18:21-22 — Matthew considerably softens the strictness of the rules.

18:18, if interpreted in relation to the community, allows to the community as a whole an authority similar to that given to Peter in 16:19b, and refers, in this case, to the action of the community in 18:17, should it decide to treat the errant brother "like a pagan or a tax collector."

18:19-20 may refer to the prayer of the community for the errant "brother," or may be a more general statement concerning the intercessory power of the Church in whose midst Christ is present (cf. 8:23-27; 1:23; 28:20).

18:21-22 sums up the whole question of dealing with the brother who has erred (whether by scandal, as in 18:5-9, or in some other way, as in 18:15-17) by demanding unlimited forgiveness for the sinner. The reference to forgiving "seventy times seven" is probably an oblique allusion to the son of Lamech in Gn 4:24. It should not be forgotten, in relation to Peter as the questioner, that Peter himself had three times denied Christ and had yet been forgiven.

18:21-35 recapitulates the teaching about forgiveness in a parable which makes the point that every Christian has been forgiven by God much more than he will ever be required to forgive a brother. The necessity of forgiveness is inculcated in a manner similar to the emphasis on "love of neighbor" in the judgment parable of Mt 25:31-46. The same teaching is found in 6:12-15.

The discourse interpreted as directed to the authorities

As already observed, the determination of Matthew's audience in ch 18 turns on the interpretation of the word "disciples" in 18:1. If Matthew means the twelve, then the discourse should be interpreted as directed to those in authority. The narrative in ch 14–17 with its emphasis on the position of Peter (cf. 16:13-20 and 17:24-27) suggests Matthew is leading up to a discussion of authority. The question with which the discourse begins suggests the same. And the context of the question in Mark 9:33-36 indicates it deals with the status of the individual Apostles in Jesus' Kingdom.

At the same time there is the difficulty that Matthew says disciples, not the twelve, and has a characteristic formula for the disciples (cf. 5:1; 13:36; 14:15; 24:3; 26:17 and passim) which is different from his formula for the twelve (cf. 10:1,2,5; 11:1; 28:16).

While some authors make a good case for interpreting "disciples" as simply "Christians,"[95] there are persuasive reasons for believing Matthew consistently means the "twelve" when he speaks of the "disciples" of Jesus.[96]

Presupposing Matthew is dependent either on Mark or a tradition similar to Mark, it is clear that in both Mark and Matthew the disciples are a small group. They are few enough to be together with Jesus in a fishing boat (cf. Mt 8:23; 14:22) or a house (cf. Mt 9:10; 13:36). They travel with Jesus as a group, and presumably a small group since they are represented as going to places where they can be "alone" with Jesus (cf. 14:13; 16:13 and passim). When Matthew speaks of others as disciples of Jesus, he uses the verb form for disciple rather than the noun (*mathētai*), e.g., 27:57, where he speaks of Joseph of Arimathaea as "*autos emathēteuthē tō Jesou*," and 28:19, where he uses the verb form when speaking of making disciples of all nations (*mathēteusate panta ta ethnē*).

Perhaps more important is how the word "disciples" is understood in Mark. According to Paul Meye in his book *Jesus and the Twelve*, "Mark describes Jesus' ministry consistently with only the twelve in view as the disciples of Jesus" (p. 210). If this conclusion is correct, then it is reasonable to believe Matthew understands and uses the term in the same way. The reason why Matthew did not consistently speak of the "twelve" when using the term "disciples" is explained by Meye as follows:

> Mark had assured the understanding that the messianic ministry had been concentrated in an authorized school of disciples; Matthew and Luke did not have to score that point. Rather they built upon it and went on to give a more extensive account of that teaching tradition which Jesus had directed to the Twelve.[97]

When understood as directed to the "twelve," the discourse becomes an exhortation and warning to the authority figures in the Matthaean community. The exhortatory parts urge them to use their authority with discretion. The warning parts remind them that a highhanded use of authority

[95] Cf. W. G. Thompson, *op cit.*, 83f; 163, 201, 247, 250, 263, 266; Bornkamm, Barth, Held, *op. cit.*, 48.
[96] Cf. P. Meye, *op. cit.*, 93-99, 216-217, 229;

W. Albright, *Matthew*, lxxiv.
[97] *Op. cit.*, 217; cf. also G. D. Kilpatrick, *The Origin of the Gospel according to Matthew*, 79; W. F. Albright, *op. cit.*, lv.

and a refusal to forgive errant brethren not only give scandal to the community but will have to be accounted for in the judgment.

On this interpretation, Mt 18:1-4 deals with the question of precedence in the community and should be understood in the context of the exalted position attributed to Peter in 17:24-27 (the payment of the shekel for Jesus and Peter together) and 16:13-20 (the founding of the Church on Peter). The reference to "the kings of the earth" in 17:25 should be remembered as part of the context also since the answer given to the question implies that authorities in the Kingdom of heaven shall not be like the "kings of the earth."

The "greatest in the Kingdom" is likened to a little child to remind the authorities that they are no different from other Christians (v 5). They are warned against scandalizing them. No specifics are indicated. But the emphasis on forgiveness in 18:21-35 and the settling of accounts between the king and his "servants" (18:23) suggest the authorities have abused their legitimate power by dealing in a highhanded manner with their fellow Christians as the forgiven debtor has with the servant in 18:28ff.

18:12-14 is an exhortation in parabolic form urging the authorities to imitate the concern of the divine Shepherd of Ez 34 for the sheep. At the same time it is a reminder of Ezekiel's condemnation of Israel's false shepherds, the kings of Israel, in Ez 34:2-10. The use of the shepherd theme from Ezekiel in Lk 15:3-7 and John 10 shows it was a well-known theme. And Matthew's consistent use of allusions to the Old Testament indicates he expects his audience to appreciate the context of his quotations and allusions. The reminder that "it is never the will of your Father in heaven that one of these little ones should be lost" would not be lost on Matthew's audience as an allusion to the words of Ez 18:32, "I have no pleasure in the death of anyone who dies, says the Lord God. Return and live!"

18:15-18 urges what has been made clear in the shepherd parable of 18:12-13, namely, that every effort should be made to win back the erring brother. At the same time the text makes clear the authority of the Church and the need for repentance on the part of the erring brother. The binding and loosing power, as in 16:19, deals with admission to the community and expulsion from the community. That this power is to be used benignly is indicated by Matthew from his manner of sandwiching the strict rules of 18:15-17 between the parable of the shepherd who searches out the stray sheep and the question of Peter about forgiveness in 18:19-20.

18:19-20 would appear to contain a general statement concerning the efficacy of prayer. When taken in the context of the question of the erring brother which is central to everything in the discourse from 18:12-35, the reminder about the efficacy of prayer may well be an exhortation to the authorities to pray for the erring brother.

18:21-22 is particularly meaningful if the discourse is directed to the authority figures in the community. Having Peter, who was given the keys of the Kingdom in 16:13-19, ask the question about forgiveness is significant. The question is asked by him whose denial of Jesus and subsequent forgiveness were well-known. If Peter is told to forgive "seventy times seven," the lesson for the authority figures in Matthew's community is obvious. It should be noted that Peter's question about forgiving balances off the solicitude of the good shepherd of 18:12-14 and indicates that the leader of the community is to be like God the Father in forgiving and searching out the sinner and like the master in the parable with which the discourse ends.

In 18:23-35 Matthew sums up the central theme of the discourse with a parable in which echoes resound by way of keywords from the preceding part of the discourse and its immediate context. The "king" (later "master") re-echoes the kings of the earth in 17:25. The servants of the king re-echo the audience who have been exhorted to forgive.[98] And the distress of the "fellow servants" (18:31) may echo the unnamed "scandal" of 18:5-10 and the warning never to "despise any of these little ones" (18:10). The principle enunciated in 18:33, "Were you not bound, then, to have pity on your fellow servant just as I had pity on you," re-echoes the experience of Peter who asked the question about forgiveness. The parable expresses in dramatic terms what was already implicit in the parable of the shepherd who searches out the stray sheep (18:12-14) and in the answer to Peter's question about the number of times he should forgive a brother (18:21-22).[99] Fittingly, the discourse ends with the keyword "brother" which is so central to everything that has been said: "And that is how my heavenly Father will deal with you unless you each forgive your *brother* from your heart."[100]

TRUE AS OPPOSED TO FALSE DISCIPLESHIP
Mt 19:1—22:46

In ch 19–22 the relationship between the narrative and the subsequent discourse in ch 23–25 is not easy to establish because Matthew has abandoned his wholesale rearrangement of Mark's material and restricted himself to minor changes and additions. As in ch 14–17, the Markan material served Matthew's purposes as it stood. In ch 19–22, therefore, the reader will have to pay special attention to the changes and additions Matthew makes in the Markan narrative.

The themes in ch 23–25 for which the reader is prepared in ch 19–22

[98] J. Jeremias, *The Parables*, 210 says: "The magnitude of the sum shows the servant is to be thought of as a satrap."
[99] The forgiveness theme is central to the covenant (cf. Jer 31:31) and is strongly inculcated by Matthew in 5:23-26; 6:12-15. See J. Jeremias, *op. cit.*, 210-214.
[100] On the tension between discipline and the love command in Mt 18, cf. V.P. Furnish, *The Love Command in the New Testament*, 78; W. D. Davies, *The Setting of the Sermon on the Mount*, 221-228.

are the following: (1) the distinction between true and false discipleship; (2) the distinction between the true and the pseudo-Israel; (3) the centrality of the love commandment; (4) the authority of Jesus as Messiah and Son of Man; (5) the end-time.

Since the material in Mk 10–12 already supported these themes, it will suffice to point out the Matthaean characteristics of the narrative and isolate those additions to, and changes in, the Markan narrative which Matthew made in order to further bolster the themes he intended to propound in the subsequent discourse.

Characteristic of Matthaean composition are: (1) departure point from Mark's text;[101] (2) prophecy with and without fulfilment formula;[102] (3) polemic against pseudo-Israel;[103] (4) concentric-circle themes: a) Jesus' authority;[104] b) doing the law (19:16-22); c) discipleship (passim); d) judgment and the end-time; (5) the number seven (cf. 22:25); (6) chiasmic balance with ch 5–7; (7) use of a subtle transition from narrative to discourse (22:41-46).

The material in ch 19–22 is chiasmically arranged in three parts: a) 19:1-30; b) 20:1–22:14; a.1) 22:15-46. The following synoptic table of Mk 10–12 and Mt 19–22 shows the material Matthew has in common with Mark, has added to Mark, has omitted from Mark, has changed in Mark.

a) 19:1-30 / Four questions

Pericopes	Mark	Matthew	Matthew's changes
Pharisees' question	10:1-12	19:1-9	Has Pharisees mention Moses[105]
Disciples' question	——	19:10-12	Only in Matthew[106]
The little children	10:13-16	19:13-15	
Rich man's question	10:17-22	19:16-26	Omits Mk 10:21[107] Adds love command[108]
Peter's question	10:23-27	19:27-30	Adds 19:28[109]

[101] Cp. Mt 19:1 with Mk 10:1ff.
[102] 21:4-5,16,42; 22:43-44.
[103] Cf. 20:1-16; 21:12-16; 22:1-46.
[104] Cf. 19:1-9; 21:12-16, 21:23-32; 22:15-46.
[105] Where Mark has Jesus ask, "What did Moses command you?", Matthew characteristically has the Pharisees ask, "Then why did Moses command . . . ?" In the Sermon on the Mount, Matthew does not have Jesus say: "Moses said, 'You shall not kill'," but, "You have learnt how it was said to our ancestors." It is Matthew's delicate way of showing respect for Moses.
[106] Matthew uses the disciples' reaction to indissoluble marriage to point up the perfection of the law of Christ as opposed to the old law. Their reaction emphasizes the radical nature of the law of Christ in the same way that Jesus' discussion with the rich young man emphasizes the perfection of the Christian way in relation to wealth. While an option appears given between following either the incomplete Mosaic law or the perfect law of Christ, the emphasis is not on the option ("Let him who can take

it, take it!") but on the difference between the two laws. The divorce pericope and the story of the rich young man serve as commentaries on the antitheses of the Sermon on the Mount (5:21-48) and on the radical nature of the response to the paradise will of God expected from true disciples.
[107] Mark is kinder to the young man than Matthew. Mark says: "Jesus looked steadily at him and loved him." Matthew omits the complimentary words because the rich young man is settling for the old law instead of the perfect law of Christ.
[108] When Christ cites the commandments in Mark, he says nothing about the love commandment. Matthew adds it to the list given by Jesus (as he did in the antitheses, see 5:43-48) because for him it is the law in the light of which all other laws are to be interpreted (cf. Mt 22:34-40; 25:31-46).
[109] Matthew, in keeping with his concern for the prestige of the Apostles, adds the statement: "You will yourselves sit on twelve thrones to judge the twelve tribes of Israel" (19:28).

b) 20:1–22:14 / True versus pseudo-Israel

Pericopes	Mark	Matthew	Matthew's changes
Parable: laborers	——	20:1-16	Only in Matthew[110]
Prophecy of passion	10:32-34	20:17-19	
Two sons and Kingdom	10:35-40	20:20-23	Changes in Mk 10:35[111]
Authority and service	10:41-45	20:24-28	
Two blind men cured	10:46-52	20:29-34	Mark has only one
Triumphal entry	11:1-11	21:1-11	Adds prophecy[112]
Cleansing and fig tree	11:12-24	21:12-22	Adds 21:15
Question re authority	11:27-33	21:23-27	
Question re two sons	——	21:28-32	Only in Matthew[113]
Parable: husbandmen	12:1-12	21:33-46	
Parable: wedding feast	——	22:1-14	Only in Matthew

a.1) 22:15-46 / Four questions

Pericopes	Mark	Matthew	Matthew's changes
Question re tribute	12:13-17	22:15-22	
Question re resurrection	12:18-27	22:23-33	
Question re greatest commandment	12:28-31	22:34-40	Adds 22:40[114] Omits Mk 12:32-34[115]
Question re Messiah	12:35-37	22:41-46	

The purpose of the narrative

Whether one adopts a vertical or a horizontal approach to the analysis of ch 19–22, the results are the same. Matthew's intention is to emphasize (1) the distinction between true and false discipleship; (2) the distinction between the true and the pseudo-Israel; (3) the centrality of the love com-

[110] The parable of the laborers, found only in Matthew, is added for two reasons. First, it balances off the concluding parable in this section, the parable of the wedding feast. Second, each parable ends with ominous words for pseudo-Israel, e.g., Mt 20:16, "Thus the last will be first, and the first, last," and Mt 21:24, "For many are called, but few are chosen."

[111] Matthew tones down Mark's emphasis on the Apostles' lack of perception. Where Mark has John and James inanely ignoring Jesus' prophecy of his death and asking for high places in his Kingdom as if it were to be a Kingdom of this world, Matthew has the *mother* of the two Apostles ask the inane question.

[112] Matthew cannot refrain from inserting the prophecy from Zechariah (9:9) which he sees fulfilled in Jesus' triumphal entry. Also, and however odd oracle and event seem aligned in this instance, Matthew has Jesus commandeer two animals, a donkey and a colt. Mark has only one, just as he has one blind man (Mk 10:46-52) where Matthew has two (Mt 20:29-34) and one demoniac (Mk 5:1-20) where Matthew has two (Mt 8:28-34).

[113] The story about the two sons may have been thrown in by Matthew to balance chiasmically with the two sons' story in 20:20-23. It serves as well, however, to emphasize the hypocrisy of the Jewish leaders and to recall to the readers' mind the condemnation of "this generation" for not listening to John (cp. Mt 21:32 and 11:16-19).

[114] Mk 12:31 has Jesus say, "There is no commandment greater than these," but Matthew goes beyond saying the love of God and neighbor are the greatest commandments. He says "the second resembles" the first (22:39) and then goes on to make the love commandment the principle of interpretation against which all laws are to be interpreted by saying: "On these two commandments hang the whole law, and the prophets also" (22:40). He had already said as much equivalently in the Sermon on the Mount (cf. 5:43-48; 7:12) and in his interpretation of the Sabbath law in ch 12:1-14. See below, pp. 150-154.

[115] Matthew omits Jesus' commendation of the scribe, mentioned by Mark: "Jesus, seeing how wisely he (the scribe) had spoken, said, 'You are not far from the Kingdom of God.' " He has nothing good to say about scribes and Pharisees.

mandment; (4) the authority of Jesus as Messiah and Son of Man; (5) the importance of the end-time judgment in relationship to true discipleship.

Adopting the horizontal approach, it is obvious that if Matthew is using Mark's text, as generally presupposed, he has added material that is pertinent to his teaching purpose and omitted material that detracts from his teaching purpose.

In relationship to true versus false discipleship, which was already the theme of Mk 10, Matthew's additions and omissions are significant. Where Mark says nothing about the Apostles' reaction to Jesus' absolute rejection of divorce, Matthew adds the negative reaction of the Apostles (Mt 19:10-12) and thereby emphasizes the perfection of Christian discipleship.[116] As Jesus says: "There are eunuchs who have made themselves that way *for the sake of the kingdom of heaven*" (19:12). The "more" of Christian discipleship is further clarified in the story of the rich young man (19:16-22), who asserts he keeps the commandments of the old law (19:20) but turns away sad when called upon to be "perfect" by selling what he owns and giving it to the poor (19:21-22).

In relation to the true versus the pseudo-Israel theme, Matthew's additions and omissions are equally significant. Mark had emphasized the same theme in his parable of the husbandmen (Mk 12:1-11). Matthew includes the parable but subtly changes the ending by using his favorite word "fruit" (cf. Mt 3:9-10; 7:15-20; 12:33) to emphasize the importance of *doing* the will of God. Compare:

> "Now what will the owner of the vineyard do? He will come and make an end of the tenants and give the vineyard to others" (Mk 12:9).
> "I tell you, then, that the kingdom of God will be taken from you and given to a people who will produce its *fruit*" (Mt 21:43).

The rejection of the pseudo-Israel, already clear in the Markan parable of the vicious husbandmen (Mk 12:1-12) is the theme of the two parables Matthew has added to the material he took from Mark. The parable of the laborers in the vineyard (the vineyard is the Isaian metaphor for Israel as God's Kingdom, cf. Is 5:1-7) ends with the words: "Thus the last will be first, and the first, last" (Mt 20:16). The parable of the wedding feast ends with the words: "For many are called, but few are chosen" (Mt 22:14). Pseudo-Israel has been rejected.[117]

Throughout the gospel, Matthew utilizes his polemic against the Pharisees both to emphasize true as opposed to false discipleship (the Pharisees are represented as the opposite of what a true disciple should be, cf. 5:20;

---

[116] See D. L. Dungan's perceptive analysis of the divorce discussion in Mt 19:1-12 as an absolute rejection of all remarriage in his *The Sayings of Jesus in the Churches of Paul*, 109-127.

[117] Matthew's parable of the two sons (21:28-32), when taken in conjunction with Jesus' rejection of pseudo-Israel in Mt 11:6-19, is another example of Matthew's subtle selection of material to emphasize the distinction between the true and the pseudo-Israel.

6:1-5,16; 23:3) and to heighten the distinction between the true and the pseudo-Israel. His additions and omissions in ch 19–22 continue the polemic.

It is not surprising, therefore, to find that in Mark's version of the "greatest commandment" (Mk 12:28-34) the scribe who questions Jesus questions in good faith, while in Matthew's version (Mt 22:34-40) the questioner has become a Pharisee lawyer and the purpose of the question is to "disconcert" Jesus (22:34). Nor is it surprising that Jesus' words of commendation for the scribe (Mk 12:34) are pointedly omitted by Matthew. He has nothing good to say about the Pharisees. The hypocritical questions (22:15-22; 22:34-40) help prepare the reader for Jesus' scathing denunciation of the Pharisees in ch 23.

In his symbolic description of the last judgment (Mt 25:31-46), Jesus makes observance of the love commandment not only the prime requirement for entrance into the eschatological Kingdom but also the essential characteristic of a true disciple. Matthew prepares the way for this teaching in two ways.

First, where Mark has Jesus say nothing about the love commandment in the list of commandments he cites for the rich young man (Mk 10:19-20), Matthew has Jesus add to the list the words "and you must love your neighbor as yourselves" (Mt 19:19). In a similar way in the Sermon on the Mount, Matthew had Jesus add the love commandment to the commandments of the decalogue (Mt 5:43-48).

Second, Matthew makes two significant changes in his version of Jesus' words about the importance of the love commandment. To begin with, he has Jesus say about love of neighbor that "the second resembles the first" (22:39). The statement puts the two on practically the same plane and prepares the way for the statement of Jesus in 25:40, "I tell you solemnly, in so far as you did this to one of the least of these brothers of mine, *you did it to me*." Matthew then goes on to have Jesus say: "On these two commandments *hang* the whole law and the prophets also" (22:40). This is clearly an addition to Jesus' statement in Mk 12:31: "There is no commandment greater than these." Matthew's version makes the love commandment not only the greatest commandment, but the commandment in the light of which all other commandments are to be interpreted. It prepares the way for the judgment scene in Mt 25:31-46 where the *only* commandment taken into consideration in the final judgment is the love commandment.

The theme of Jesus' authority as Messiah and authoritative Son of Man was already a prominent theme in Mark's material.[118] By including the Markan material, especially the account of Jesus' authoritative stance in

118 Cf. Mk 10:1-12; 10:41-45; 11:1-10; 11:15-18; 11:27-33; 12:13-37.

relation to the four questions in 19:1-30 balanced off with the four questions in 22:15-46, Matthew more than adequately underlined the authority of Jesus.

His addition to the Markan text dealing with Peter's question about renunciation[119] is significant. When Peter asks Jesus, "What about us? We have left everything and followed you. What are we to have then?", Matthew has Jesus answer as the authoritative Son of Man: "I tell you solemnly, when all is made new and the Son of Man sits on his throne in glory, you shall yourselves sit on twelve thrones to judge the twelve tribes of Israel" (Mt 19:28).

Jesus' claim of absolute authority as Son of Man anticipates his declaration of 28:18, "All power in heaven and on earth has been given to me," and prepares the way for the similar claim in 24:30 and 25:31-33, "When the Son of Man *comes in his glory*, escorted by all the angels, then he *will take his seat* on his throne of glory."

It is in this context that we can best understand Matthew's end pericope in 22:41-46. While Jesus gives no answer to his own question, Matthew's intimation is that Jesus is the Son of Man. The identification is made by combining the promises of Ps 110:1 and Dn 7:13 and applying them to Jesus (cf. all the references to the Son of Man in ch 24–25 and especially the wording of Jesus' reply to the High Priest in Mt 26:64).[120]

DISCIPLESHIP AND THE SON OF MAN
Mt 23:1–25:46

The last great discourse[121] has the usual Matthaean characteristics: (1) departure point from Mark;[122] (2) "seven" woes against the Pharisees; (3) concentric-circle themes;[123] (4) chiasmic balance with the Sermon on the Mount;[124] (5) an ending pericope which focuses the central message of the discourse;[125] (6) the customary closing formula.[126]

Authors dispute whether the discourse begins in ch 23 or ch 24. The

[119] Cp. Mk 10:28-31 with Mt 19:27-30.
[120] Cf. N. Perrin, *The Kingdom of God in the Teaching of Jesus*, 143, n. 3; *Rediscovering the Teaching of Jesus*, 175-185.
[121] Cf. W. F. Albright, *op. cit.*, 276-310; Bornkamm, Barth, Held, *op cit.*, 21-24; 60-62; R. Schnackenburg, *God's Rule and Kingdom*, 195-214; N. Perrin, *Rediscovering the Teaching of Jesus*, 154-206; L. Hartman, *Prophecy Interpreted;* W. G. Kummel, *Promise and Fulfillment;* J. A. T. Robinson, *Jesus and His Coming;* W. D. Davies, *Introduction to Pharisaeism.*
[122] Compare Mt 23:3-7 and Mk 12:38-40.
[123] Jesus' authority as Son of Man, doing the law, and the theme of the end-time dominate the thought of the whole discourse.
[124] Ch 23–25 and ch 5–7 balance in length, having 109 and 136 verses respectively. Each is given on a mountain — the Mount in Galilee

(5:1) and the Mount of Olives (24:3). Jesus is seated magisterially in both discourses. The one opens with beatitudes, the other with woes. The Sermon on the Mount ends with the words: "Not everyone who says to me, Lord . . ." (7:21-23); the last discourse ends with the words of the damned: "Lord, when did we see you hungry . . ." (25:44).
[125] The judgment parable in 25:31-46 sums up the themes of discipleship, the law of love, the coming of the Son of Man, and the end-time.
[126] Compare 26:1, "Jesus had now finished *all he wanted to say . . .*," and 28:20, "teaching them to observe *all I commanded you.*" The teaching has been in the discourses. As K. Stendahl says: "Matthew achieves his picture of Jesus the Teacher by his editorial arrangement of the famous five discourses, partly by the use of Q material" (*op. cit.*, ix).

change of place and audience in ch 24 suggests the discourse begins there. But the same change is observable in ch 13, and no one disputes the unity of ch 13.[127] For the following reasons, we shall presume the discourse begins with ch 23. First, the themes of ch 23 are continued in ch 24–25. Second, the first words of ch 23 indicate the opening of a discourse: "Then addressing the people and his disciples, Jesus said . . ." (23:1). Third, without ch 23 the balance would be lost with the Sermon on the Mount. Fourth, if ch 23–25 is broken into two discourses, the structure of the gospel according to narrative followed by discourse would be disrupted.

Matthew composed the discourse as he did the Sermon on the Mount by bringing together material from sundry sources, but primarily from Mark and the Q source. The following outline shows what is peculiar to Matthew, what he found in Mark, and where the common Q material is found in Luke. A synopsis should be consulted for a closer and more detailed comparison.

Pericopes	Matthew	Mark	Luke
Introduction	23:1-12[128]	12:38-39	11:46; 20:45-47
Woes	23:13-36[129]	———	11:42-52
Lament over Jerusalem	23:37-39	———	13:34-35
Departure from the Temple	24:1-3	13:1-4	21:5-7
End of the world	24:4-14	13:5-9a,13b	21:8-11
Fall of Jerusalem	24:15-22	13:14-20	21:20-24[130]
Coming of the Son of Man	24:23-31	13:21-27	17:23-24,37; 21:25-28
The fig tree as a parable[131]	24:32-36	13:28-32	21:25-33
As in the days of Noah	24:37-41	———	17:26-30,34-35
As when a burglar comes	24:42-44	———	12:39-40
As with a faithful servant	24:45-51	———	12:42-46
As with bridesmaids	25:1-13	———	
As with talents	25:14-30	———	19:12-27
As with sheep and goats	25:31-46	———	

[127] The parable discourse begins outside the house (13:1-2). The first part is addressed to the crowds and the disciples (13:3-35). The second part (13:36-51) is addressed to the disciples alone inside the house (13:36).
[128] Matthew has taken his departure point, as usual, from Mark (cf. Mk 12:38-39).
[129] Matthew uses the Q material for his "woes" against the Pharisees. In Luke, the same material is found in a completely different context.
[130] Luke's description of the fall of Jerusalem is written for non-Jews and as a consequence is much clearer in terminology.

[131] The last part of the discourse, which is made up mostly of Q material, found in completely different contexts in Luke, is used by Matthew, along with material peculiar to him alone (25:1-13 and 25:31-46), to create a balance with ch 23. The two chapters flanking the apocalyptic discourse about the end of the world, the destruction of Jerusalem, and the coming of the Son of Man in judgment, are thus concentrated on the theme of warning in relationship to true and false discipleship. Ch 23 has seven woes; ch 24:32–25:46 has seven warnings.

The audience

The last, like the first, discourse is Matthew's, not Jesus' composition. It presupposes as past events the passion, death, and resurrection of Jesus and the hectic years between 30 and 80 A.D., during which the Jews suffered the destruction of Jerusalem and the Temple by the Romans, and the Christians suffered persecution from the Jews. The discourse envisions, as a consequence, not the situation of Jesus in 30 A.D. but the situation of Matthew and his community in the eighties. It is from that perspective alone that it makes sense.

Speaking to the situation of his Jewish Christian community in the eighties, Matthew has Jesus speak first to the crowds and the disciples in the Temple area and then to the disciples alone on Mount Olivet. As in the Sermon on the Mount, the discourse has the disciples (or more properly Matthew's community) as its primary audience and as its secondary audience those readers, particularly Jews tending toward Christianity, who could not make up their minds about leaving Judaism and the leadership of the Jamnian Pharisees. The castigation and condemnation of the Pharisees in 23:1-36 is directed in a particularly pointed way to this secondary audience.[132] The apocalyptic discourse in ch 24 is for both audiences but especially the primary audience.

Structure

The discourse has three parts: the first (23:1-39) deals with the condemnation of the Pharisees and the prediction of the fall of Jerusalem; the second (24:1-31) with the end of the world, the destruction of Jerusalem, and the second coming of Jesus; the third (24:32–25:46) with seven warnings in parabolic form advising Christians to use well the time intervening before the second coming. The discourse is divided as follows:

1) *23:1-39 / Warnings and condemnations*

    a) 23:1-12   Warning not to be like the Pharisees.
    b) 23:13-36   Condemnation of the Pharisees.
    c) 23:37-39   Condemnation of Jerusalem.

2) *24:1-31 / The apocalyptic discourse*

    a) 24:1-3   Departure from the temple and disciples' questions.
    b) 24:4-14   Answer to question about the end of the world.
    c) 24:15-22   Answer to question about the destruction of Jerusalem.
    d) 24:23-31   Answer to question about Jesus' second coming.

3) *24:32–25:46 / Seven parousia parables*

    a) 24:32-36   As with the fig tree.
    b) 24:37-41   As in the days of Noah.

---

[132] The first "woe" threatens the scribes and Pharisees because they are preventing people from entering the Christian community: "You who shut up the kingdom of heaven in men's faces, neither going in yourselves nor allowing others to go in who want to" (23:13).

c) 24:42-44   As when a burglar comes.
d) 24:45-51   As with a faithful servant.
e) 25:1-13   As with bridesmaids awaiting the bridegroom.
f) 25:14-30   As with talents.
g) 25:31-46   As with sheep and goats.

1) 23:1-39 / Warnings and condemnations

The first part of the discourse becomes more understandable if the reader recognizes that Matthew has utilized the literary technique of casting Jesus in the role of a prophet. The technique is a variant of the technique in the Sermon on the Mount where Matthew had Jesus speak as the legislator "greater than" Moses. Here Jesus speaks as the last and the greatest of the prophets.[133]

Like the prophets, Jesus brings God's message of judgment on Israel, threatens "woes",[134] foretells the coming of "the day of the Lord,"[135] promises blessings for obedience and curses for disobedience,[136] and predicts the destruction of the Temple (23:37-39; 24:15-22).[137] It is not unlikely that Matthew sees Jesus as the prophet like Moses (cf. Dt 18:18) whom Jewish tradition predicted would come to introduce the eschatological age.[138] Jesus' words in ch 23–24 reflect Matthew's understanding of this concept. Matthew's Jesus–Moses parallels in ch 1–4 suggest the same.

a) 23:1-12 / Warning not to be like the Pharisees

In 23:1ff Matthew takes as his departure point the saying of Mk 12:38, "In his teaching he said: 'Beware of the scribes'." Matthew develops this warning at length. But he begins, as in the Sermon on the Mount, by clarifying the issue. Jesus, speaking through Matthew, is not against the law of Moses (cf. 5:17-19) which the scribes and Pharisees teach from "the chair of Moses," but against those teachers who do not do what they teach (23:3 and cp. 5:17-19) and who, even when they do what they teach, do not do it for the glory of God but for their own aggrandizement (23:4-7 and cp. 6:1-5).

In 23:8-12 Matthew directs himself to Christian teachers.[139] They are not to be like the Pharisees and scribes who focus attention on themselves as teachers. They are to remember there is only "one teacher, the Christ" (23:10). There is nothing, therefore, independent about Christian teachers.

[133] The historical Jesus did, of course, speak as a prophet. A form critical analysis of the material from the tradition used by Matthew in ch 23 confirms this contention. What is new (and literary) about ch 23 is that Matthew composes for Jesus out of isolated sayings in the tradition a complete prophetic discourse similar in many ways to those found in the books of the prophets.

[134] Cf. Am 5:7,18; 6:1; Is 5:8-23; 10:1-4. In Is 5:8ff, there are, as in Mt 23:13-35, "seven" woes.

[135] Cf. Am. 5:18-20; Is 9:1; Zeph 1:15-18; Mal 3:19ff.

[136] Cf. Jer 11:1ff and passim in the prophetic books and Deuteronomy.

[137] Cf. Jer 7; 26; Ez 8–11.

[138] Cf. H. Teeple, The Mosaic Eschatological Prophet; T. F. Glasson, Moses in the Fourth Gospel.

[139] Cf. W. F. Albright's statement: "Nothing illustrates better than these five verses (7-11) our contention that what we have in this gospel is a very substantial amount of private teaching addressed to the inner circle of the disciples. These five verses are totally misunderstood if they are interpreted as being addressed to the whole community" (op. cit., 279).

They are to teach only what Jesus has taught them (cf. 28:19, "teaching them to observe *all I have commanded you*").

b) 23:13-36 / Condemnation of the Pharisees[140]

The seven woes recapitulate and reinforce almost every charge made by Matthew against the Pharisees. They are hypocrites (cf. 6:2, 5, 16; 15:7). They are blind guides (cf. 15:14). They are a brood of vipers (cf. 3:7; 12:34).

What Matthew condemns through the mouth of Jesus is that multiplication of laws which makes law an unbearable burden, that minutial casuistry which brings law, even the law of God, into disrepute, and that cold legalism which considers law more important than people (cf. 11:28–12:14). The Jesus who said, "My yoke is easy and my burden light" (Mt 11:30), was opposed not only to the scribes and Pharisees but to all who make the will of God, as expressed in law, an intolerable burden. Matthew's indictment of the Pharisees in the seven woes, therefore, is not only directed against a particular group of men during a brief period of history but likewise against that class of men in any age who, out of selfishness sometimes and out of blindness frequently, make the yoke of God's law an unsupportable burden.

Several redactional elements of 23:13-36 are worthy of note. First, there is the suggestion of J. C. Fenton that Matthew has not only balanced off the woes at the beginning of this last discourse with the beatitudes at the beginning of the first discourse but that he even went so far as to "put the woes in such an order that each one paired off with one of the blessings, taken in the reverse order: i.e., first woe with last beatitude, second with seventh beatitude, etc. Thus:[141]

THE WOES	THE BEATITUDES
1. you shut the Kingdom of heaven	8. theirs is the Kingdom of heaven
2. child of hell (*huion geenēs*)	7. sons of God (*huioi theou*)
3. blind . . . blind . . . blind	6. they shall see God
4. mercy	5. mercy . . . merciful
5. the outside of the cup and of the plate	4. hunger and thirst
6. tombs . . . dead men's bones	3. those who mourn
7. that upon you may come all the righteous blood shed on earth	2. they shall inherit the earth

Second, if we have been correct in seeing as Matthew's secondary audience those Jews hesitating to adopt Christianity because of the pressure put on them by the Pharisees of the local synagogues, then the first woe

---

[140] Cf. W. D. Davies, *Introduction to Pharisaeism*; W. F. Albright, *op. cit.*, cxv-cxxiii, 278-283; S. Van Tilborg, *The Jewish Leaders in Matthew*; J. Jeremias, *Jerusalem in the Time of Jesus*, 233-253; J. Neusner, *The Rabbinic Traditions about the Pharisees before 70 A.D.*

G. Baum, *The Jews and The Gospel*; D. R. A. Hare, *The Theme of the Jewish Persecution of Christians in the Gospel according to St Matthew.*

[141] Cf. J. C. Fenton, *Saint Matthew*, 368.

(23:13), "You who shut up the kingdom of heaven in men's faces, neither going in yourselves nor allowing others to go in who want to," [142] takes on added significance. The pressure would be the persecution alluded to in ch 10:31b-42.

Third, the fourth woe, against those who "have neglected the weightier matters of the Law — justice, mercy, good faith" (23:23), takes on added significance in view of Matthew's contention in 22:37-40 that the law of love is the over-riding law in the light of which all other laws are to be interpreted.

Fourth, the seventh woe (23:29-32) which speaks of the Pharisees as "the sons of those who murdered the prophets," already looks forward to the death of Jesus in the statement: "Very well then, finish off the work your fathers began" (23:32).

Fifth, the epithets in 23:33, "Serpents, brood of vipers, how can you escape being condemned to hell," serve as an inclusion-conclusion with the similar words of the Baptist at the beginning of the gospel (cf. 3:7).

Sixth, Jesus' words, "I am sending you prophets and wise men and scribes — some you will slaughter and crucify, some you will scourge in your synagogues and hunt from town to town" (23:34), recall what Jesus said to the Apostles about persecution in 5:11-12 and in 10:17-25.[143] At the same time the declaration, "I am sending you prophets," looks forward to the final missionary mandate in 28:18-20 where Jesus commissions the Apostles as his prophets just as Yahweh in the Old Testament commissioned the prophets.

Seventh, in characteristic fashion Matthew uses the final pericope of this part of the discourse to prepare the way for what will follow in ch 24. Jesus says: "Your *house* will be left to you *desolate*, for, I promise, you shall not see me any more until you say: 'Blessings on him *who comes* in the name of the Lord' " (23:38-39). In ch 24 Jesus will speak about the destruction of the Temple and about the coming of the Son of Man.

2) 24:1-31 / The apocalyptic discourse

The central part of the last great discourse continues to resist adequate explanation and is acknowledged by all to be the most difficult section of the whole gospel. We shall restrict ourselves, therefore, to a brief discussion of the most significant literary and redactional elements and ask the reader to consult the commentaries.[144]

The apocalyptic discourse becomes more understandable when the reader

---

[142] A comparison with Luke's version of this woe: "Alas for you lawyers who have taken away the key of knowledge! You have not gone in yourselves, and have prevented others going in who wanted to" (Lk 11:52) shows how Matthew has rephrased it to fit the situation of the Church in his time.

[143] The threefold reference to innocent "blood"

in 23:35-36 will be taken up again in 27:6, ". . . it is blood money," and in 27:25, "His blood be on us and on our children."

[144] H. Wansbrough in *A New Catholic Commentary on Holy Scripture* and J. Fenton in his *Saint Matthew* are particularly good. W. F. Albright's *Matthew* has much good information but is redactionally deficient.

realizes Matthew, following Mark (Mk 13), has presented it in the literary form known to both Greeks and Jews as the farewell address.[145] Biblical examples of the form are Jacob's farewell discourse (Gn 47:29–49:33), Josue's (Jos 23–24), David's (1 Chron 28–29), and the last supper discourse of Jesus in John's gospel (Jn 13–17). A classic example in Greek literature is the farewell address of Socrates as given by Plato in his *Crito* and *Phaedo*. To these should be added the apocalyptic farewell address of Mark (Mk 13) and the farewell addresses of Matthew (Mt 24:1-31) and Luke (Lk 21:5-36) which are dependent on the earlier farewell address of Mark's gospel.

The literary characteristics of the farewell address are well-known. The writer places himself in the position of a great man in the days or hours immediately preceding his death. He then pictures the great man gathering his followers around him to give them encouragement, instructions, and warnings which will assist them after his departure. The encouragement consists in the assurance of ultimate success or victory despite opposition, persecutions, and overwhelming odds. The instructions deal with what is to be done by the great man's followers in the days and years following his death, how they are to comport themselves as worthy disciples, how they are to deal with the opposition, and how they are to know the signs which herald the day of victory. The warnings deal with the fate of their enemies, the need for the followers to persevere, and the necessity of carrying on faithfully the work begun by the great man himself. In the biblical farewell addresses, it is also customary for the great man to speak of a sucessor who will assist his followers in carrying out their mission.

In Mt 24 most of these characteristics are verified. Jesus takes his Apostles aside to a site (Mt Olivet) overlooking Jerusalem. He encourages, instructs, and warns them concerning what will happen after his death. And he speaks, in the wide sense at least, about a successor.[146]

The verification of the literary characteristics of a farewell address in Mt 24 suggests but does not prove that the discourse as we have it now is the composition of Matthew rather than an actual historical discourse delivered by Jesus. While it is true that Jesus could have delivered such a discourse and that farewell discourses are sometimes composed by gathering together the actual sayings of a great man before his death in such a way that the discourse is made to constitute his last will and testament, it is equally true that it is almost impossible to identify which sayings derive from the great man and which from the author who composed the discourse.

[145] For a discussion of the farewell address as a literary form, cf. R. Brown, *The Gospel according to John*, Vol. II, 597-601.
[146] The Paraclete is Jesus' successor in John's farewell discourse. In Matthew's gospel, the coming "Son of Man" is a successor only in the wide sense since Jesus promises that he himself will be with his Apostles to the end of time (Mt 28:20).

The farewell discourse composed for Jesus by the author of the fourth gospel in Jn 13–17 points up the difficulty.

In John's gospel, Jesus is represented as giving his last discourse inside a house, in the course of a supper, and on the night preceding his death. In the synoptic gospels, Jesus' farewell address is independent of the last supper. It is given outside on Mount Olivet. And it is dated at least one day earlier than John's discourse (cf. Mt 26:2,17,20).

The differences suggest three possibilities. First, Jesus actually delivered two farewell addresses. This is unlikely on a literary and psychological basis. Second, he delivered no farewell address at all, and the discourses attributed to him are the literary compositions of John and Mark respectively. This is unlikely but possible. Third, Jesus spoke some words of farewell at the last supper and these were remembered and used at a later time by John and Mark in their composition of a farewell address for Jesus. This is the most likely explanation of the provenance of the farewell discourses in John and Mark.

On this supposition there is a possibility of explaining not only the historical basis for some kind of an actual farewell discourse delivered by Jesus but also the glaring differences that appear in the Johannine and synoptic versions of the farewell discourse.

The actual farewell words of Jesus would be found in the synoptic accounts of the last supper (Mk 14:12-42; Mt 26:17-46; Lk 22:7-46). When John came to compose his farewell discourse for Jesus, he chose to situate the discourse at the last supper and as a consequence incorporated in his discourse some of the sayings of Jesus recorded by the synoptics as spoken by Jesus at the supper. The synoptic authors, on the other hand, for reasons that go back to the author of the Markan apocalyptic discourse, retained the last sayings of Jesus in their account of the supper and the agony in the garden, and chose to situate the farewell discourse one day before the last supper and on Mount Olivet instead of in the supper room.

Ultimately, the divergences in the Johannine and synoptic farewell discourses in place, time, setting, and literary style can be traced to the literary liberties taken by each author. The author of the Johannine address preferred to model Jesus' last discourse on Moses' farewell address in Deuteronomy. The synoptics, but more accurately the author of the Markan farewell address upon whom Matthew and Luke depend, preferred to model Jesus' last discourse on the prophetic literature, particularly Ez 7–11 and Dn 7–9.

In short, the farewell address of Jesus in the synoptics pertains to two literary *genres* — the apocalyptic *genre* and the farewell discourse *genre*. Since the apocalyptic *genre* leans heavily on the motif of God's victory over his enemies and the associated motifs of persecution and retribution, the author of the Markan farewell discourse chose to situate the discourse on Mount Olivet and have Jesus speak about the imminent destruction of Jerusalem just as Ezechiel, in 587 B.C., had Yahweh look down at Jerusalem and the Temple and speak about their destruction (cf. Ez 7–11). Since the situation, content, and style of the synoptic farewell discourses lean so heavily on the apocalyptic *genre*, we shall have to speak about apocalyptic before taking up the question of Matthew's dependence on Mark and the redactional differences between the farewell discourses of Mark and Matthew.

The apocalyptic tradition and form (best exemplified in Ez 38–39; Is 24–27; Joel 3–4; Zech 9–14; Dn 7–12; Mt 24; Mk 13; Lk 21; 1–2 Thess; Rev.) concentrates on one aspect of Israel's covenant theology: namely, the certain and effective success of the covenant King's implementation of his plan for the salvation of Israel and the world.

Apocalyptic borrows from the traditions that preceded it. It takes up the design of history elaborated in the salvation histories and in messianic theology, the element of judgment in the prophetic discourses, and the general wisdom attempt to synthesize in a grand plan. Out of all of these it forges a new literary form.

The new form has distinctive characteristics which flow, for the most part, from the psychological situation of the authors and their audiences when the works were written, from the theological traditions out of which the apocalyptic viewpoint was born, and from the literary devices adopted and developed to express the new viewpoint.

From the psychological situation of the authors and their audiences — a situation of frustration and disillusionment induced by captivity, persecution, and politico-religious crisis in general — the form acquired such secondary characteristics as the following: (1) an invincible confidence in God and faith in the inspired books; (2) a refined appreciation for the superiority of the true faith; (3) a heightened hatred for the forces of evil both in the individual moral sphere and in the misguided materialism of the dominant political powers.

From the prophetic tradition,[147] the wisdom tradition,[148] and the postexilic theological emphasis on the transcendence of God, the form drew what may be considered its four primary characteristics:[149] (1) an overall concern with eschatology; (2) a deterministic outlook on history; (3) a relative or mitigated dualism; (4) an overemphasis on transcendentalism.

From the biblical literature as a whole, but particularly from Amos, Isaiah, Ezechiel, Joel, and Zechariah, and perhaps from Persian mythology,

[147] Cf. *JBC* 20:15-24; and B. Vawter, "Apocalyptic: Its Relation to Prophecy," *CBQ* 22 (1960), 33-46.
[148] Cf. G. von Rad, *Old Testament Theology*, Vol II, 301-315.
[149] On the differences between the prophetic and the apocalyptic view of eschatology, cf. J. Moltmann, *The Theology of Hope*, 135ff.

the apocalyptic authors drew such literary characteristics as the following: [150]
(1) symbolism — names, numbers, beasts, colors, etc; (2) an extensive
angelology; (3) bizarre descriptions of cosmological upheavals; (4) a sys-
tematized presentation of historical events; (5) pseudonymity; (6) eso-
tericism; (7) the repetition of the same basic message through the presentation of grand symbolic historical tableaus.

As a literary medium apocalyptic is the strangest and to some persons
the most repulsive of literary forms. Its message, however strange the
medium, is basically simple and can be expressed succinctly in the words of
the Gospel: "In the world you will have affliction. But have courage. I
have overcome the world" (Jn 16:33).

Authors are agreed that Mt 24:4-31 is apocalyptic in form.[151] His discourse has all the major, and most of the minor, characteristics of apocalyptic literature. It is eschatological and transcendental. It is relatively
deterministic. And it smacks faintly of a mitigated dualism. It is pseu-
donymous in as much as Matthew speaks through the mouth of Jesus.
It envisages future events such as the destruction of Jerusalem, the end of
the world, and the coming of the Son of Man in judgment. It describes
these events in terms of cosmological catastrophes. It has a cast of angels
and the customary apocalyptic trumpets.

Granting all this, it follows that Matthew's apocalyptic discourse
should be interpreted in the same way as other apocalyptic writings. As
with all other figurative language, the symbolic and cosmological language should be demythologized. Historical events clearly "predicted" by
the author should be identified with events which preceded the time of the
author, since the form allows the author to speak in the name of the one
who preceded him and to "predict" what has happened in the interim. These
events in Matthew's discourse would be the destruction of Jerusalem and
the Temple in 70 A.D. and the persecution of the Christians by the Jews
and the Romans up to and including the time of Matthew. The "immediacy"
of other events not verified by the time of the author, e.g., the end of the
world and the coming of the Son of Man should not be pressed in relation
to the imminence or urgency of the events, since it is characteristic of
apocalyptic literature to exaggerate the imminence of God's intervention to
save his own from the forces of evil.

The discourse as we have it in Matthew seems dependent on Mk 13,
however much Matthew revised and expanded it. Although it is much
debated whether Mark or someone before Mark composed the apocalyptic
discourse in Mk 13,[152] there is one factor that makes it highly probable the

[150] On the characteristics of apocalyptic literature, cf. D. S. Russell, The Method and Message of Jewish Apocalyptic; H. H. Rowley, The
Relevance of Apocalyptic; P. F. Ellis, The Men
and the Message of the Old Testament, 506-
530; L. Morris, Apocalyptic.

[151] Cf. A. Feuillet, Dict. de la Bible Suppl.,
6 (1960) 1347-1350; W. F. Albright, op. cit.,
286-289; L. Hartman, Prophecy Interpreted.
[152] Cf. V. Taylor, The Gospel according to St.
Mark, 500-524.

original discourse is the work of Mark, namely, the location of the discourse on Mount Olivet. In Ez 8–11 the prophet pictures the "glory of God" leaving the Temple, resting on Mount Olivet, and from there directing the destruction of the Temple and the city. In Mark's gospel, the author sees the Romans' destruction of Jerusalem and the Temple in 70 A.D. as a repeat of what happened in the time of Ezechiel. He evokes the similarity between the earlier and later catastrophes by having Jesus leave the Temple (Mk 13:1), go to Mount Olivet (Mk 13:3), and from there predict the destruction of the city (13:14-20). Since Mark is by common agreement the most apocalyptic of the gospels[153] and it is entirely unlikely that Mark, Matthew and Luke would all have independently chosen to situate Jesus' farewell discourse on Mount Olivet, the most likely candidate for the original discourse would be Mark.

In Mark's apocalyptic discourse, Jesus predicts the destruction of the Temple (Mk 13:2) and the disciples ask only the one question — when will that destruction take place? (Mk 13:4). In the discourse that follows, however, Jesus not only answers the question about the Temple (Mk 13:14-20) but speaks as well about the end of the world (Mk 13:5-13) and about the coming of the Son of Man (Mk 13:24-27). Mark concludes the discourse with the parable of the fig tree and Jesus' solemn words: "But as for that day or hour, nobody knows it, neither the angels of heaven, nor the Son; no one but the Father" (Mk 13:23-32).

Matthew, for the sake of clarity, has the Apostles ask three questions corresponding to the three subjects Jesus will speak about — the end of the world, the destruction of Jerusalem, and the coming of the Son of Man (Mt 24:3).

In addition to changing Mark's introduction, Matthew also changes his conclusion. Instead of one parable, the parable of the fig tree (cf. Mk 13:23-32), Matthew expands the conclusion to embrace a series of seven parables,[154] and thus balances off the seven parables of the third part of the last great discourse (24:32–25:46) with the seven woes of the first part (23:13-32). Matthew's discourse divides as follows:

Introduction (24:1-3)
a) 24:1-2   Jesus predicts the destruction of the Temple.
b) 24:3   The Apostles ask three questions: (1) about the destruction of the Temple; (2) about the sign of the coming of the Son of Man; (3) about the end of the world.

The apocalyptic discourse (24:4-31)
a) 24:4-14   Answer to the third question — *re* the end of the world.
b) 24:15-22 Answer to the first question — *re* the destruction of the Temple.

---

[153] Cf. J. M. Robinson, *The Problem of History in Mark.*

[154] Matthew had done the same thing in his parable discourse (Mt 13). Where Mark had only five parables in his lakeside discourse (Mk 4), Matthew expanded the number to seven.

c) 24:23-31 Answer to the second question — *re* the sign of the coming of the Son of Man.

Conclusion (24:32–25:46)

a) 24:32-36 The fig tree as a parable of the coming of the Son of Man.
b) 24:37-41 As in the days of Noah.
c) 24:42-44 As when a burglar comes.
d) 24:45-51 As with a faithful servant when his master returns.
e) 25:1-13 As with bridesmaids awaiting the bridegroom.
f) 25:14-30 As with talents given to servants to work with.
g) 25:31-46 As with sheep and goats separated by the shepherd.

The apocalyptic section (Mt 24:15-31) of the last great discourse has met with conflicting interpretations. A. Feuillet interprets the whole discourse in the light of the destruction of Jerusalem by the Romans in 70 A.D.[155] W. Albright interprets everything in relation to the coming of Jesus to glory via the passion and resurrection and denies any reference whatsoever to a second coming.[156] D. R. A. Hare asserts the discourse says nothing at all about the fall of Jerusalem and believes Matthew's purpose in the discourse is to "prepare Christians for enduring faithfullness during the indefinite period that remains" by answering the second of the questions asked by the disciples in 24:3, "What is the sign of your coming and of the end of the world."[157]

We have preferred to interpret the discourse as dealing with three questions posed in 24:3, (1) the question of the end time (vv 4-14); (2) the question about the fall of Jerusalem (vv 15-22); (3) the question about the coming of the Son of Man at the parousia (vv 23-31). We have done so for reasons almost entirely redactional. First, because Matthew appears to use his ending pericope transitions in this section in the same way he has used them throughout the previous parts of the gospel. Second, because in his habitual manner he has used his narrative material to prepare for the subjects of the subsequent discourse. Third, because he has expanded Mark's conclusion to the apocalyptic discourse in a very significant way (cp. Mk 13:28-37 with Mt 24:32–25:46).

Matthew's transitions, as we have seen, invariably look forward to what follows in his discourses. In ch 19–22, the concluding pericope of the narrative deals with the question put by Jesus to the Pharisees about the Messiah: "Whose son is he?" (22:41-46). The answer to the question is not given in 22:41-46. It is only implied in the quotation from Ps 110:1, "The Lord said to my Lord: Sit at my right hand until I make your enemies the footstool for your feet." A twofold answer, however, is given in the following dis-

[155] See A. Feuillet, "Le Sens du Mot Parousie dans l'Evangile de Matthieu: Comparaison entre Matth. 24 et Jac. 5:1-11," *The Background of the New Testament and its Eschatology*, ed. W. D. Davies and D. Daube (1956) 261-280.

[156] Cf. Albright-Mann, Matthew, 290-299.
[157] Cf. D. R. A. Hare, *The Theme of Jewish Persecution of Christians in the Gospel according to Matthew*, 178-179.

course. In ch 23, Matthew has Jesus speak as a prophet. He condemns the pseudo-Israel of the Pharisees (23:13-36) and he concludes by predicting the destruction of the Temple (23:37-39). In substance, Matthew's answer is that Jesus is the eschatological prophet of Dt 18:18.[158]

In ch 24–25, Matthew gives a second answer to the unanswered question of 22:41-46 by presenting Jesus as the Son of Man who will come at the end time to judge all nations. Matthew's emphasis on Jesus as the Son of man is continued, as we have seen,[159] in the passion narrative and in the final missionary mandate of 28:18-20.

In addition to using this subtle transition from his narrative in ch 19–22 to his discourse in ch 23–25, Matthew uses two other ending pericope transitions within the discourse itself. First, the ending pericope of the prophetic discourse in ch 23 contains Jesus' prediction about the destruction of the Temple (23:37-39) and prepares the reader for the allusions to this event in 24:15-20. Second, the ending pericope of the apocalyptic discourse in 24:4-31 concludes with the statement that the "sign of the Son of Man will appear in heaven . . ." and all the nations "will see the Son of Man coming on the clouds of heaven with power and great glory" (24:30-31). In each case the section of the discourse which follows the ending pericope deals with the subject indicated in the ending pericope transition. This is certainly true for ch 24:31–25:46 which deals with the coming of the Son of Man to judge the nations. It is equally true for the disputed reference to the destruction of the Temple and Jerusalem in ch 24:15-25. As we have seen, Matthew invariably takes up the subject indicated in his transition pericope and develops it in what follows. If he says nothing in the apocalyptic section about the destruction of the Temple and Jerusalem, as D. R. A. Hare claims,[160] the least one would have to say is that he departed markedly from both his methodology and his style.

We believe Matthew's transitional pericopes (22:41-46; 23:37-39; 24:29-31) provide the clearest key to the interpretation of the discourse as a whole and especially for the interpretation of the apocalyptic section of the discourse. There is additional evidence, however, from the narrative which precedes the discourse. In characteristic Matthaean fashion, the audience is prepared in the narrative section (ch 19–22) for the subjects treated in the discourse section (ch 23–25), namely: (1) the condemnation of the Jews (ch 23); (2) the destruction of Jerusalem and the coming of the Son of Man to judge (ch 24–25); and (3) the emphasis on the love commandment.

The condemnation of the Jews in ch 23 is anticipated obscurely in the

---

[158] It is difficult to prove, but it is not unlikely that Matthew wishes to represent Jesus in 23 as the eschatological prophet predicted by Moses in Dt 18:18. Moses predicts a "prophet like me." Matthew has already shown in ch 1–7 that Jesus is like Moses. Moses also specifies that the eschatological prophet will "teach." In Mt 23:10 Jesus says: ". . . you have only one teacher, the Christ."

[159] Cf. p. 77.

[160] Cf. *op. cit.*, 177-178.

parable of the vineyard in the words: "Now when the owner of the vineyard comes, what will he do to those tenants? They answered, 'He will bring those wretches to a wretched end . . .' " (21:40-41). It is anticipated clearly in the allegorizing parable of the wedding feast (22:1-14), where Jesus says: "The King was furious. He dispatched his troops, destroyed those murderers, and *burnt their town*" (22:7). The identity of Jesus as the Son of Man is anticipated in the third prophecy of the passion (20:17-19) and in the discussion about the use of authority (20:28). The emphasis on the love command, which anticipates the last judgment parable of 25:31-46, is unequivocal in 22:34-40 where Jesus responds to the question about the greatest commandment by citing the love commands of Dt 6:5 and Lev 19:18.

In addition to Matthew's ending pericope transitions in 22:41-46; 23:37-39; 24:29-31 and his narrative preparation in ch 19–22 for the subjects of the subsequent discourse, there is the significant redactional evidence provided by Matthew's expansion of the conclusion to Mark's apocalyptic discourse (Mk 13:28-37). Matthew has expanded Mark's brief warnings by assembling seven parables (two from Mk 13:28-37 and five from his own source material) to form a conclusion which by itself is as long as ch 23 and ch 24 taken together. There are thirty eight verses in Jesus' prophetic discourse (23:2-39); twenty eight in Jesus' apocalyptic discourse (24:4-31); and *sixty six* in Matthew's conclusion (24:31–25:46). Matthew's version of the apocalyptic discourse is decidedly bottom heavy!

The significance of the expanded conclusion lies in its emphasis on the impossibility of knowing the time of the end judgment and the consequent necessity of using well the in between time. Such an emphasis provides an excellent clue to Matthew's thinking about the time element in the apocalyptic discourse of 24:4-31 and to the purpose he had in mind for the discourse as a whole.

The purpose of the discourse, as D. R. A. Hare rightly says, is to "prepare Christians for enduring faithfulness in the indefinite period that remains." [161] It is for this reason that the discourse begins by dealing with the end time (*synteleia tou aiōnos*) in 24:4-14 instead of with the first question of 24:3 which concerns the fall of Jerusalem. Matthew wants to make two points categorically clear: (1) "the man who stands firm to the end will be saved" (24:13); (2) the end time will come only after the gospel has been proclaimed to the whole world" (24:14 and cp. 28:19).[162]

In the following two sections, Matthew speaks about what will happen from the time of Jesus down to the end time. In 24:15-22, he speaks obliquely about the destruction of the Temple and, implicitly, of Jerusalem in 70 A.D. in order to disabuse his readers of any idea that the end time was meant to

[161] Cf. *op. cit.*, 177.
[162] It is sometimes said that the New Testament theologians delimited the time of the parousia and the end of the world. Against this view, see the excellent study of A. L. Moore, *The Parousia in the New Testament*, 108-159.

follow immediately upon the fall of Jerusalem. The fall of the city was a sign, but only one sign among many.

In 24:23-31, Matthew warns his readers not to be confused by the claims of impostors (24:23-26). He then goes on to say that the coming of the Son of Man "will be like lightning striking in the east and flashing far into the west" (24:27). It will be entirely unpredictable and it will be followed by the judgment when "all the peoples of the earth will . . . see the Son of Man coming on the clouds of heaven with power and great glory" (24:30 and cp. 25:31-33).

As Matthew used the ending pericope (23:37-39) of the prophetic discourse in ch 23 to lead into the apocalyptic discourse in 24:4-31, so here he uses the ending pericope (24:29-31) of the apocalyptic discourse to lead into his conclusion for the discourse as a whole (24:32–25:46). By speaking about the coming of the Son of Man to judge all the nations, Matthew uses his ending pericope to introduce the central theme of the conclusion — the theme of preparing for the end time judgment by using well the intervening time and by making it a time of works and particularly works of charity toward one's neighbor.

3) 24:32—25:46 / Seven parousia parables

The seven parousia parables[163] in Matthew's conclusion all deal in one way or another with three interrelated themes: (1) the coming of the Son of Man to judge all men; (2) the time of the coming; (3) the necessity of being prepared for the judgment. All seven, however, emphasize the third theme. As G. Bornkamm has shown, the theme of judgment at the end time is extraordinarily prominent in Matthew's gospel and no place more so than here.[164]

In passing, it should be noted that Matthew has done to the conclusion of Mark's apocalypse (Mk 13:23-37) what he earlier did to Mark's parable discourse (Mk 4:1-34). Where Mark had five parables, Matthew expanded his discourse to contain seven parables (Mt 13:1-52). In a similar way, where Mark had but two parousia parables in his conclusion to the apocalyptic discourse, Matthew has expanded his conclusion to contain seven parousia parables. The expansion creates, as we have seen, a balance with the seven woes against the Pharisees at the beginning of the final great discourse (23:13-32). Both the predilection for the number seven and the love of balance are characteristic of Matthew. So also is the use of key words such as 'day' and 'hour' in 24:32–25:46.

What is important in Matthew's conclusion is his intimation that the end

[163] See J. Jeremias, *The Parables of Jesus,* 48-66. The term "parousia parables" is borrowed from Jeremias' comment: ". . . both evangelists [Mt and Lk] have inserted them [the parables of the House-breaker and the Servant placed in authority] in a larger collection of *Parousia* parables (Mt 24:32–25:46; Lk 12:35-59)" *op. cit.,* 94.
[164] Cf. Mt 7:21-23; 10:14-15, 40-42; 2:36-37; 13:24-30, 36-43, 47-50; 16:27; 18:23-35, and see Bornkamm, Barth, Held, *op. cit.,* 15-24.

time judgment is not necessarily imminent. He had already intimated as
much in his statement that the end time would come only when the gospel
had been preached to all the nations (24:14). He will intimate the same
even more forcefully in the final missionary mandate when Jesus proclaims
that the work of the Church is to "Disciplize all nations" (23:19). Matthew's
understanding is that there will certainly be a second coming of the Son of
Man — a parousia — but that the parousia will be delayed!

The first parable, the parable of the Fig Tree (24:32-36), with its reference to summer which is harvest time in Palestine and as such symbolic of
judgment since the gathering of the elect is frequently likened to a harvest,
concludes with the categorical statement: "But of that *day* and *hour* no one
knows,[165] not even the angels of heaven, nor the Son, but only the Father"
(24:36). In other words, they may indeed see all the signs which indicate
that "he (the Son of Man) is near, at the very gates" (24:33), but no one
knows for certain the day or the hour when he will come. It is necessary,
therefore, to be ready at all times.

In the second and third parables, the parable of Noahs' day and the parable
of the burglar (24:37-44), Matthew plays on the key words 'day and 'hour.'
The second parable makes the point that the coming of the Son of Man will
be as sudden "as it was in Noah's *day*" (24:37-41). The third parable warns
the householder that the Son of Man's coming will be as unexpected as the
coming of a burglar who comes "at an hour you do not expect" (24:42-44).
The fourth parable, the parable of the honest and dishonest servants (24:45-
51), continues the play on words by concluding with the statement: ". . .
his master will come on the *day* he does not expect and at an *hour* he does
not know" (24:50).

The fifth parable, the parable of the bridesmaids (24:1-13), makes the
point that the coming of the Son of Man may well be delayed a long time.
The bridesmaids without oil are called foolish, not because they fall asleep —
all ten bridemaids fall asleep — but because they did not count on and prepare for a long delay. As J. Jeremias says: ". . . the 'tarrying' of the bridegroom (v. 5) is the postponement of the *Parousia*."[166] The parable concludes
with a repetition of the key words: ". . . you never know the *day* or the
hour" (24:13 and cp. 24:36, 37, 42, 44, 50).

The sixth parable, the parable of the talents (25:14-30), makes the same
point as the previous parable, for the master returns to settle accounts with
his servants only after a long time (*meta de polyn chronon*) (25:19).

The seventh parable, the sheep and the goats (25:31-46), repeats much
already said in the other parables: the coming of the Son of Man, the judgment, the division into good and wicked; but it also omits much: namely,

---

[165] It should be noted that Matthew repeats
regularly the key words 'day' and 'hour' (cf.
24:36,37,42,50; 25:13) and thus unifies all his
material in 24:32–25:46.
[166] Cf. J. Jeremias, *op. cit.*, 51.

the warnings to be watchful and the regular references to the day and the hour. The reasons for the repetitions and omissions are self-evident. In the last judgment parable, there is no more time. There is no longer occasion to be watchful. The Son of Man has come, and it is the time for judgment. The day and the hour that no one knew, not even the Son, but only the Father (24:36) has arrived!

The parable concentrates on only one point — the criterion according to which the good are judged blessed and the wicked accursed. All are agreed the one criterion is the love commandment.[167] Not all are agreed, however, on the meaning of the significant statement: "Whatsoever you do to the least of my brethren, you do to me" (25:40, 45).

They are not agreed because "the least of my brethren" can be interpreted in at least two ways. It can mean: (1) Christians in general, and the preachers of the gospel in particular; (2) any and every man in any circumstances and at any time.

J. Lambrecht has argued that "the least of these my brethren" (25:40, 45) refers to missionaries and that the nations are judged according to the manner in which they treated the disciples sent to preach the gospel.[168]

This conclusion is based for the main part on the similarities with Mt 10, particularly Mt 10:40-42, a chapter very much concerned with the mission to Israel rather than with the mission to the world commanded in 28:19.

However, even if "the least of my brethren" is not restricted to missionaries and is extended to embrace all Christians in general, the meaning would still be too limited for the context of Matthew's gospel. The immediate context is the end time when all men will be judged and when presumably the gospel has been preached to all the nations (cf. Mt 24:14; 28:19). Such a judgment requires a universal norm.[169] The context of the gospel as a whole is clearly universalistic. The universal mission is foreshadowed: in the visit of the Magi (2:1-12); in the words "you are the salt of the earth" (5:13); "you are the light of the world" (5:14); in the cures of the centurion's servant (8:5-13), the gadarene demoniacs (8:28-34), the Canaanite woman's daughter (15:21-28); and in the parable of the darnel where "the field is the world" (13:38). The universal mission is explicit in 28:19 and 24:14.

Along with the argument from the context, one must include the Matthaean insistence on the love command as the greatest command and the criterion in the light of which all other commands are to be interpreted.[170] Certainly

[167] Cf. J. Jeremias, *op. cit.*, 206-210, especially 209; Bornkamm, Barth, Held, *op. cit.*, especially 23-24; C. G. Montefiore, *The Synoptic Gospels*, 257-322; P. Furnish, *The Love Command in the New Testament*, 79-84.

[168] Cf. J. Lambrecht, "The Parousia Discourse: Composition and Content in Mt XXIV–XXV," *L'Evangile selon saint Matthieu: redaction et theologie* (ed. M. Didier) 333-350. See also, L. Coupe, "Matthew XXV:31-46 — The Sheep and Goats Reinterpreted," *NovT* 11 (1969) 32-44.

[169] As D. R. A. Hare says: "The universality of the judgment requires a universal norm; not all men can be judged on the basis of the treatment accorded a small group of Christians. Indeed the view that the eternal destiny of all men will depend upon their treatment of Christians is essentially immoral!" (*op. cit.*, 124).

[170] See pp. 150-154.

the great command is for all men and is an apt and adequate norm of judgment for all men.

On the redactional level, two elements should be taken into consideration. First, in characteristic fashion, Matthew has prepared his audience to accept the love command as the universal norm for judgment by including in his foregoing narrative block (ch 19–22) the scene with the Pharisees in which Jesus declares and promulgates the overriding importance of the love command (22:34-40). Second, in equally characteristic fashion, Matthew has used the last judgment parable as his ending pericope for the final great discourse and has thus summed up under the love command everything said about 'doing' and 'not doing' in 23:3-36 and 24:45–25:30.

Finally, it can hardly be held that the centrality of the love command did not rank high among all the things that Jesus taught his Apostles. In Matthew's mind, as a consequence, when Jesus is shown commissioning his Apostles to disciplize all nations "teaching them to observe all I have commanded you" (28:19), the love command must certainly have been considered central to all Jesus commanded. The idea, therefore, that all men at the end time would be judged on their observance or non-observance of the command: "You shall love your neighbor as yourself" (a command which by definition [cf. 24:14] has been preached to all men) can hardly have been alien to Matthew's mind. As P. Furnish says:

> . . . in 25:32 "all the nations" gathered before the Son of Man must be *evangelized nations*, the worldwide "kingdom" out of which the unrighteous will be separated.
>
> Since this is the scene presupposed, it is futile to debate the question whether "the least of these my brethren" is a reference to Christians only, and not the world at large. In light of Matthew's expectations for the eschaton the question is irrelevant. At that time all men will be within the kingdom in the sense that formally they will have received the gospel. They all stand finally under the claim and the judgment of the gospel of love.[171]

THE PASSION, DEATH, AND RESURRECTION OF THE SON OF MAN
Mt 26:1—28:20

The authority of Jesus as the Son of Man foretold by Daniel (cf. Dn 7:13) dominates the seventh and final discourse of the gospel[172] (28:18-20). In ch 26–28, Matthew's frequent references to the Son of Man indicate

---

[171] Cf. P. Furnish, *The Love Command in the New Testament*, 82-83.

[172] See H. Conzellmann, "History and Theology in the Passion Narratives of the Synoptic Gospels" *Interpretation* 24 (April 1970) 192-194; R. Fuller, *The Formation of the Resurrection Narratives*; P. Benoit, *The Passion and Ressurrection of Jesus Christ*; G. Barth, *Tradi-

tion and Interpretation in Matthew*, 143-147; A. Vanhoye, *Structure and .Theology of the Accounts of the Passion in the Synoptic Gospels*; E. Blair, *Jesus in the Gospel of Matthew*; R. Martin, "St. Matthew's Gospel in Recent Study" *Expository Times* 80 (5, 1969), 132-136; F. Hahn, *Mission in the New Testament*; W. Marksen, *The Resurrection of Jesus*.

his narrative is to be interpreted by its goal, which is the enthronement of Jesus in 28:18.[173]

The narrative contains the usual Matthaean characteristics: (1) departure point from Mark's narrative;[174] (2) prophetic prediction texts with and without the fulfilment formula;[175] (3) the propensity for the number seven;[176] (4) the polemic against pseudo-Israel;[177] (5) concentric-circle themes;[178] (6) the use of an ending pericope as a subtle transition to the subsequent discourse. [179]

As in his two previous narrative sections (ch 14–17 and ch 19–22), Matthew takes the bulk of his material from Mark. It will be necessary again, therefore, to note the material Matthew has added to or omitted from the Markan text and to analyze the changes Matthew has introduced into the Markan narrative.[180]

The following synoptic table of Mk 14–16 and Mt 26–28 shows the material Matthew has in common with Mark, has added to Mark, has omitted from Mark, has changed in Mark.

Pericopes	Mark	Matthew	Matthew's changes
Conspiracy against Jesus	14:1-2	26:2-5	Mt adds vv 3-4 [181]
Woman anoints Jesus' head	14:3-9	26:6-13	No change [182]
Judas betrays Jesus	14:10-11	26:14-16	Subtle change *re* money [183]

[173] As Conzellmann says: "The passion is a stage on the way that runs like a straight line to the enthronement — (Mt 28:16-20)" (*art. cit.*, 192).

[174] Cp. Mt 26:2-5 with Mk 14:1-2.

[175] Cf. Mt 27:9 (Jer 32:6-15 and Ze 11:11-13) and 26:31,54,56,64.

[176] Note the sevenfold reference to "silver pieces" (27:3-10).

[177] Matthew leaves no doubt the leaders of the pseudo-Israel were responsible for the death of Jesus (cf. 26:3-5, 59-68; 27:1,11-26,41-43,51, 62-66).

[178] E.g., the authority of Jesus (passim); discipleship (passim); universality (cf. 26:13, 28).

[179] Matthew's resurrection account (28:1-11) is skillfully composed to prepare the way for the meeting of the Apostles with Jesus on the Mount in Galilee from which Jesus will proclaim his authority as Son of Man and the authority of the Apostles as his prophets (28:16-20).

[180] H. Conzellmann's conclusion concerning Luke's composition of the passion narrative is perfectly applicable to Matthew's passion narrative: "Although the use of new material by Luke cannot be disputed, the most important alterations are the result of Luke's editorial work and are the expression of his own views" (*Theology of Luke*, 200).

[181] Matthew makes two significant changes in Mark's account: (1) Instead of a simple, "It was two days before the Passover . . . ," as in Mark, Matthew has Jesus link the time element with a prediction about the Son of Man:

"It will be Passover, as you know, in two days' time, and the Son of Man will be handed over to be crucified." The prediction emphasizes the foreknowledge of Jesus. The linking of the Passover and the death of Jesus is probably an allusion to the new Passover and the New Covenant (cf. 26:28). Matthew introduces the title "Son of Man" because it is his aim to emphasize that Jesus is the authoritative Son of Man of Dn 7:13 and also, perhaps, to form an inclusion-conclusion with 28:18. (2) Matthew's addition of the verb "assembled" looks like an allusion to Ps 2:2, "The rulers take counsel together against the Lord and his anointed." The same language is repeated in 27:1 and 28:12 and in each case recalls Ps 2:2. In 28:12 Matthew introduces the story of the guards who are bribed with "silver" as Judas was bribed in 26:14-16. His intention seems to be, as in 27:3-10 where Judas returns the thirty pieces of "silver," to emphasize official Judaism's rejection and betrayal of Christ. Thus, at the beginning (26:3), in the middle (27:1), and at the end of his narrative (28:12), Matthew lays the blame for Jesus' death at the feet of the leaders of the Jews.

[182] The statement, "wherever in all the world this Good News is proclaimed," is taken from Mark, but it serves to prepare the reader for the later command to the Apostles to "disciplize all nations" (28:19).

[183] Mark has "money" (*argurion*). Matthew specifies "thirty pieces of silver" (*arguria*) because he is preparing the way for his quotation and fulfilment formula in 27:9-10.

Preparation for Passover	14:12-16	26:17-19	Simplifies by omitting [184]
Judas' treachery predicted	14:17-21	26:20-25	Key text from Mk 14:21a [185]
The Eucharist and the covenant	14:22-25	26:26-29	Adds v 28 [186]
Peter's denials predicted	14:26-31	26:30-35	Emphasizes v 32 [187]
Gethsemane	14:32-42	26:26-46	
Betrayal and arrest	14:43-52	26:47-56	Adds vv 52-54 and omits Mk 14:51-52 [188]
Sanhedrin condemns Jesus	14:53-65	26:57-68	Allusion to Ps 2:2; Ps 110:1; and Dn 7:13 [189]
Peter denies Jesus	14:66-72	26:69-75	Addition [190]
Blood money	——	27:3-10	Only in Matthew [191]
Jesus before Pilate	15:1-15	27:1-26 and 11-26	Matthew adds 27:19 and 27:24-25 [192]
The crown of thorns	15:16-20	27:27-31	

[184] Matthew omits Mk 14:12b, "when the Passover lamb was sacrificed," possibly because he looks upon Christ as the Passover lamb and knows he will not be sacrificed until the next day. He simplifies by leaving out the "man carrying a pitcher of water" (Mk 14:13b-15).

[185] For Matthew, Jesus' statement, "The Son of Man is going to his fate, as the Scriptures say he will" (Mt 26:24 = Mk 14:21a), is crucial for the understanding of the passion. Matthew's emphasis on Christ's foreknowledge, his willingness to fulfill the Scriptures, the almost inevitableness of Judas' betrayal, the Jews' rejection of Jesus, and Pilate's impotence to save Jesus, has as its goal to show that Christ perfectly fulfills the will of the Father as revealed in the Scriptures (cf. 26:2,12,18,21,26-28,31,45,53-54,56a, 64; 27:9). Matthew adds v 25 to further emphasize Jesus' foreknowledge.

[186] Matthew adds v 28b, "for the forgiveness of sins," because he sees Jesus as the "suffering servant" of Is 53, because he wishes to emphasize the theme of forgiveness (cf. 6:12-25; 18:12-35), and because of Jer 31:34 where forgiveness is a primary characteristic of the New Covenant.

[187] The words, "after my resurrection I will go before you to Galilee," are pivotal for Matthew's account of the passion. Like Mark (Mk 16:7), Matthew repeats the promise (Mt 28:7), but unlike Mark, Matthew not only describes the meeting of Christ and the Apostles in Galilee (Mt 28:16-20) but makes it the climax of his gospel.

[188] The reference to the "twelve legions of angels" recalls Dn 7:10, "thousands upon thousands (of angels) were ministering to him," and serves, along with Matthew's many other references to the Son of Man of Dn 7:13 who will receive "dominion. glory, and kingship" (cf. 26:64 and 28:18). Mk 14:51-52 is omitted because irrelevant.

[189] In 26:57 Matthew changes the verb in order, as in 26:2; 27:1 and 28:12, to allude to the priests and elders as those "assembled against the Lord and his anointed" (Ps 2:2). In 26:64 he follows Mark (14:64) in combining the allusion to Ps 110:1, "you will see the Son of Man seated at the right of the Power," with an allusion to Dn 7:13, "and coming on the clouds of heaven." The double allusion expresses perfectly Matthew's interpretation of the passion as Christ's way to enthronement as authoritative Son of Man (cf. 26:2,24,29,53-54).

[190] Matthew adds "bitterly" to "Peter wept," thus putting Peter in a better light.

[191] Only Matthew has the incident. But it is not a mindless intrusion and its main point is not the death of Judas. Matthew had prepared for the incident by changing Mark's "money" (argurion) to the more precise "thirty pieces of silver" (cp. Mk 14:12 and Mt 26:15). The purpose of the story is to highlight the guilt of the Jews in rejecting Jesus. The thirty pieces are mentioned seven times. And Matthew has the Jews admit "it is blood money" (27:6b). It is Matthew's way once again of showing that official Judaism's rejection of Jesus constitutes them the pseudo-Israel. Matthew indicates by his reference to Zech 11:12-13, "And they took the thirty silver pieces, the sum at which the precious One was priced by the children of Israel," that Jesus' rejection by his own people was already predicted in the Scriptures.

[192] Matthew's editing of Mark's text shows again his intention of emphasizing the responsibility of pseudo-Israel for Jesus' death. Pilate's unwillingness to execute Jesus is stressed in order to emphasize by contrast pseudo-Israel's rejection of Jesus. To leave no doubt, Matthew adds to Mark's text the words, "And the people, to a man, shouted back, 'His blood be on us and on our children' " (27:24-25).

Jesus is crucified	15:21-27	27:32-38	
Jesus is mocked	15:29-32	27:39-44	Adds "Son of God" twice
Jesus dies	15:33-41	27:45-56	Adds 27:51b-53 [193]
Jesus is buried	15:42-47	27:57-61	Adds allusion to Is 53
Guards and sealing of tomb	——	27:62-66	Only in Matthew [194]
Women and the resurrection	16:1-8	28:1-10	Great changes [195]
Conspiracy with guards	——	28:11-15	Only in Matthew [196]
Enthronement of the Son of Man	——	28:16-20	Only in Matthew [197]

[193] From the crowning to the burial, Matthew's account is almost indistinguishable from Mark's. In 27:51-53b, however, Matthew makes a significant addition. Using apocalyptic language to express the significance of Jesus' death, he explicates the "from this time onward" (*ap' arti*) of Jesus' words in 26:64. The purpose of the addition is to show that with the death of Jesus, the old era and the Old Covenant are finished and the new age and the New Covenant have begun. Beginning with the rending of the veil of the Temple, which even in Mark symbolized the end of the old era and the beginning of the new, Matthew goes on to mention two classic apocalyptic signs of the arrival of the messianic era: the earthquake and the resurrection of the dead (27:52; cp. Is 24:19-20; 26:19; Dn 12:2-3). Cf. P. Benoit, *The Passion and Resurrection of Jesus Christ*, 199-204.

[194] Matthew again alludes to Ps 2:2 by having the priests and the Pharisees "assemble" (*sunexthesan* — same verb as in 26:3,57; 28:12) to persuade Pilate to post guards and seal the tomb. The seals may be an allusion to Daniel in the lions' den where the king had seals put on "the stone that had been brought to block the opening of the den" (Dn 6:18). At a later date, Daniel in the lions' den became a symbol of the resurrection. Matthew's allusion here may be the origin of the symbolism. In either case, the allusion fits with Matthew's frequent allusions to the book of Daniel. As in Dn 6, where Daniel's enemies were foiled in their accusation (Dn 6:11-16) and later punished (Dn 6:25), so here Matthew may be intimating something similar for the Jews responsible for Jesus' death. Cf. P. Benoit, *op. cit.*, 226-227.

[195] Matthew ends his final narrative with a transition passage which introduces the subsequent seventh discourse. Since Mark showed the women silent and said nothing about the fulfillment of Jesus' promise to meet with his Apostles in Galilee, Matthew had to make a wholesale revision of the Markan narrative to make it into a suitable transition passage. His changes make good sense when considered in the light of his purpose, which is to prepare his readers for the enthronement of Jesus in 28:16-20. Preserving Mark's visit of the women to the tomb and the angel's message to the Apostles (Mk 16:1,6-7), Matthew makes the following changes:
(1) Omissions: a) he omits Salome from the list of women, perhaps because the Torah called for "two witnesses." b) He says nothing about the women's intention to "anoint" the body of Jesus (Mk 16:1), probably because he considered the anointing already done at Bethany (26:6-13). c) He omits the discussion about rolling back the stone (Mk 16:3-4) because he provides an earthquake to take care of it. d) He omits the silence of the women (Mk 16:8).
(2) Additions: a) he provides an apocalyptic earthquake to accompany the angel who opens the tomb (cf. Dn 6:23) and to provide evidence for the guards. 26:66 and 28:11) who witness the earthquake and the angel (28:4). b) Unlike Mark (16:8), who has the women say nothing to anyone, Matthew has them turn "to tell the disciples" (28:8). The message is essential to Matthew's preparation for the meeting on the mountain in Galilee (28:16). c) Finally, Matthew adds the meeting of the women with Jesus, their falling down before him (like the Magi in Mt 2:11), and Jesus' repetition of the message: "Tell my brothers that they must leave for Galilee; they will see me *there*."

[196] The conspiracy with the guards is found only in Matthew and again, as in 26:3; 27:1,62, Matthew alludes to Ps 2:2 by using the same verb (*sunexthesan*), attributing to the leaders of the Jews the continued opposition of pseudo-Israel to Christ and pointedly remarking "to this day that the story told among the Jews" (28:15).

[197] The relationship of the final discourse of Jesus to the preceding transitional narrative is made unmistakeable in Matthew's introduction to the missionary mandate of the enthroned Christ. The statement, "Meanwhile the eleven disciples set out for Galilee, to the mountain *where Jesus had arranged to meet them*" (28:16), recalls not only the double message about meeting Jesus in Galilee (28:7,10) but also the earlier prediction of Jesus: "After my resurrection I shall go before you to Galilee" (26:32).

Conzellmann's conclusion seems inescapable: "The passion is a stage on the way that runs like a straight line to the enthronement (Mt 28:16-20)."[198] Jesus identifies himself with the Son of Man from the beginning to the end (cf. 26:2,24,46,53,64; 28:18). He three times speaks of the meeting in Galilee with his Apostles (26:32; 28:7,10). He tells the assembled Sanhedrin, "*From this time onward* you will see the Son of Man seated at the right hand of the Power and coming on the clouds of heaven" (26:64), and then in 28:18 speaks of himself in language from Dn 7:13-15, "All authority in heaven and on earth has been given to me." For the Jews who have eyes to see (i.e., believe), it should be clear that Jesus has been raised from the dead and "seated at the right hand of the power."

For the observant reader, the conclusion to Matthew's gospel swarms with inclusion-conclusions which look back to the beginning of his gospel: (1) The Jews, the guards, and Pilate (27:62-66) are as incapable of obstructing Jesus as Herod and his soldiers (Mt 2:1-18). (2) The women prostrate themselves before the risen Christ (28:9) as the Magi had prostrated themselves before the infant Jesus (Mt 2:11). (3) The *light in Galilee* foretold by Isaiah (Is 9:1 = Mt 4:14-16), which is seen first on the mount of the beatitudes (Mt 5:1ff), then on the mount of the transfiguration (Mt 17:1-7), is seen finally on the mountain in Galilee "where Jesus had arranged to meet them" (28:16). (4) The last words of Jesus, who had been named Emmanuel (Mt 2:22-23), echo the name "God-with-us." He declares: "And know that *I am with you* always; yes, to the end of time" (Mt 28:20). (5) The gospel begins with the Gentile Magi coming from the ends of the earth to do obeisance to the infant God (Mt 2:1-11). It ends with the Jewish Apostles sent out to the ends of the earth to disciplize all nations and have them do obeisance to the enthroned Son of Man and Son of God by observing all he has commanded (Mt 28:19-20).

[198] *Art. cit.*, 192.

Part Three

THEOLOGICAL MATTHEW

It has been the contention of this book that Matthew, like Paul before him and John after him, theologized on the didache of Jesus and developed his own inspired theology. The results of his theologizing constitute what we call Matthaean theology as distinct from Pauline, Lukan, Markan, or Johannine theology.[1]

MATTHAEAN THEOLOGY

In our study of Matthew's theology, the reader should always keep in mind that it is *Matthew's* theology that is under consideration, not the theology of his predecessors or even the theology of Jesus. An analysis of the theological teaching of Jesus belongs properly to the sphere of the quest for the historical Jesus.[2] An analysis of the theology of Matthew's predecessors in the oral tradition belongs properly to the sphere of form criticism.[3] A redaction or composition study of Matthew's gospel of itself goes no further than the mind and the theology of Matthew.

Properly speaking, our analysis aims to discover what the evangelist himself believed and taught about Christ and the Church in the last quarter of the first century. It aims, if we may paraphrase the question of Jesus at Caesarea Philippi, to ask Matthew: Who do you say that Jesus is? What do you say about the relationship between the Israel of the Pharisees and the Israel of the Christian community? What do you say about the law as taught and interpreted by the Pharisees and as taught and interpreted by Christ?

[1] As G. Bornkamm says: ". . . the first three Gospels are documents expressing a definite, though in each case very different theology, which gives to each of them, without detriment to what they have in common, a more or less consistently and systematically developed theme, which makes it possible to recognize as their background, different communities with their particular problems and views" (Bornkamm, Barth, Held, *op. cit.*, 11).

[2] A number of attempts have been made to sift out the precise historical didache of Jesus. Cf. particularly, G. Bornkamm, *Jesus of Nazareth*; N. Perrin, *The Kingdom of God in the Teaching of Jesus*; *Rediscovering the Teaching of Jesus*; and the works of J. Jeremias, especially *New Testament Theology*.

[3] See R. Bultmann, *The History of the Synoptic Tradition*; H. Conzellmann, *An Outline of the Theology of the New Testament*; J. Jeremias, *The Parables of Jesus*.

What do you say about the authority and mission of the Apostles and the Church? Other questions might be asked, but these are the central questions. Matthew's answers, as presented in his gospel, constitute what we consider to be his theology.

Two observations are in order before entering upon a study of Matthew's theology. First, Matthew's gospel belongs to a class of literature known as *Klein-literatur*. It is a type of literature addressed to a narrow and familiar audience which the author knows intimately and with which he shares not only the same faith but the same general attitudes, feelings, and problems. It is an audience which knows the author so well that it can read between his lines, resonate to the implications of his symbolism, innuendoes and loaded words, and fill in for itself what the author knows and takes for granted it will fill in and understand. We must remember that for such an audience, much that appears puzzling and ambiguous to us was more than adequately clear.[4]

Second, Matthew's theology like all theology is conditioned in its presentation and content by the theological needs of his audience. Such needs necessitated emphases on matters which sometimes have little relevance for us in the twentieth century. We are little concerned, for example, about the Pharisees' opposition to Matthew's claim for Jesus' messiahship, for the authority of Jesus over Moses, and for the Church as the true Israel. We take these for granted. It was quite different in Matthew's time and in Matthew's situation. It will be necessary, therefore, to distinguish between what is normative and what is time-conditioned in Matthew's theology.

At the same time, it will be necessary to remember that no matter how irrelevant some elements of the gospel may be in themselves, they may be extremely relevant in some other way. The Pharisees, for example, are of little interest to us in themselves. But it is nonetheless true that Matthew's gospel was written in reaction to them. As a consequence, Matthew's theology can be appreciated in depth only to the degree that one knows the Pharisees and their teachings.[5]

With regard to methodology in studying Matthew's theology, several points established in our redaction study of the gospel are of particular importance. First, Matthew's concentric-circle form of presentation makes it essential, if we are to understand fully the theological concepts of Matthew, that we synthesize what is said about each concept in each concentric-circle presentation. This will require repetition of much that has already been said in our redaction study of the gospel. It will be necessary, however, because Matthew does not present his theology in the linear

[4] W. Albright's contention that Matthew uses his quotations from Scripture in the light of their Old Testament context, if correct, would mean that Matthew knew his audience well enough to expect them to be able to supply the Old Testament context and thus understand his message far more fully than we who are not so well acquainted with the Old Testament (*op. cit.*, lxi).

[5] Cf. J. Neusner, *The Rabbinic Traditions about the Pharisees before 70 A.D.*

fashion we are accustomed to in our modern theological works. He does not take up a subject, develop it, and then move on to another subject. In Semitic fashion he keeps returning to the same subject in different concentric-circle presentations. Synthesis, therefore, is essential.

Second, it has been observed that Matthew chooses carefully his ending pericopes. Since the ending pericopes of his narratives usually look forward to and serve as an immediate transition to the discourse that follows, it will be advisable to study them carefully.[6] The ending pericopes of the discourses, on the other hand, do just the opposite. They look back to the discourse just terminating and emphasize a central theme of the discourse.[7] In every case the ending pericopes provide evidence for ascertaining the direction of Matthew's thinking.

Third, it has been established that the gospel as a whole leads up to and is summarized by the final discourse of Jesus in Mt 28:18-20. An analysis of each term in the discourse in the light of the gospel as a whole should, as a consequence, provide an insight into the major themes of Matthew's theology.

Keeping in mind the necessity of synthesizing the concentric-circle presentations of each theme and the importance of the end pericopes, we shall use Matthew's summary in 28:18-20 as a guide to his theology. We shall study his Christology in the light of his statement in 28:18, "All authority in heaven and on earth has been given to me." The statement implies such questions as: (1) Who is Jesus that all authority should be given to him? (2) Is he the Messiah? (3) Is he the Son of God? (4) Is he the Son of Man? It is upon Matthew's affirmative answer to these questions that his Christology rests.

We shall study his ecclesiology in the light of the missionary mandate in 28:19-20. The mandate implies such questions as: (1) To what corporate body of men is this authority and mission given? (2) What is the authority of the twelve Apostles in this corporate body? (3) What authority does Peter have in relation to the other Apostles and the Church as a whole? (4) What precisely is the mission of the Church in the world? (5) What is the meaning of "teach them to observe all that I have commanded you"?

MATTHEW'S CHRISTOLOGY

To understand Matthew's Christology, it will be necessary to say something about the purpose and methodology of Christology in general. It will

---

[6] Mt 4:23-25 prepares the way for the Sermon on the Mount; 9:36-37 for the missionary discourse; 12:43-50 for the parable discourse; 17:24-27 for the community discourse; 22:41-46 for the last great discourse; and 28:1-10 for the missionary mandate discourse in 28:16-20.

[7] On this basis, a central theme of the Sermon on the Mount is the doing of the radical will of God (7:21-27); a central theme of the missionary discourse is the authority of the Apostles (10:40); of the parable discourse, understanding Jesus (13:52); of the community discourse, forgiveness (18:23-35); of the last discourse, the importance of the love command (25:31-46).

then be possible to analyze Matthew's Christology and come to some conclusions about his viewpoint on the nature and person of Christ. We shall begin with a discussion of Christology in general. We shall then attempt to subsume, under the three titles, Messiah, Son of God, and Son of Man, the substance of Matthew's Christology.

Christology in general is the science which aims to elucidate the answers the New Testament theologians gave to the question put by Jesus himself: "Whom do men say that I am?"[8] More precisely, the central question of New Testament Christology is the question: "How explain the 'uniqueness' of Christ? How explain to Jew and Gentile that *this* man is different from other men; that he is, indeed, *more* than man?" In short, New Testament Christology aims to discover what the New Testament theologians believed and taught about the nature and person of Christ. It is a positive, not a speculative science.

To understand New Testament Christology as a positive science, it is necessary to realize that the early preachers and the later evangelists were forced by the nature of the Christ event and by the demands of their audiences to pose to themselves — and answer in terms intelligible to their audiences — the question: "How is Jesus not only different from other men but even more than man?"

In order to explain the "uniqueness" of Christ, the early preachers as well as St. Paul, the Synoptic theologians, and John, made use of certain titles for Christ and certain concepts already known by their audiences from the Jewish, Roman, or Hellenistic background of the particular society and culture in which they lived.[9]

Since the gospel was first preached to Jews in the ambiance of Palestinian Judaism, scholars presuppose that the earliest concepts and titles used to explain the uniqueness of Christ's person and work were those already known and familiar from the Old Testament and from rabbinical discussion and speculation about the Kingdom of God and the Messiah.

It is presupposed that the following titles would be particularly meaningful for Jews with a Palestinian background: (1) the title "Messiah" and the background of the Old Testament teaching on the coming of the Mes-

[8] Cf. W. Marksen, *The Beginnings of Christology*; R. Brown, *Jesus, God and Man*; O. Cullmann, *Christology of the New Testament*; R. Fuller, *Foundations of New Testament Theology*; W. Pannenburg, *Jesus God and Man*; N. Perrin, *The Kingdom of God in the Teaching of Jesus*; *Rediscovering the Teaching of Jesus*; J. Jeremias, *New Testament Theology*; *The Prayers of Jesus*; *The Problem of the Historical Jesus*; J. M. Robinson, *A New Quest of the Historical Jesus*; "The Recent Debate on the New Quest" *JBR* 30 (1962) 198-208; H. C. Kee, *Jesus in History*; H. K. McArthur, "From the Historical Jesus to Christology," *Interpretation* 23 (1969) 190-206;

In Search of the Historical Jesus; G. Bornkamm, *Jesus of Nazareth*; E. Kaesemann, *Essays on New Testament Themes*; *The Testament of Jesus*; R. Bultmann, *Theology of the New Testament*, Part I, 1-189; H. Conzellmann, *An Outline of the Theology of the New Testament*; J. McIntyre, *The Shape of Christology*; H. Boers, "Where Christology is Real," *Interpretation* 26 (July 1972) 300-327; R. N. Longenecker, *The Christology of Early Jewish Christianity*; C. C. Anderson, *The Historical Jesus: A Continuing Quest*. B. Vawter, *This Man Jesus*.
[9] Cf. R. H. Fuller, *op. cit.*, 1-141; O. Cullmann, *op. cit.*, 1-12, 315-328.

siah, the messianic Kingdom, and the messianic age. With this title would
go other titles associated with the development of messianic theology,
namely, "Son of David," flowing from the promise to David in 2 Sm 7;
"Son of God," flowing from the usage in 2 Sm 7 and Pss 2 and 110, according to which each Davidic king was considered to be the "adopted
Son of God"; and "King," flowing from the same Old Testament background; (2) the title "suffering servant" (more often implicit than explicit)
from the Servant Canticles of Isaiah in general but particularly from the
fourth canticle (Is 52:12–53:13); (3) the title "Son of Man" from Dn 7
and Ez (passim); (4) the title "Prophet" (more properly the "eschatological
prophet") from Dt 18:18.

For Jews who lived outside Palestine in such Hellenistic cities as Alex-
andria, Athens, Antioch and the like, the titles utilized by the preachers and
evangelists would be similar to those used in Palestinian Judaism for the
most part, but different in some aspects because of the different background
of the Hellenistic Jews. Titles familiar to Hellenistic Jews would be the
following: (1) the title "Son of God" in the sense of a very holy, God-
fearing man, as used in Wis 2:13,16-18; 5:5; (2) the title "wisdom" (usually
implicit) flowing from the quasi-apotheosis of wisdom in such texts as
Prov 8:22-31; Sir 24:3-22; Wis 7:22–8:18; (3) the title "first or heavenly
man" (usually implicit) as developed in the theology of Philo and the
rabbis in their speculation concerning the "man" in Gn 1:26 and 2:7; (4)
the title "logos" flowing from certain aspects of Old Testament speculation
concerning the "word of God" and certain aspects of Hellenistic philosophy
to which Jews of the diaspora were drawn.[10]

For the Gentiles who knew little or nothing about the titles familiar to
Jews of a Palestinian background and Jews of a Hellenistic background,
the preachers and evangelists had to make do for the most part with the
above-mentioned titles. There were other titles, however, familiar from the
pagan background of the Gentiles which could be used. With these the
evangelists and preachers could tailor their message to the capacity and
background of their audiences by using the titles in a new and more nuanced
context.

These additional titles were: (1) titles flowing from the imperial cultus,
i.e., the ruler worship which had begun with Alexander the Great and his
successors and was eventually picked up by the Roman emperors, e.g.,
"Lord" (*Kyrios*), "God" (*theos*), "Son of God" (*huios tou theou*), and
"savior" (*sotēr*); (2) titles and concepts which were beginning to be popular
in pagan society such as the concept of the "divine man" (*theios anēr*) who
was held to be able by means of an indwelling divine power to prophesy,
work miracles, and in general perform stupendous feats beyond the capaci-

---

[10] Cf. C. H. Dodd, *The Interpretation of the Fourth Gospel*, 263-285.

ties of ordinary men, and the concept of the Gnostic redeemer and the Gnostic redeemer myth to the degree that it can be proved they existed prior to the beginning of the second century.[11]

In view of what has been said, the methodology for a scientific study of Christology involves a succession of difficult steps. Since the New Testament writings made use of traditions which flowed initially from preaching to Jews of the Palestinian milieu, then from preaching to Hellenistic Jews, and finally from preaching directed to Gentiles, a scientific methodology for the study of New Testament Christology would involve the following: (1) the determination of the audience and background of each title-bearing unit in the New Testament along with a grasp of the original audience's understanding of the title; (2) the determination of the writer's audience along with a grasp of the writer's use of the title in relation to his audience; (3) the attempt to discover if and in what sense Christ himself used the title predicated of him by the New Testament writer. It is here that the investigator touches upon the question of the "historical Jesus" and his self-consciousness which is the ultimate and absolute foundation of New Testament Christology.[12]

Scholars have not yet adequately analyzed Matthew's Christology. And, considering the monumental problems such a task poses, it is perhaps not too much to say that it will be some years before a definitive study appears. The scope of the present work precludes any attempt at such a study. We shall limit ourselves, therefore, to an analysis of the titles: Messiah, Son of God, and Son of Man. Our aim will be equally limited. We shall say something about the background of each title, its use by Matthew, and the reasons for Matthew's use of the title. For the form critical evaluation of each title, the reader is urged to consult the major studies on New Testament Christology mentioned above.

Our study will show that Matthew and his community believed firmly in Jesus' right to the titles Messiah and Son of Man. It will show as well that they hailed Jesus as the Son of God in a unique sense. It will be difficult, however, to prove that this unique sense included the ultimate sense of divinity and equality with the Father in an ontological meaning of the terms. This is not to say that they did not believe in the divinity of Jesus. They did. But the belief and the expression of the belief are different things. The one can be certain. The other is always subject to the ambiguity of language and the extreme difficulty of expressing so lofty a belief in incontrovertably clear terminology.

[11] Cf. R. Brown, *The Gospel According to John*, Vol. I, lii-lv.
[12] Cf. N. Perrin, *Rediscovering the Teaching of Jesus*; H. C. Kee, *Jesus in History*; G. Bornkamm, *Jesus of Nazarth*; H. K. McArthur, "From the Historical Jesus to Christology" *Interpretation* 23 (1969) 190-206; R. H. Fuller, *op. cit.*, 102-141; N. J. McEleney, "Authenticating Criteria and Mk 7:1-23," *CBQ* 34 (Oct. 1972) 431-460.

Jesus is the Messiah

The background of the title Messiah has been adequately analyzed.[13] The title means the "Anointed" (Hebr. *mashíach*). It has its background in the centuries long expectation of a unique descendant of King David who would realize for Israel the promises made to her by God in the course of her two millennia old history.

The title is linked with the whole of Israel's expectation of a great destiny in the history of the world. This expectation went through three broadly conceived phases and periods. In the first period, sometimes referred to as the period of soteriological messianism (from the Greek *soteria*, salvation), stretching from the time of Abraham down to the time of David (c. 1800 to 1000 B.C.), Israel looked to God himself for the fulfilment of her promised destiny.

In the second period, sometimes referred to as the period of dynastic messianism, stretching from the time of David to the time of the Babylonian captivity (c. 1000 to 587 B.C.), Israel looked to the kings of the Davidic dynasty for the fullfilment of her hopes. The expectation was based upon the prophet Nathan's revelation to David that the Davidic dynasty would be eternal (2 Sm 7:14). The promise is expressed by retrojection in such texts as Gn 3:15; 49:8-12; Nm 24:17-19. It is expressed clearly in the psalms (Pss 2; 45; 72; 89; 110; 132) and in the oracles of the prophets (cf. Mi 4–5; Is 7–11).

In the final period, sometimes referred to as the period of personal messianism, stretching from the time of the Babylonian captivity down to the time of Christ (c. 587–30 A.D.), Israel abandoned her hope in the dynasty as a whole and began to believe in the eventual birth of a unique son of David who would inaugurate a period of unending fidelity to God and thereby fulfill God's plan for Israel and the world. It is disputed when this more limited expectation began, but it is generally credited to the period following the Babylonian captivity (587-537 B.C.); possibly beginning as early as the time of Isaiah and Micah (c. 700 B.C.), but more likely beginning with the oracles of Jeremiah in the early sixth century B.C. The most significant oracles are: Jer 23:5-6; 30:8ff; 33:15-16; Ez 34:23-24; 37:24-25; 17:22-24; Zech 9:9.

As a consequence of its broad background, the title Messiah embraces not only the anointed king but such other titles as: son of David, King, and Son of God in the sense of one adopted by God as the Davidic kings were considered to be adopted as God's sons (cf. 2 Sm 7; Pss 2; 72; 89; 110).

The title Messiah undoubtedly arose in Palestinian Judaism and at an

[13] Cf. R. H. Fuller, *op. cit.*, 23-31, 62-65, 109-114, 158-164, 188-197; S. Mowinckel, *He That Cometh*; O. Cullmann, *op. cit.*, 109-136; P. F. Ellis, *The Men and Message of the Old Testament*, 312-342; H. Riesenfeld, *The Gospel Tradition*, 75-93; R. N. Longenecker, *op. cit.*, 63-82.

early stage of the apostolic preaching. The reasons for this deduction are cogent: (1) because the need existed to prove that Christ was indeed the predicted Messiah; (2) because the title testified to the continuity of Salvation History; (3) because, despite its ambiguities and proneness to misinterpretation, the title nevertheless testified to much that was true about Jesus — his Davidic descent, his position in the eschatological Kingdom as God's vicar (cf. 1 Cor 15:21ff), his claim to rule not only Israel but all mankind, his claim to be the giver of the messianic Torah.[14]

While it is true that in the time of Jesus there were many in Israel who looked for a political, nationalistic Messiah, it is equally true that there were many whose concept of the Messiah was not only universalistic and eschatological but deeply spiritual as well.[15] It will be Matthew's contention that Jesus fulfilled all that was best in Israel's patrimony of messianic expectation. He supports this contention in a number of ways.

First, he entitles Jesus Messiah fourteen times.[16] Second, he uses for Jesus a number of other titles which are the equivalent of Messiah: (1) son of David;[17] (2) Emmanuel (1:23); (3) King;[18] (4) "He who is coming" (11:3). Third, in by far the majority of the cases where Matthew uses the fulfilment formula, the formula is used in reference to Jesus fulfilling the messianic predictions of the prophets.[19]

In addition to his use of the title Messiah fourteen times and its equivalent titles seventeen times, Matthew has a number of other ways in which he testifies to his belief in the messiahship of Jesus. (1) He begins his gospel with a genealogy which establishes Jesus' descent from David (cf. 1:1-25). (2) He takes pains to establish the authenticity of John the Baptist as a true prophet and indeed as the Elijah figure who would arrive in messianic times to introduce the Messiah.[20] (3) He presents Jesus as the promulgator of the definitive messianic Torah (cf. 5:17–7:27). (4) He constructs a whole narrative section (ch 8–9) in such a way that the miracles recounted recall the miracles foretold by Isaiah for the messianic age (cf. 11:2-5). (5) In his description of Jesus' entry into Jerusalem (21:5-11), he emphasizes precisely those details which illuminate its messianic character. (6) Finally, in his passion narrative he three times alludes to the words of Ps 2:2, "The princes conspire together against the Lord and against his anointed," in his descriptions of the chief priests and the elders of the people who assemble together to plot against Jesus.[21]

The reasons for Matthew's frequent use of the title Messiah and its equivalents are not difficult to deduce. Like all early Christians, Matthew

[14] Cf. N. Perrin, *The Kingdom of God in the Teaching of Jesus*, 76-78.
[15] Cf. R. H. Fuller, *op. cit.*, 28-31; O. Cullmann, *op. cit.*, 115-117; H. Riesenfeld, *The Gospel Tradition*, 75-93.
[16] Cf. 1:1,16,17,18; 2:4; 11:2; 16:16,20; 22:42; 23:10; 26:63,67; 27:17,22.
[17] Cf. 1:1; 9:27; 13:24; 15:22; 20:30-31, 21:9, 15.
[18] Cf. 2:2; 21:5; 27:11,29,37,42.
[19] Cf. 1:22; 2:5,23; 4:14; 8:17; 11:2-6; 11:10; 12:17; 13:14,35; 15:7; 21:4,16,42; 26:54; 27:9.
[20] Cf. 3:1-12; 11:7-19; 17:9-13; 21:23-31.
[21] Cf. 26:3; 27:1; 28:12.

and his community believed firmly that Jesus was the promised Messiah.[22] The apologetic foundation of this belief would pertain to the area of Scripture studies popularly known as "the quest for the historical Jesus" and may be by-passed here. It will be sufficient to observe that the faith of the early Christians rested upon Jesus' own proclamation that in him the Kingdom of God was at hand (cf. Mt 4:17 and parallels), upon Jesus' miracles, especially his resurrection from the dead, and upon the fulfilment in his life of so much that the Old Testament prophets had predicted about the Messiah.

The question of Matthew's belief in the messiahship of Jesus is not an issue. What is important is to discover why he went to such lengths to establish in an almost apologetic manner that Christ was indeed the expected Messiah. The movement of the gospel as a whole and the counter propaganda of the Jews suggest an answer.

The gospel moves steadily toward the authoritative declaration of Jesus in ch 28:18, "All power in heaven and on earth has been given to me . . .," and toward the Matthaean thesis that flowed from that authority, namely, that the unrepentant Jews had been rejected and that henceforth the true Israel was to be found in the Christian Church. While it is true that in Matthew's theological presentation the authority is given to Jesus as Son of Man, it is equally true that it was inconceivable to both Christians and Jews alike that the recipient of such power could be anyone other than the Messiah. It is presupposed, therefore, that by Matthew's time at least and probably much earlier, the title Son of Man had become another title for the Messiah. Matthew's emphasis on Jesus as the Messiah of Israel, therefore, is just one more way he uses to establish the authority of Jesus and the true Israel designated by Jesus.

The counter propaganda of the Jews must also be taken into consideration. It is mentioned expressly only in Mt 27:62-66; 28:11-15, but the Jews' designation of Jesus as "this impostor" (Mt 27:63) would certainly have included the denial of his messiahship.[23] It was against such counter propaganda that Matthew directed his genealogy of Jesus as son of David (Mt 1:1-17), his account of Jesus' adoption by Joseph (1:18-25), his designation of John the Baptist as the Elijah figure who would precede and announce the coming of the Messiah and the messianic age, his frequent use of the fulfillment formula in relation to the predictions of the prophets, and his account of Jesus' acceptance of the title Messiah in 26:63-64.

[22] The same faith in the messiahship of Jesus is expressed in the Pauline letters (passim), in Mark's gospel (cf. 8:27–11:11 and passim), in Luke's gospel (cf. ch 1–2 and passim), and in John's gospel (cf. 1:19-51; 4:26; 7:25-31,40-44; 11:27). As Luke observes, "It was at Antioch that the disciples were first called 'Christians' " (Acts 11:26). Since 'Christians' is the equivalent of Messianites, it is no arduous deduction to claim that the early Christians must have been quite convinced of, and insistent upon, the messiahship of Jesus.

[23] Note the heated disputes between Jesus and the Jews concerning the origin of the Messiah in John's gospel (cf. Jn 7:25-31,40-44), a gospel very similar in its refutation of Jewish propaganda to Matthew's gospel.

A subtler reason for Matthew's emphasis on the messiahship of Jesus was his conviction, reiterated throughout the gospel, that through Jesus Salvation History had come to its climax.[24] It may safely be presupposed that Israel's Salvation History could not possibly have reached its climax without the fulfillment of the promise made to Abraham that in him all the nations would be blessed (Gn 12:2-4) and the promise to David that his dynasty would be perpetual (2 Sm 7:14). The two promises were the pillars upon which Israel's hope rested. It was inconceivable to Matthew and the early Christians, therefore, that Jesus would be anyone but the Messiah. It was this conviction more than anything else that led them to scour the Old Testament for messianic prophecies and to show that in Jesus these prophecies had been fulfilled.

It is this conviction as well — probably grounded in the ministry of Jesus himself — that explains Matthew's insistence that Jesus preached only to the Jews and that he sent his Apostles to preach only to the Jews (cf. Mt 10:5). Since the Messiah had been promised to Israel, it was demanded by the Scriptures that he manifest himself first to them and thereby fulfill the requirements of Salvation History. Matthew shows that Jesus was faithful to the requirements of Salvation History. It is only after the resurrection that Jesus sends his Apostles to announce the gospel to the Gentiles (Mt 28:18-19).[25]

It should be noted as well that Matthew, like Mark before him, has carefully qualified the nature of Jesus' messiahship to prevent any political as opposed to theological interpretation of Jesus' messianic character. The misinterpretation of Jesus' messiahship as political is ruled out explicitly by Matthew's temptation narrative (Mt 4:1-11), by his description of Jesus as a "suffering servant" Messiah (passim), by the discussion on the use of authority (Mt 18; 20:24-28), by the description of Jesus entering Jerusalem as the humble Messiah of Zech 9:9 (Mt 21:1-9), and by the account of Jesus' arrest where Jesus forswears force by his words, "Put your sword back, for all who draw the sword will die by the sword" (Mt 26:52). It is implicitly ruled out by Jesus' proclamation of the beatitudes and by his self-description in Mt 11:29, "Learn from me, for I am gentle and humble in heart."

Jesus is the Son of God

Faith in the divinity of Jesus as the only begotten Son of God is not a late development in Christian theology. The Pauline epistles witness to the divinity of Jesus in the fifties of the first century.[26] At the end of the first

---

[24] Cf. 5:17-20; 26:26-29; 27:51-54.
[25] Paul's practice of preaching first in the synagogues and his insistence on "Jews first, but Greeks as well" (Rom 1:16; 2:10; 3:9,22; 9:30-33; 10:12; 11:25,32) betrays a similar grasp of the demands of Salvation History.
[26] Cf. Phil 2:6-11; Rom 1:4; 1 Cor 8:6.

century, the Johannine school of theology gave massive witness to the belief.[27] It is nevertheless true that the title Son of God is ambiguous when taken by itself in the New Testament.[28]

The ambiguity of the title is the result of its history. It had been used for centuries in pagan religions to designate kings who were thought to be begotten by the gods. The pharoahs of Egypt, Alexander the Great, and the later Roman emperors are only the better known of many examples. In addition to kings, the title was given to such famous men as Apollonius of Tyana and other miracle workers of antiquity, sometimes known as *theoi androi* (divine men).

In the Old Testament, kings of the Davidic dynasty were given the title "Son of God" (in an adoptive sense) almost from the beginning.[29] Angels were referred to as "sons of God."[30] Israel as a nation was referred to as "Son of God" (cf. Ex 4:22; Hos 11:1). And in the later wisdom literature, it was not uncommon to designate a truly holy man a "Son of God" (cf. Wis 2:16-18; 5:5).

It is not the title itself, therefore, that is decisive in Matthew's gospel, but the context in which it is used and indeed the context of the gospel as a whole. In short, what the title meant against its pagan or Old Testament background, or even in Matthew's sources, is not nearly so important as what it meant according to the intention of Matthew. The convergence of testimony in Matthew's gospel, direct and indirect, by title and by implication, and even by innuendo, is what ultimately convinces us that Matthew believed in and intended to give witness to his belief in the divinity of Jesus.

Matthew uses the title Son of God of Jesus nine times. On three occasions the demons address Jesus as Son of God (Mt 4:3,6; 8:29). The Apostles use the title twice (14:33; 16:16). The high priest asks Jesus if he is the Son of God (26:68). The scoffers beneath the Cross twice refer sarcastically to Jesus as the Son of God (27:40,43). And at the death of Jesus the centurion says: "Indeed this was the Son of God" (27:54).

In all of these cases, it is almost impossible to determine what each speaker meant in using the title. It is easier and more rewarding, however, to determine what Matthew would have understood them to mean (whether they meant it or not) and what he himself wished to express by recording the speakers' statements.

The clearest indication of Matthew's understanding of the title Son of God is found in his baptismal formula (28:19). The dispute about the

[27] Cf. Jn 1:1-18; 5:17-18; 8:58; 10:33-38; and passim.
[28] Cf. O. Cullmann, *op. cit.*, 270-314; R. H. Fuller, *op. cit.*, 31-33; 65; 68-71; 114; 162-164; 192-202; 243-269; W. Pannenburg, *Jesus God and Man*; J. Jeremias, *The Central Message of the New Testament*, 9-30; R. Brown, *Jesus, God and Man*; H. Conzellmann, *An Outline of the Theology of the New Testament*, 76-84, 127-129.
[29] Cf. 2 Sm 7:14; Pss 2; 45; 72; 89; 110; 131.
[30] Cf. Gn 6:2; Job 1:6; 2:1; Pss 29:1; 89:6; Dn 3:25.

origin of the formula, whether the words are a formulation of the community or a genuine saying of Jesus, is important but irrelevant to the question of Matthew's understanding of it. The formula puts the Son on the same level as the Father and the Holy Spirit and at the very least suggests equality. The words of the formula presuppose the equality of the Son with the Father implicit in 11:25-27, "Everything has been entrusted to me by my Father; and no one knows the Son except the Father, just as no one knows the Father except the Son and those to whom the Son chooses to reveal him."

The baptismal formula presupposes as well the pre-existence of Jesus implicit in the statements about Jesus as the one who has been "sent"[31] and as the one who has "come."[32] More than anything else, it is the baptismal formula with its implications of the equality of the Father and the Son that explains the unique relationship implicit in the way Jesus speaks about the Father as "my Father."[33] None of these sayings should be understood as attempts to explain in a philosophical manner the equality of the Father and the Son. Nonetheless, they give every indication of implying such an equality and as such have ontic connotations.

The ontic connotations are reinforced by the Matthaean presentation of Jesus' self-consciousness. Matthew presents Jesus as one conscious of a unique authority. In 28:18 Jesus commissions his Apostles in a manner purposely modeled on the way Yahweh commissioned the Old Testament prophets. In the Sermon on the Mount, Jesus speaks with sovereign authority about the Old Law, derogating from some of its commands and radicalizing it as a whole (5:17-48). He speaks of the law as "my yoke" (11:28-30), interprets the law with sovereign authority (12:1-14; 15:1-20; 22:34-40), declares himself master of the Sabbath (12:8), and asserts his authority to forgive sins (9:1-8). He has foreknowledge of events.[34]

Equally significant is the fact that Jesus calls upon men to make a "decision" for him.[35] One who can command a decision for himself is in the position of usurping a divine prerogative. The fact that Jesus does so in Matthew's gospel and does so without the least trace of an apology goes far toward explaining Matthew's understanding of the person of Jesus.

Two other pericopes, of lesser weight exegetically but hardly irrelevant, give further support to the ontic connotations of the title Son of God. First, in the trial account Matthew makes it reasonably clear that Jesus was condemned for proclaiming himself the Son of God. The adjuration of the High Priest, "Tell us if you are the Christ, the Son of God" (26:63), is in itself ambiguous as to the precise meaning of the title Son of God. The

[31] Cf. 10:40; 15:24; 21:37.
[32] Cf. 10:34; 11:19.
[33] Cf. J. Jeremias, *The Central Message of the New Testament*, 9-30. For a divergent exegesis of the significance of the "Abba" name used by Jesus for the Father, see H. Conzellmann, *op. cit.*,

101-106.
[34] Cf. 8:15; 12:40; 16:21; 17:22-23; 20:18-19; 24:2ff; 26:2,12,13,23,32,34.
[35] Cf. 5:11; 7:21-27; 10:22,32--33,37-39, 42; 19:21, 27-29.

ensuing accusation of blasphemy leveled against Christ by the High Priest, however, indicates the true sense of the title at least as understood by Matthew and possibly as understood by the High Priest. Until a better reason for the accusation of blasphemy is forthcoming, it will have to be presumed that the High Priest, or at least Matthew, understood Jesus to be claiming he was the Son of God in a sense which presumed divinity.[36]

Second, Jesus' question to the Pharisees, "What is your opinion about the Christ? Whose son is he?" (Mt 22:41-46), introduces, although without an explicit answer, the question of the nature of Jesus' "sonship." Jesus' answer to his own question, "If David can call him Lord, then how can he be his son?", implies Jesus is much more than the Messiah.[37] The implication is borne out that Jesus is infinitely superior to David. Jesus is addressed as "Lord" or refers to himself as "Lord" directly or indirectly at least thirteen times in Matthew's gospel,[38] and in a number of places the title is far from being a simple term of conventional courtesy.[39] In conjunction with the title Lord, with its implications of divinity, it should be noted that Matthew regularly speaks of men worshipping Jesus,[40] whereas Mark uses the verb worship (Greek-*proskunein*) only once (Mk 5:6). For Matthew, Jesus is more than the Messiah and more than the Son of Man. He is the Son of God and one with the Father.

Jesus is the Son of Man

Because of its importance in the New Testament and its long history in biblical and extra-biblical literature, few titles have been so exhaustively investigated as the title "Son of Man."[41] The results of the investigation remain inconclusive. There is consensus neither on the ultimate origin of the title nor on its precise development in Judaism.

The most probable remote background of the title is the Canaanite culture of Ugarit.[42] The most probable immediate background is the apocalyptic literature of the two centuries immediately preceding the time of Christ. The title is used in Dn 7:13ff (c. 165 B.C.), in *Ethiopian Enoch* (c. 175-163 B.C.), and in IV Ezra (c. 70 A.D.).[43]

[36] W. F. Albright, *Matthew*, 332, says: "Whatever views the ruling party might have on the coming of the Messiah, it should be emphasized that the act of claiming to be the Messiah was not one which was in itself blasphemous. We have no evidence of what view was taken in ruling circles about the use of God's Son."
[37] Cf. N. Perrin, *Rediscovering the Teaching of Jesus*, 23f.
[38] Cf. Mt 7:21-22; 8:25; 14:28,30; 15:25; 16:22; 17:4; 18:21; 22:45; 25:11,37,44.
[39] See, particularly, 8:25; 14:28,30; 22:45; 25:37,44.
[40] Cf. 2:2,8,11; 8:2; 9:18; 14:33; 15:25; 20:20; 28:9.
[41] Cf. F. H. Borsch, *The Son of Man in Myth and History*; H. E. Todt, *The Son of Man in the Synoptic Tradition*; A. J. B. Higgins, *Jesus and*

the Son of Man; R. Scroggs, *The Last Adam*; N. Perrin, *The Kingdom of God in the Teaching of Jesus*, 90-111; H. Teeple, "The Origin of the Son of Man Christology," *JBL* 84 (1965), 213-260; C. Colpe, "Son of Man" in *TDNT* Vol. VIII; R. H. Fuller, *op. cit.*, (passim); O. Cullmann, *op. cit.*, 137-192.
[42] Cf. C. Colpe, *art. cit.*, R. N. Longenecker, *op. cit.*, 82-93.
[43] R. H. Fuller (*op. cit.*, 42) concludes: "There is a body of evidence which, on a plausible interpretation, indicates that the figure of the Son of Man as the pre-existent divine agent of judgment and salvation was embedded in the pre-Christian Jewish apocalyptic tradition. This tradition provides the most likely source for the concept of the Son of Man as used by Jesus and the early Church."

The use of the title in Judaism is difficult to document, but it seems not unlikely it proceeded somewhat as follows: (1) in some source earlier than Dn 7:13ff, the title Son of Man came to be attached to an individual. *Ethiopian Enoch* (c. 175-163 B.C.) attributes the title to a pre-existent divine being and therefore takes for granted it refers to an individual. (2) Jesus spoke about the Son of Man, but in what specific sense is difficult to determine. (3) The Christian community in Palestine, under the influence of apocalyptic literature and the recollection of Jesus' use of the title, was the first to link the Son of Man sayings with Jesus himself. Two sayings about the Son of Man in Mark's gospel (Mk 2:10,28) indicate the community's part. (4) Mark then linked the Son of Man sayings of the community, which had arisen as a development of Jesus' own use of the title, under the aspect of authority and thus conceived Jesus as the authoritative Son of Man who suffers, dies, and rises, and does all with eschatological power and authority. (5) Finally, Matthew came along, took over the Markan teaching concerning the authority of Jesus as the Son of Man of Daniel, emphasized it further, pointed to the resurrection as the confirmation of Jesus' authority as Son of Man, and explicitly attributed to Jesus the authority of the Danielic Son of Man by having Jesus declare: "All authority in heaven and on earth has been given to me" (Mt 28:18).[44]

Matthew's use of the Son of Man title, seen in the light of his concept of Jesus' full authority and in the context and movement of his gospel as a whole, is impressive and significant. He uses the title a grand total of thirty times,[45] more than twice as many times as Mark.[46] Of the fourteen occurences of the title in Mark, all but two are found in Matthew.

Mark's dependence for the title upon Dn 7:13ff seems more than obvious. In Matthew the dependence upon Dn 7:13ff is certain. He uses the title 30 times, uses it in the context of the whole Daniel episode, and makes additional references to Daniel confirming his designation of Jesus as Daniel's authoritative Son of Man.[47]

The additional references do not use the title Son of Man, but they suggest it so strongly that it is impossible to doubt Matthew was not thinking of the Danielic Son of Man. Jesus' words in 26:53, "Do you not think that I cannot appeal to my Father who would promptly send more than twelve legions of angels to my defense," elicit immediately the Danielic vision of the Ancient of Days surrounded by legions of angels (Dn 7:9ff). Jesus' words in 28:18, "All authority in heaven and on earth has been

---

[44] Cf. R. H. Fuller, *op. cit.*, 36-39; H. E. Todt, *op. cit.*, 222; H. Boers, *art. cit.*, 302-315; R. Scroggs, *op. cit.*, 116-122.

[45] Cf. Mt 8:20; 9:6; 10:23; 11:19; 12:8,32,40; 13:37,41; 16:13,27,28; 17:9,12,22; 19:28; 20:18, 28; 24:27,30[bis],37,39,44; 25:31; 26:2,24[bis],45, 53,64.

[46] Cf. Mk 2:10,28; 8:31,38; 9:9,12,31; 10:33,45;

13:26; 14:21,41,62.

[47] In addition to Matthew's twenty-one usages of the title which are paralleled in either Mark or Luke, there are usages found only in Matthew (cf. Mt 10:23; 13:37,41; 16:13,28; 17:12; 19:28; 25:31; 26:2). In six of these nine, the text points unmistakably to Dn 7:13ff as the background (cf. 10:23; 13:37,41; 16:28; 19:28; 25:31).

given to me . . . ," recall the words of Dn 7:13-14, "I saw one like a son of man coming on the clouds of heaven. When he reached the Ancient One and was presented before him, he received dominion, glory, and kingship."

Matthew's reason for emphasizing the title Son of Man is both simple and provocative. He had already emphasized the authority of Jesus as messianic Son of David, promulgator of the messianic Torah, doer of the messianic miracles, and fulfiller of the messianic prophecies. Son of Man provided him with still another title emphasizing the extraordinary authority of Jesus.

Matthew's use of the title in the context of Dn 7:13ff indicates that for him the Jesus who "speaks with authority" (Mt 5–7), "acts with authority" (Mt 8–9), and bestows his authority upon the Apostles (10:1-5; 28:18-20), does so because he is the authoritative Son of Man of Daniel's apocalyptic vision.

His use of frequent references to the Son of Man in the passion narrative[48] and especially his use of the resurrection account to prepare the way for the missionary mandate of 28:18-20 indicate that for him Jesus takes the passion upon himself in full authority as the Son of Man and that it is at the resurrection that his authority as Son of Man is confirmed as an objective reality.

Matthew's apologia for the authority of the Church as the true Israel over against the pseudo-Israel of the Pharisees rested on two convictions: (1) Jesus had received all authority from the Father; (2) Jesus had delegated this authority to his Apostles. The words of Jesus to his Apostles in the missionary discourse presuppose these convictions: "He who welcomes you welcomes me, and he who welcomes me, welcomes him who sent me" (Mt 10:40).

MATTHEW'S ECCLESIOLOGY

There is no controversy about the ecclesiastical tone of Matthew's gospel. No other New Testament writing has so much to say about the Church. No other gospel has been so shaped by concern for the Church. And no other gospel has had so normative an influence on the development of the Church from New Testament times down to the present.

It might be expected that a correct understanding of Matthew's ecclesiology would clear up our modern problems concerning the nature of the Church, the position and authority of the bishops, the primacy of Peter and the papacy, and the use of authority in the Church. But it is not easy to arrive at a correct understanding of Matthew's ecclesiology.[49]

It is not easy because Matthew did not use our terminology. His key

---

[48] Cf. 26:3,24[bis],45,53,64.
[49] Cf. R. Schnackenburg, *The Church in the New Testament*, 69-76; J. L. McKenzie, *Authority in the Church*; Bornkamm, Barth, Held, *op. cit.*, 15-51.

word is "authority," but he does not distinguish between moral and disciplinary authority, between primacy of jurisdiction and primacy of honor, between personal authority and constitutional authority. Our terminology has a background in Roman law and Greek philosophy. Matthew's background is Jewish and his terminology comes out of Old Testament thought forms and literature. The differences are considerable.

It is not easy for another reason. Matthew did not write his gospel in view of our problems but in view of the problems of his own community. Modern problems are the outcome of divisions among Christians. Some question the institution of an authoritative church. Some accept the institution but question its nature, its constitutional form, and the extent and use of its authority in the internal and external forums. Some opt simply for a moral union of Christians based on faith in Christ and belief in the inspiration of the Bible.

Matthew, in the eighties, faced no immediate problem of divisions between different Christian groups. Unlike Paul at Corinth, Matthew did not have different groups saying: "I am for Paul, I am for Apollos, I am for Cephas, I am for Christ" (1 Cor 1:12). Nor did he have the problem of heresy alluded to by the author of 1 Jn 2:19, "Those rivals of Christ came out of our own number, but they had never really belonged."

Matthew's problem was with Judaism. His ecclesiology is framed more in terms of the question, "Who is the true Israel?", than in terms of the question, "Which Christian group represents the true Church of Christ?" It is true that there existed in Matthew's time dissident groups of Christians who claimed to be the true Church or the true followers of Jesus;[50] nevertheless, Matthew's ecclesiology is characterized primarily by its claim that the true Israel is to be found, not in Jamnian Judaism led by the Pharisees, but in the Christian Church founded on Peter and led by the Apostles and their successors. Matthew will have much to say about true and false discipleship in the Church, but his ecclesiology is only secondarily concerned with this distinction.[51] He writes to convince Christian Jews and Pharisee-led Jews that the Christian community alone represents the true Israel of God — that Israel founded on Sinai by Moses and brought to completion by Christ, the inaugurator of the New Covenant and the guarantor of all that Yahweh had promised to Israel and the world.[52]

It will be Matthew's contention (1) that Judaism has rejected Christ; (2) that Christ has rejected Judaism, which becomes, as a consequence, only a pseudo-Israel; (3) that the Christian Church constitutes the true Israel; (4) that Christ by virtue of his supreme authority as Messiah, Son

[50] Cf. 1 Cor 1:12; 1 Jn 2:19; Rev 2:1–3:22.
[51] Cf. K. Stendahl, *The School of St. Matthew* (1968 edition) xi-xiv.
[52] For Matthew, there is no break in continuity between the true Israel of the Old Covenant and the true Israel of the New Covenant. Matthew would agree with Paul that the Jews had heard the gospel and rejected it and by so doing had cut themselves off from the true Israel of God (cf. Rom 9–11).

of Man, and Son of God has invested the Apostles with authority to be the leaders of the true Israel in place of its old leaders, the Pharisees and elders; (5) that among the Apostles Peter and his successors are to enjoy a primacy of authority; (6) that the true Israel led by the Apostles has been commissioned to disciplize all nations, initiating them into the Church by baptizing and teaching them to observe all that Jesus commanded concerning the will of the Father.

Matthew keeps these ecclesiological contentions in mind throughout the gospel. The positive elements recur as concentric-circle themes. The negative elements recur as motifs and counterpoints to the positive elements.[53] For example, it will be Matthew's contention that the Jews' rejection of Jesus led to Jesus' rejection of the Jewish leaders and the consequent designation of the Apostles as the new leaders of Israel. Similarly, it will be Matthew's contention that the Jews' rejection of Jesus' messianic Torah led to Jesus' instruction of the Apostles in order to prepare them for their mission of teaching the perfect Torah to all men.

The force of Matthew's argumentation, therefore, can be felt not only in his concentric-circle presentation but in the movement of his gospel as a whole. The gospel which begins with foreshadowings of the Jews' rejection of Jesus ("At this news King Herod became greatly disturbed, and with him all Jerusalem.") and of the Apostles' designation as the new leaders of Israel ("I will make you fishers of men.") moves on to the authority of Jesus in ch 5–9 and the authority of the Apostles in the missionary discourse of ch 10. This discourse is then followed with a narrative account of the rejection of the Jews (ch 11–12) followed by the discourse on the Kingdom (ch 13) in which a distinction is drawn between the true Israel led by the Apostles and the pseudo-Israel led by the Pharisees. From this point onwards in the gospel (ch 14), Jesus turns away from the Jews and concentrates his attention on the Apostles. In the passion narrative (ch 26–27), the Jews definitively reject Jesus ("His blood be on us and on our children."). Finally, in the mission mandate (28:18-20), Jesus definitively commissions the Apostles as the leaders of the true Israel with a mission which embraces all humanity.

Matthew's mode of presentation is to foreshadow, then clarify his foreshadowing, and finally formulate. The reader as a consequence must attend not only to the movement of the gospel as a whole, but to Matthew's foreshadowings, clarifications, and formulations. Since the positive message is not given by means of a linear exposition but by means of concentric-circle

---

[53] R. Schnackenburg, (*op. cit.*, 71) says: "Jesus' sharp attacks on the scribes and Pharisees must probably in the evangelist's perspective also be directed against the unbelieving Judaism of his time. His positive ideas about the Church are only fully intelligible against the background of this polemic; consequently the fundamental concept of his gospel can scarcely be better summarized than by the ideogram 'the true Israel,' even though the new people of God is never actually designated by the term Israel (even in 19:28)."

presentation, the reader must also endeavor to make a synthesis of the teaching presented on each point in each concentric circle.

The Jews' rejection of Jesus

Matthew foreshadows the Jews' rejection of Jesus in the infancy narrative. When the Magi come to Jerusalem with news of the infant king of the Jews, Jerusalem is "perturbed," not overjoyed (2:3). Subsequently, the attempt is made to put Jesus to death — an attempt that will be successful in Jerusalem when the chief priests and the elders assemble and make "plans to arrest Jesus . . . and have him put to death" (26:3).

The foreshadowing of 2:3 is not clarified until ch 11, but it underlies and explains for Matthew's audience the Baptist's unconcealed animosity toward the Pharisees and Sadducees and his virulent epithet "Brood of vipers" (3:7-11) — an epithet which Jesus himself will later use for the Pharisees (23:33). It underlies and explains as well Jesus' highly critical attitude toward the Pharisees in the Sermon on the Mount (cf. 5:20; 6:2,5,16).

In 11:18-19 the foreshadowing is clarified in Jesus' statement: "For John came, neither eating nor drinking, and they say 'He is possessed.' The Son of Man came, eating and drinking, and they say, 'Look, a glutton and a drunkard, a friend of tax collectors and sinners'." The statement presupposes the Jews' rejection both of Jesus' messianic teaching (ch 5–7) and Jesus' messianic works (ch 8–9). Matthew makes the rejection even more clear by recording the Pharisees' accusation against Jesus: "The man casts out devils only through Beelzebul, the prince of devils" (12:24). In the subsequent parable discourse (ch 13), it is the Jews' rejection of Jesus that explains Jesus' statement that the "mysteries of the kingdom are not revealed to them" (13:11).

The Jews' rejection of Jesus is alluded to in several ways in ch 14–25. It is implicit in Jesus' three passion predictions (16:21; 17:22; 20:18). It becomes a central element in the parables of the wicked husbandmen (21:33-46) and the wedding feast (22:1-14). It is summed up in Jesus' poignant lament: "Jerusalem, Jerusalem, you that kill the prophets and stone those who are sent to you! How often have I longed to gather your children, as a hen gathers her chicks under her wings, and you refused!" (23:37).

In Matthew's passion account (ch 26–27), the Jews' rejection of Jesus is played up as in no other gospel. The Jews assemble three times to plot against Jesus (26:3-5; 27:1; 27:62). In the Jews' dealing with Judas, the thirty pieces of silver (26:14-16) are mentioned seven times, and Matthew has the Jews admit, "It is blood-money" (27:6), prior to asserting that in this transaction the Jews were fulfilling the words of Scripture which predicted their rejection of the Messiah: "And they took the thirty silver pieces, the sum at which the precious One was priced by the children of Israel" (27:3-10).

In the trial before the Sanhedrin (26:57-66), the Jews' answer to the question concerning Jesus' guilt is: "He deserves to die" (26:66). In the trial before Pilate (27:11-26), Matthew plays down the guilt of Pilate and plays up the guilt of the Jews. When Pilate says to the Jews, "I am innocent of this man's blood. It is your concern," Matthew has the Jews express their rejection of Jesus in the words: "His blood be on us and on our children" (27:24-26).

The problem posed by the Jews' rejection of Jesus is a matter of theological concern to John (Jn 12:37-50), to Luke (Acts 28:23-28), and to Paul (Rom 9–11). For Matthew, the theological problem is no great concern. He sees it as something foretold in Scripture.[54] What is important to Matthew is the ecclesiological aspect of the Jews' rejection of Jesus. Because the Jews have rejected Jesus, Jesus rejects the Jews.

With the rejection of the Jews, and particularly the Jewish leaders, it becomes a foregone conclusion that new leaders must be designated for leaderless Israel. The Church is distinguished from the pseudo-Israel in many ways but in none so manifestly as in the designation of the Apostles as the leaders of the true Israel. Thus, Matthew's emphasis on the Jews' rejection of Jesus is made to serve the ecclesiological purpose of his gospel.

Jesus' rejection of pseudo-Israel

Jesus' rejection of pseudo-Israel is foreshadowed in ch 1–10, made explicit in ch 11–13, and taken for granted in the rest of the gospel. It is foreshadowed broadly in the Baptist's brief discourse to the Pharisees and Sadducees (3:8-12), and specifically in his warning that "Even now the axe is laid to the roots of the trees" (3:10). It is again foreshadowed in Jesus' words to the centurion: "I tell you many will come from the east and west to take their places with Abraham and Isaac and Jacob at the feast in the kingdom of heaven, *but the subjects of the kingdom will be turned out into the dark*" (8:10-12).

In ch 11–13, the rejection is explicit. Pseudo-Israel is condemned as "this generation" which refuses to listen to either the Baptist or Jesus (11:6-24) and as the "evil and unfaithful generation" that refused to heed a "greater than Jonah" and a "greater than Solomon" (12:34-42). The spiritual condition of this perverse generation is then described graphically in the parable which describes the pseudo-Israel as a house filled with "seven" evil spirits! (12:43-45).[55]

The whole of the narrative in ch 11–12 has as its redactional purpose

---

[54] Cf. 13:10-15; 15:7-9; 21:39-46; 27:3-10.   [55] Cf. J. Jeremias, *The Parables of Jesus*, 197f.

to draw the lines between the true and the pseudo-Israel. The lines are first drawn in 11:25-27 when Jesus says: "I bless you, Father, Lord of heaven and of earth, for hiding these things from the learned and the clever and revealing them to mere children." The learned and the clever represent pseudo-Israel, and the mere children, the true Israel.

Following the condemnation of pseudo-Israel in the parable of the return of the "seven" unclean spirits (12:43-45),[56] the lines are definitively drawn when Jesus asks the question, "Who is my mother? Who are my brothers?", and then "stretching out his hand toward his disciples" declares; "Here are my mother and my brothers. Anyone who does the will of my Father in heaven, he is my brother and sister and mother" (12:46-50).

In the parable discourse (ch 13), the lines already drawn are now taken for granted. Pseudo-Israel is presented as "those outside the house" (13:1) to whom Jesus speaks in parables because, as he tells his disciples, "the mysteries of the kingdom are revealed to you, but they are not revealed to them" (13:11) and because "they (pseudo-Israel) look without seeing and listen without hearing or understanding" (13:13). The true Israel is presented as those "inside the house" (13:36), who have revealed to them "the mysteries of the kingdom" (13:11), and to whom it can be said: "Happy are your eyes because they see, your ears because they hear" (13:16).

In the remainder of the gospel (ch 14–28), Jesus concentrates on the instruction of the Apostles, the future leaders of the true Israel; the rejection of the pseudo-Israel is taken for granted. In 15:7-9 Jesus says to the Pharisees and scribes: "Hypocrites! It was you Isaiah meant when he so rightly prophesied, 'This people honors me only with lip-service, while their hearts are far from me'."

In 15:13-14, in language reminiscent of the Baptist's warning about the "axe already laid to the roots" (3:10), Jesus says of the Pharisees: "Any plant my heavenly Father has not planted will be pulled up by the roots. Leave them alone. They are blind men leading blind men; and if one blind man leads another, both will fall into a pit."

In 16:12, when Jesus warns his Apostles to "beware of the yeast of the Pharisees and Sadducees," they understand his words as a warning "against the teaching of the Pharisees and Sadducees."

Finally, Jesus' rejection of pseudo-Israel is presupposed in the parable of the vineyard laborers which ends with the words: "The last will be first, and the first, last" (20:1-16); in the parable of the two sons (21:28-32); in the parable of the wicked husbandmen (21:33-46), especially the words: "I tell you that the kingdom of God will be taken from you and given to a people who will produce fruit" (21:43); and in the parable of the wedding

[56] W. F. Albright (*Matthew*, 160) rightly interprets Mt 12 as "containing in microcosm the judgment of Jesus on contemporary Israel."

feast (22:1-14), especially the words: "The wedding feast is ready, but as those who were invited proved to be unworthy, go to the crossroads in the town and invite everyone you can find to the wedding" (22:8).

In the last great discourse (ch 23–24), Jesus' seven "woes" against the Pharisees (23:13-38), ending with the words, "So be it! Your house will be left to you desolate" (23:38), constitute a bill of indictment against pseudo-Israel. The eschatological discourse (ch 24), with its prediction of the destruction of the Temple, seals the indictment and leaves it to history. By the time pseudo-Israel utters her own self-condemnation with the words, "His blood be upon us and upon our children" (27:25), Matthew has closed his case.

The Church is the true Israel

Matthew's case against the Jews is important for an understanding of his gospel as a whole and especially for his ecclesiology. But it is subject to misinterpretation in a number of ways. It is certainly misinterpreted if it is taken to be a repudiation of Old Testament revelation, faith and spiritual values or of Old Testament Salvation History. It is grossly misinterpreted if it is taken to be a condemnation of all individual Jews, whether Jews of the time of the historical Christ, or Jews contemporary with Matthew in the eighties, or all Jews down the centuries. Some have so interpreted the words: "His blood be on us and on our children" (27:25).[56a]

Matthew is not anti-Semitic. He himself is a Jew. His community is predominantly Jewish. It is a community of *'anawim* (cf. 5:3-10). It practices the same "righteousness" (*dikaiosunē*) as the true Israel of old (cf. 5:20).[57] It is the "New Covenant" Israel predicted by Jeremiah (Jer 31:31). It is the Israel to which and for which the promises of old were made and fulfilled. It is the Israel which has accepted the Messiah and the messianic Torah, has Jewish Apostles as its prophets, teachers, and leaders, and has Simon-Peter, a Jew, as its foundation stone.[58] It is the Israel which is in continuity with the "remnant of Israel," the "seven thousand who did not bend the knee to Baal," the faithful of Israel from the time of Abraham to the time of Jesus and Matthew himself. It is in short the "true Israel."[59]

As a consequence Matthew does not speak of a "new" Israel, or a "new" law. His respect for Moses is so great that he parallels the life of Jesus with the life of Moses (ch 1–4), has Jesus deliver the charter discourse of the New Covenant from a "new Sinai," and has Jesus at the Transfiguration

[56a] C. G. Montefiore rightly says of these often misinterpreted words: "This is one of those phrases which have been responsible for oceans of human blood, and a ceaseless stream of misery and desolation" (*The Synoptic Gospels*, vol. I, 346).

[57] Cf. Bornkamm, Barth, Held, *op. cit.*, 31-32.

[58] When Christ commissions Peter (16:17-19), he speaks of "my church." The opposition should be noted between "*my* church" and "*their* synagogues" (cf. 4:23; 9:35; 10:17; 12:9; 13:54) as well as "their scribes" (cf. 7:29).

[59] Entrance into the true Israel is by way of baptism "in the name of the Father, the Son, and the Holy Spirit" (28:19). Nothing is said anywhere in the gospel about circumcision. It has been superceded by baptism as Judaism has been superceded by Christianity.

flanked on one side by Moses and on the other by Elijah. Jesus himself declares he has come, not to destroy, but to fulfill the Law and the Prophets. And Jesus is nowhere shown to be opposed to or lacking in respect for Moses.

Matthew's condemnation, therefore, is in no sense a condemnation of Israel as a whole, since this would include not only the true Israel of the Old Covenant but the true Israel of the New Covenant as well. He does not condemn the "little people." He condemns the leaders of that group in the nation of Israel which, like the false Israelites of old excoriated by the prophets, continues resisting God and continues persecuting Christ's prophets, the Apostles, "as they persecuted the prophets" before them (cf. 5:12; 23:33-36).[60]

Matthew certainly lamented the fact that the Jewish nation as a whole did not accept Christ, but he does not theologize about the problem the way Paul did (Rom 9–11) and he no more condemns individual Jews than did Paul. His concern is not with those many Jews to whom the gospel was never preached, but with those Jews, particularly their leaders, to whom the gospel was preached by Christ and by whom it was rejected in such a way that "by default" the true Israel was left without leaders.

Matthew's emphasis on the rejection of the Jews can be seen in sharper perspective if it is evaluated as a redactional technique whose purpose is to highlight Jesus' selection of the Apostles to be the new leaders of the true Israel. As Matthew says: "When Jesus saw the crowds he felt sorry for them because they were harassed and dejected, like sheep without a shepherd" (9:36). The words of Jesus to his Apostles in 10:6, "Go to the lost sheep of the House of Israel," express not only Jesus' attitude toward the Jews as a people but Matthew's as well. They are "lost sheep" for whom it is necessary to appoint new and faithful shepherds.[61]

The true Israel, therefore, which consists of Jews and non-Jews, is defined (1) by contrast with the Pharisees; (2) by a "justice" which exceeds that of the Pharisees (5:20); (3) by its acceptance of Jesus as Messiah, Son of Man, and Son of God; (4) by its acceptance of the Apostles as leaders (10:40); (5) by its faith in Jesus (10:31b-33); (6) by its acceptance of Jesus' law (5:21-48; 11:28-30); (7) by its acceptance of the way of the Cross signified by baptism "in the name of the Father, the Son, and the

---

[60] For Matthew, that part of the Israelite nation led by the Pharisees constitutes the "pseudo-Israel" precisely because it is continuous with the pseudo-Israel of old of which "gave lip-service to the law" (Mt 15:17 quoting Is 29:13), "persecuted the prophets" (23:33-36), rejected the Messiah, the messianic Torah, and the New Covenant, rejected John the Baptist as the promised Elijah (21:23-32), did not produce "fruits worthy of repentance" (3:8-12; 5:20; 21:41-43), and

brought about the death of Jesus (ch 26-28 passim).

[61] In the mission mandate the ministry of the Apostles will be extended to all nations (28:19). During the ministry of Jesus, the Apostles, as Jesus himself, go to the lost sheep of Israel (10:5-6) in accordance with the dictates of Salvation History which required that the gospel be preached first to the Jews.

Holy Spirit" (28:19); and (8) by its acceptance of the love commandment as the supreme commandment (22:34-40).

The leaders of the true Israel

With regard to the Apostles as the leaders of the true Israel, three factors should be kept in mind in analyzing Matthew: (1) the influence of the Jamnian Pharisees; (2) the movement of the gospel as a whole; (3) Matthew's method of presentation, beginning with foreshadowing of his teaching, proceeding to clarification of his foreshadowings, concluding with the formulation of his teaching.

It is a truism of history that action begets reaction, that conflicting claims beget definitions of positions, and that contradiction begets clarification and reformulation of teaching. It is now generally agreed that the claims of the Jamnian Pharisees to be the leaders of the true Israel, the interpreters of the true law, and the protectors of orthodoxy against the claims of Christ and the Church, provided the major catalyst for the writing of Matthew's gospel.[62] The claims of the Pharisees in Matthew's time stimulated Matthew's theologizing as surely as the claims of Paul's opponents at Thessalonica, Corinth and Galatia stimulated Paul's theologizing. It was the Jamnian claim to be the true Israel that prompted Matthew's demonstration of Judaism's rejection of Christ and Christ's consequent rejection of Judaism. It was the Jamnian claim that the Pharisees were the legitimate leaders of Israel that prompted Matthew's presentation of the Apostles as the authoritative leaders of the true Israel.

The movement of the gospel as a whole runs unerringly toward the authoritative mission mandate in ch 28:18-20. It begins with the preliminaries to the mandate in the authority of Jesus as Messiah, one "greater than Moses," promulgator of the messianic Torah, and doer of the messianic works. It is one of the major functions of ch 1–9, as we have shown in the redaction study of these chapters, to establish the authority of Jesus before recording in ch 10 the designation of the twelve Apostles as the delegates of Jesus in proclaiming the gospel and performing the works of the messianic era. It is against the background of the rejection of the Jews in ch 11–12 that we are shown in ch 13 the distinction between the pseudo-Israel led by the Pharisees and the true Israel led by the Apostles. "The mysteries of the kingdom of heaven," as Jesus says to his Apostles, "are revealed to you, but they are not revealed to them" (13:11).

It is against this same background — the rejection of the Jews — that we see Jesus instructing his Apostles in the way of the Cross and the way of discipleship in ch 14–27. It is against this background and the back-

[62] Cf. G. D. Kilpatrick, *op. cit.*, 109-123; K. Stendahl, *op. cit.*, xi-xiv; W. D. Davies, *The Setting of the Sermon on the Mount*, 256-314; R. Schnackenburg, *op. cit.*, 69-75; J. Rohde, *Rediscovering the Teaching of the Evangelists*, 99-106.

ground of Matthew's Christology that we see Jesus authoritatively commission the Apostles, as Yahweh had commissioned the prophets of old, to disciplize all nations and bring about the establishment of the reign of God in the world (28:18-20).

It is only in the light of the gospel as a whole, therefore, that the reader can appreciate to the full the significance of the individual texts dealing with the Apostles as leaders of the true Israel.[63] Matthew uses his texts to fill in the picture provided by the movement of the gospel as a whole, first by foreshadowing the leadership of the Apostles, then by clarifying the foreshadowing, and finally by formulating it.

The leadership of the Apostles is foreshadowed in the programmatic text: "Follow me and I will make you fishers of men" (4:19).[64] The text is programmatic because it links the future commission of the Apostles ("I will make you") and their mission ("fishers of men") with the following of Christ. The Apostles will be prepared for their future work by "following" Christ. The "following" is not independent of the "and I will make you fishers of men."

The terminology "fishers of men" is in contradistinction to the previous vocation of the Apostles. They have fished for fish. In the future they will fish for men. The expression is obviously metaphorical.[65] It will be explained as the gospel goes on as a work similar to the work of Jesus — a work of sacrificial love for men and a work of preaching-teaching.[66]

That the "follow me" and the work of being "fishers of men" are intimately associated is made clear by Matthew almost immediately. Following the beatitudes, Jesus says to his Apostles: "Happy are you when people abuse you and persecute you and speak all kinds of calumny against you on my account. Rejoice and be glad, for your reward will be great in heaven; this is how they persecuted the prophets before you" (5:11-12 and cf. 23:33-36; 10:17-25).

It is further clarified by the words: "You are the salt of the earth. *But if salt becomes tasteless*, what can make it salty again? It is good for nothing, and can only be thrown out to be trampled underfoot by men" (5:13). If they "follow" Jesus in the way of the Cross, they will be, as Christ is, "the salt of the earth and the light of the world." In the apostolic college, only Judas, who gave up following Jesus, was to lose his savor.

The suffering entailed in "following" Jesus is again clarified in the three

---

[63] To concentrate on the texts, apart from a redaction criticism of the gospel as a whole, would put the reader in the position of those described by E. V. Rieu as crippled by form criticism: "Yet, as a preliminary to the study of the gospels, too large a dose of form criticism might well reduce one to the condition of a man who stands before a Raphael and keeps on asking where the artist got his paints" (*The Four Gospels: A New Translation from the Greek*, xi).
[64] The formulation is taken from Mk 1:17. Mat-

thew goes beyond Mark in his clarification of the implications of the text, but for his understanding of the passion-discipleship theology of the words, "Follow me," he is almost entirely dependent on Mark's theology.
[65] Cf. W. Wuellner, *The Meaning of "Fishers of Men"*; R. P. Meye, *Jesus and the Twelve*, 100-110.
[66] As R. P. Meye says (*op. cit.*, 108): "The fullest meaning of the expression, 'fishers of men,' is to be found in *a work similar to that of Jesus*."

stories on discipleship in ch 8:18-27, the prediction of scourgings in the synagogues, delations to governors and kings, death and hatred in ch 10:17-25, and the passion predictions of Jesus followed by the declaration: "If anyone wants to be a follower of mine, let him renounce himself and take up his cross and follow me" (cf. 16:21-28; 17:22-23; 20:17-28).

The work of preaching-teaching is implicit in the declarations, "You are the light of the world . . . You are the salt of the earth" (cf. 5:13-14), and in the admonition, "The man who infringes even one of the least of these commandments and teaches others to do the same will be considered the least in the kingdom of heaven; but the man who keeps them and teaches them will be considered great in the kingdom of heaven" (cf. 5:19 and see 18:1-4). The preaching apostolate is explicit in the missionary discourse (ch 10) in the words: "And as you go, proclaim that the kingdom of God is at hand" (cf. 10:6 and see the similar formulation for the preaching of the Baptist [3:2] and Jesus [4:17]). The work is formulated in the explicit mandate of 28:19, "Going, therefore, disciplize all nations, teaching them . . . ."

The third element of the programmatic text, the "I will make you," is partially clarified in 5:11-16 and fully clarified in 10:1-5; 28:19.[67] M. J. Suggs suggests "that 5:11-16 has been constructed by Matthew so as to form the first commissioning saying in the gospel."[68] He compares it with the commissioning of Peter in 16:17-19 which consists of three parts: (1) a benediction; (2) the bestowal of a symbolic name; (3) the commission proper. In 5:11-16 there is the same sequence: (1) the benediction: "Blessed are you when men revile you and persecute you" (5:11-12); (2) the bestowal of symbolic names: "You are the salt of the earth . . . You are the light of the world" (5:13-15); and (3) the commission proper: "Let your light so shine before men, that they may see your good works and give glory to your Father who is in heaven" (5:16). The commission seems to have been arranged by Matthew to conform to the pattern of Peter's authoritative commission in 16:17-20, but the ambiguity of audience in the Sermon on the Mount makes the commission itself ambiguous.

Whatever the ambiguity in 5:13-16, the commission of the Apostles is clear in 10:1-5. Following the demonstration of Jesus' authority as Messiah (ch 1-2), as one "greater than Moses" (passim in ch 1-7), as promulgator of the messianic Torah (ch 5-7), and doer of the messianic deeds (ch 8-9), Matthew begins the missionary discourse with the words: "He summoned his twelve disciples, and gave them authority" (10:1ff). To appreciate the significance of the mandate, the reader should recall the ending pericope of the preceding narrative. Jesus feels compassion for the

---

[67] Mt 19:28 may well be a clear indication of the appointment of the Apostles, but there is some dispute about the precise meaning of the text in relation to the time element. It is better to consider it another Matthaean foreshadowing.

[68] *Wisdom, Christology, and Law in Matthew's Gospel*, 122-127.

multitude because they are "like sheep without a shepherd" (9:36). He then urges his disciples to "ask the Lord of the harvest to *send laborers* to his harvest" (9:37). Matthew means his audience to recognize the Apostles as the laborers sent by God to his harvest, but sent by the authority and designation of Jesus.

The designation and the authority of the Apostles as the new leaders of the true Israel is unequivocal in the final mission mandate on the mount in Galilee. The risen Jesus declares that all authority in heaven and on earth has been given to him and then commissions the Apostles with the words: "Going, therefore, disciplize all nations . . . baptizing . . . teaching . . . and I will be with you." As mentioned earlier,[69] the full significance of the commission can be appreciated only if the reader takes into consideration the implicit allusion to Dn 7:13-15 and to the Old Testament literary form of the mission mandate.

The allusion to Dn 7:13-15 grounds the authority of Jesus in prophecy. The literary format consciously reproduces the commissioning of the prophets by Yahweh.[70] The implication is clear. Jesus enjoys divine authority. He commissions his Apostles with the same sovereign authority with which Yahweh had commissioned the Old Testament prophets. The Apostles are the prophets of the New Testament Israel. They speak with the authority of Jesus as the Old Testament prophets spoke with the authority of Yahweh.[71]

It is sometimes asserted that the unique authority of the Apostles died with the Apostles. To some extent this is true. But it is not true to say that their successors in the Church did not enjoy a genuinely hierarchical authority. To deny the authority of the successors of the Apostles would be to eviscerate Matthew's argumentation for the new leaders of the true Israel. His argument is that the Apostles and their successors are for the Church what the Pharisees are for the pseudo-Israel. He makes this clear by equating the Pharisees of his own time with the Pharisees of the time of Jesus. There is a similar continuity with the Apostles and their successors. Moreover, Matthew, wrote at a time when most of the Apostles were dead. His argument would be senseless if it did not include the successors of the Apostles. If it did not, then Matthew's Church would be leaderless.

Not only would his Church be leaderless in its opposition to the Pharisees of Jamnia, but the missionary mandate would make no sense. The mandate called for disciplization of the whole world. There is no indication in the gospel that Matthew considered the goal already accomplished.

The promise of Jesus to be with his Apostles "till the end of time" would be equally senseless if it did not extend to the successors of the Apostles. There is no indication that Matthew viewed the end of the world

[69] pp. 22-24, 51-53.
[70] Cf. Jer 1:1ff; Is 6:1ff; Ez 3:1-10.
[71] The conception of the Apostles as the prophets of the New Testament is not restricted to the mission mandate. It is quite explicit in 5:11-12 and 23:33-36.

as imminent. He occasionally cautions Christians to be ready for the end-time (cf. ch 24–25), but he nowhere says the end-time is on the horizon.

It is true that there was a sort of parousiac fever in the early church and that first generation Christian writings reflect this fever, particularly the early Pauline letters, e.g., 1-2 Thess and 1 Cor. But even in the Pauline letters, the temperature drops considerably between 1-2 Thess and Gal, and it is almost normal by the time Paul writes Romans. Matthew's gospel belongs to the second generation of Christian writings. It was written anywhere from fifty to seventy years after the resurrection and at least twenty years after Romans. It is as little afflicted with parousiac fever as the gospel of John, the gospel of Luke, or the epistle to the Ephesians, all equally late writings.

A leaderless Church in Matthew's time or a Church without authoritative leaders would make incomprehensible the monarchical episcopate of the second century. Bishops such as Ignatius of Antioch (c. 115) would have to be almost *ad hoc* creations. All the evidence indicates just the opposite. They considered themselves the authoritative successors of the Apostles. That they did so is no small testimony to the theological claims made for them by Matthew.[72]

THE PRIMACY OF PETER

Few texts in the New Testament have been so exhaustively scrutinized as Matthew's testimony to the primacy of Peter in his account of the Caesarea Philippi episode (16:17-19).[73]

The testimony, of course, is not limited to Matthew. Jesus' "feed my sheep" command to Peter in John's gospel (Jn 21:15-17) is concerned with the primacy of Peter.[74] So also are Jesus' words to Peter in Luke's gospel: "I have prayed for you, Simon, that your faith may not fail, and you in your turn must strengthen your brothers" (Lk 22:31-32).[75]

The four gospels, Luke in Acts, and even Paul in Galatians (Gal 2:11-14) give ample testimony to the unique position of Peter among the Apostles as a group and in the early history of the apostolic Church.

The difficulties of the primacy passage preclude exhaustive treatment. Its importance, however, demands it be discussed within the limits we have set for ourselves. It will be our view, in the light of the prominence given to Peter throughout the gospel, the redaction history of the gospel, the movement of the gospel, and the significance of the Petrine promise in

[72] Cf. K. Rahner, *The Episcopate and the Primacy*; E. H. Maly, *The Priest and Sacred Scripture*, 18-39; A. Ehrhardt, *The Apostolic Succession*.

[73] Cf. O. Cullmann, *Peter: Disciple, Apostle, Martyr*; G. Bornkamm, "The Authority to 'Bind' and 'Loose' in the Church in Matthew's Gospel" in *Jesus and Man's Hope*, Vol. I, 37-50; R. Schnackenburg, "The Petrine Office: Peter's Re-

lationship to the other Apostles" *TD* 20 (Summer 1972) 148-152; K. L. Schmidt, "Church" in *TDNT*; D .W. O'Connor, *Peter in Rome*; O. Karrer, *Peter and the Church. An Examination of Cullmann's Thesis*.

[74] Cf. R. Brown, *The Gospel According to John*, Vol I, 302; Vol. II, 1088-1092; 1112-1122.

[75] Cf. O. Cullmann, *op. cit.*, 26f.

itself, that Matthew utilized the theological dialogue between Jesus and Peter in 16:13-19 in order to testify to his belief in the primacy of Peter and his successors in the Church founded by Jesus.

In our discussion, we shall presuppose that (1) the preeminence of Peter in the apostolic Church is an assured datum of apostolic tradition and history; (2) the triple testimony of Mt 16:17-19, Lk 22:31-32, Jn 21:15-18, in addition to Jesus' bestowal of the name "rock" on Peter suffice to prove that Matthew was dependent for the core of his belief in the Petrine primacy on an actual saying of Jesus to Peter; (3) it is practically impossible to prove or disprove the total verbal authenticity of any of the primacy texts; (4) the absence of a primacy promise in Mk 8:27ff can be adequately explained in the light of Mark's theological purposes; (5) either Jesus, or Matthew himself, or Matthew's Palestinian tradition formulated the wording for the primacy text of 16:17-19 by playing on the name "rock" and by introducing a barely veiled allusion to the significant saying of Isaiah concerning the nature of vicarious authority (Is 22:20-22); (6) Matthew has gone out of his way to emphasize the primacy of Peter; (7) our problem is to explain on redactional and theological grounds why Matthew has done this.

The pre-eminence of Peter

The four gospels, the Acts of the Apostles, and even the Pauline epistles[76] testify unanimously to Peter's pre-eminence in the apostolic church and among the Apostles. His name is always first in the listing of the names of the Apostles.[77] He is consistently represented as the spokesman of the Apostles as a group and, in Matthew's gospel, more so than in the others. Jesus tells him his name will be changed to "rock."[78] And in three of the four gospels,[79] Jesus expressly assigns to Peter a position of unique eminence in relation to the Church as a whole and the Apostles as a group.[80] As W. F. Albright says: "To deny the pre-eminent position of Peter among the disciples or in the early Christian community is a denial of the evidence."[81]

Based on Jesus' words

That Matthew, like Luke and John, was dependent for the core of his belief in the primacy of Peter on an actual saying of Jesus to Peter seems the only reasonable explanation of the evidence. All three testify to the

---

[76] Concerning Gal 2:11-14, R. Schnackenburg says: "The days when people following the lead of F. C. Baur set up an irreconcilable opposition between Petrine and Pauline early Christianity are presumably over. The controversy nowadays has focused on the manner in which Peter's primacy is to be understood, above all whether it was only a personal privilege of limited duration and validity, or whether it possessed fundamental and more far-reaching significance" (The Church

in the New Testament, 34).
[77] Cf. Mt 10:2; Mk 3:16; Lk 6:14; Acts 1:13.
[78] Cf. Jn 1:42; Mt 10:2; 16:17; Mk 3:16; Gal 1:18; 2:11,14.
[79] Cf. Mt 16:17-19; Lk 22:31-32; Jn 21:15-17.
[80] Peter's position in relation to the Church as a whole is far more clear than his position in relation to the other Apostles.
[81] Cf. W. F. Albright, op. cit., 195.

same fact but in entirely different terms. One can only deduce that such testimonies given by three evangelists of diverse tendencies and styles, writing at different times and for different audiences and with different theological perspectives, are either all authentic or, if not, could not have arisen except on the basis of some very definite statement by Jesus. It is doubtful that the form critics will ever be able to establish all three testimonies as based on the actual words of Jesus, but it is equally doubtful that any of the three would have arisen without a dominical statement.

For three such different independent testimonies to have emerged without any basis in fact defies all logic and experience. The Apostle who denied Jesus three times and whose betrayal was known by all was the least likely candidate for the nickname "rock" and the least likely of all the Apostles for three different "inventors" of the primacy to seize upon independently as their unanimous candidate for the primacy.

In fact, all three assert Peter's primacy despite his lack of faith in Christ. In Luke's testimony (Lk 22:31-32) and in John's (Jn 21:15-17), it is expressly noted that the primacy is given to Peter despite his lack of faith in Christ. In Matthew's testimony (Mt 16:17-19), the conferring of the primacy follows shortly after Peter's loss of faith in Jesus while walking on the waters and within earshot of Jesus' rebuke to Peter: "Man of little faith! Why did you doubt?" (Mt 14:31).

Authenticity

It is practically impossible to prove or disprove the total, verbal authenticity of any of the above-mentioned primacy texts. The mere fact that all three are different makes it even more difficult to determine what is original.

At most, form criticism can show that John's testimony (Jn 21:15-18) seems to have been expanded to set the primacy conferral in contrast with the triple denial of Jesus by Peter.[82] It can also cast doubt on it to a certain extent by showing that in relation to Jesus' Good Shepherd discourse in Jn 10, the "feed my sheep" motif of Jn 21:15-18 smacks suspiciously of a play on the theme of Jesus as the Good Shepherd in Jn 10. The discourse in Jn 10 seems less the discourse of Jesus than of John and to that extent casts doubt on the genuineness of the "feed my sheep" analogy in Jn 21:15-18. But it may be that Jn 21:15-18 is original and that the discourse in Jn 10 is a homiletic development of Jesus' statement to Peter about "my sheep."

The Lukan testimony (Lk 22:31-32) has all the earmarks of a genuine saying of Jesus. But its setting at the last supper and in the context of Peter's denial of Jesus makes it sound contrived and makes it difficult to explain

---

[82] Cf. R. H. Fuller, *The Formation of the Resurrection Narratives*, 152; but see also the suggested explanation of R. E. Brown for the three- fold form of the primacy statement (*op. cit.,* 1112-1113).

how all the other evangelists, who pay so much attention to what Jesus said to Peter at the last supper, could have omitted so important a saying.

The Matthaean testimony (16:17-19) is genuinely suspicious on only one count — and that only if one interprets "Son" in an ontic rather than in a relational sense. If understood relationally with reference to the Father or as a practical equivalent to "messiah," it would not attribute to Peter a profession of Jesus' divinity, which is extremely unlikely prior to the resurrection. Apart from this obvious expansion and the allusion to Is 22:20-22, which sounds so typically Matthaean, there is no good reason why Matthew's version could not rest upon the actual words of Jesus.[83]

Some have argued that the absence of these words in the parallel Markan pericope (Mk 8:27ff) proves Matthew did not have them in his Markan source and must have added them from elsewhere. He did not, of course, have them in his Markan source if Mark was indeed his source. But this does not mean that Jesus' words to Peter about the primacy were not a part of the whole Caesarea Philippi episode. There is good reason to believe that Matthew's version is more faithful to the common tradition than Mark's and that Mark suppressed Jesus' words to Peter for valid redactional purposes while Matthew retained them for equally valid redactional purposes.

Absence in Mk 8:27ff

The absence of a primacy promise in Mk 8:27ff has usually been explained as indicating there was no such promise in the tradition as Mark knew it. In the light of what is now known about Mark's redactional techniques and purposes, this reasoning can no longer stand up.

Mark's attitude toward the Apostles has been the subject of a number of studies.[84] Two authors, in particular,[85] have adverted to Mark's use of the motif "the obtuseness of the Apostles" as a redactional technique aimed at impressing upon his audience both the importance and the difficulty of comprehending how essential it is for true discipleship to "take up the cross and follow Jesus." The motif "the obtuseness of the Apostles" runs all through Mark's gospel, beginning in ch 1–8 (cf. 4:13,41; 5:31; 6:49-52; 7:17-18; 8:15-21) and reaching a climax in 8:31–10:45, where Jesus three times foretells his passion and death and each time the Apostles totally misunderstand the meaning of his words. That the motif "the obtuseness of the Apostles" is a literary ploy can be seen from the unambiguously redactional arrangement of the material in Mk 8:31–10:45:

a) 8:31   *First* prophecy of the passion
    8:32-33   *Obtuseness* of the Apostles
    8:34–9:29   *Instruction* on discipleship

[83] But see R. H. Fuller, *op. cit.*, 166-177 and O. Cullmann, *op. cit.*, 175-184.
[84] Paul Meye's, *Jesus and the Twelve* is particularly good. T. J. Weeden's, *Mark—Traditions in Conflict* has much good material, but is vitiated by simply incredible conclusions.
[85] Q. Quesnell, *The Mind of Mark*, 161-176; D. J. Hawkin, "The Incomprehension of the Disciples in the Marcan Redaction," *JBL* 91 (March 1972), 491-500.

b) 9:30-31   *Second* prophecy of the passion
   9:32-34   *Obtuseness* of the Apostles
   9:35–10:31   *Instruction* on discipleship
c) 10:32-34   *Third* prophecy of the passion
   10:35-40   *Obtuseness* of the Apostles
   10:41-45   *Instruction* on discipleship

It cannot be proved that the tradition upon which Mark based his gospel contained the promise to Peter found in Mt 16:17-19. But if it did, Mark's wholehearted emphasis on the redactional motif of the "obtuseness of the Apostles" makes it perfectly obvious why he would suppress it. Jesus' words, "Simon son of Jonah, you are a fortunate man! It was not flesh and blood that revealed this to you but my Father in heaven," would have clashed violently with the whole tenor of the "obtuseness of the Apostles" motif and substantially vitiated its redactional purpose. This redactional "discovery" enhances considerably the probability that the common tradition used by Mark and Matthew is more faithfully preserved by Matthew than by Mark. It suggests as well that Peter's profession of Jesus' messiahship might well have been the situation in which Jesus uttered the words upon which the primacy of Peter was based by Matthew, Luke, and John.

The formulation of Mt 16:17-19

We presuppose that Mt 16:17-19 as a whole derives from a Palestinian tradition and was formulated either by Matthew himself or by the tradition he inherited.[85a] We do not exclude the possibility that at least in part it may go back to the historical Jesus, if the object of Peter's testimony is taken to be Christ's messianic mission, not his divinity.

Evidence for a Palestinian, i.e., Aramaic or Semitic formulation is compelling. First, there is the typical use of parallelism and strophic structure (there are three strophes of three lines each), both of which are characteristically Semitic.[85b] Second, there is a very high incidence of Aramaic expressions, e.g., the macarism, "Blessed are you, Peter . . ."; the expressions "Bar-Jonah" (in reference to Peter's father), "flesh and blood," "bind and loose," and "the gates of Hades." Third, the play on the word "rock" is perfect in the Aramaic but flawed in the Greek by the change from *Petra* to *Petros*; cp.:

Aramaic: "You are *Kepha* and upon this *Kepha* I will build my church."
Greek: "You are *Petros* and upon this *Petra* I will build by church."
Fourth, there is a direct parallel in rabbinical literature for the idea of building on a man as on a "rock" — in this case Abraham of whom it is said: "When God looked upon Abraham, who was to appear, he said: Behold I have found a rock upon which I can build and base the world. Therefore he

---

[85a] See O. Cullmann, *op. cit.*, 158-210; R. Brown et al., *Peter in the New Testament*, 83-101.

[85b] A similar strophic pattern is found in other sayings of Jesus (cf. 6:9-13; 11:7-9, 25-30).

called Abraham a rock."[85c] Finally, it is hardly a coincidence that so Semitic a formulation should be found in the most Jewish of the four gospels.

The Palestinian origin of the formulation, as a consequence, is not seriously disputed. The origin of the formulation, however, is another matter. If interpreted messianically, it could well go back to Jesus; but if taken as Peter's premature testimony to the divinity of Jesus, it would suggest a later formulation. Most often it is credited to those who formulated the tradition Matthew inherited and used in his gospel. The formulation, it is suggested, took place in the church at Antioch where Peter appears to have been highly esteemed as early as Paul's letter to the Galatians (cf. the indirect testimony to Peter in Gal 2:11-14), which is usually dated in the early fifties.

While this is the most probable explanation of the formulation, there are nevertheless cogent reasons for suspecting the formulation may be the work of Matthew himself. There are, to begin with, a number of expressions used in the formulation which are typically Matthaean, e.g., "Blessed are you . . . ,"[85d] "Father in heaven,"[85e] and "the kingdom of heaven." There is, in addition, the Matthaean reference to "special revelation" (cf. 16:17 and cp. 11:25-27); the use of the "rock" analogy, used earlier in the gospel (cf. 7:24); and the use of the implicit quotation from Is 22:22 in the words "I will give you the keys of the kingdom" (16:19).[85f]

These indications taken alone are not sufficient to establish Matthaean formulation of the Petrine promise. There are other indications, however, which, though less controllable, when combined with the above strongly suggest it might well have been Matthew who formulated the promise as we have it now. To appreciate these less controllable indications, we have to remember that Matthew does not hesitate to compose discourses, both long and short, for Jesus. It is not un-Matthaean therefore for the author who composed the final missionary mandate of Jesus in 28:18-20 to compose a short discourse such as the words of Jesus to Peter in 16:17-19. In addition, we have already noted in our analysis of Matthew's redaction that he frequently utilizes quotations from Isaiah and Daniel, sometimes direct and sometimes indirect quotations. A closer look at the content of the Petrine promise shows that beneath the surface of the text there is discernible an indirect quotation of Is 22:22 and an allusion to Dn 7:13-15.

The indirect quotation of Is 22:22 is in the words: "I will give you the keys of the kingdom." To ears attuned to the Old Testament and particularly to Isaiah (the prophet most regularly quoted by Matthew and presum-

[85c] Cf. Strack-Billerbeck, Vol. I, 733; and see Is 51:1-2.
[85d] Matthew uses beatitudes or macarisms regularly (13 times in all), where the other evangelists rarely use them, and Mark not at all.
[85e] Matthew uses the same expression in his version of the Lord's prayer (cf. 6:9).

[85f] Considering Matthew's redactional emphasis on "their synagogues" throughout the gospel and particularly in ch 13 where the dividing line is drawn between "their synagogues" and 'ours,' it may well be that the words "my church" in Mt 16:18 can be credited to Matthew's formulation.

ably popular with his audience), the words would immediately elicit a remembrance of the text and context of Is 22:15-25, particularly vv 20-22:

> On that day I will summon my servant Eliakim, son of Hilkiah;
> I will clothe him with your robe, and gird him with your sash,
>   and give over to him *your authority.*
> He shall be a father to the inhabitants of Jerusalem
>   and to the house of Judah.
> I will place *the key of the House of David on his shoulder*;
>   when he *opens*, no one shall *shut*,
>   when he *shuts*, no one shall *open.*

The significance of the indirect quotation from Is 22:22 can be appreciated fully only when the reader realizes, as Matthew's audience undoubtedly did, that it comes in the context of a passage which describes the dismissal of King Hezekiah's master of the palace, Shebna, and his replacement by Eliakim. It describes in short the appointment of a man who is to function as the prime minister or, more properly, the vizier of the Davidic king. As R. de Vaux says:

> The Egyptian vizier's instructions are described in a very similar fashion. Every morning 'the vizier will send someone to open the gates of the king's house, to admit those who have to enter, and to send out those who have to go out.' One is reminded of our Lord's words to Peter, the Vizier of the Kingdom of Heaven (Mt 16:19). Like the Egyptian vizier, the master of the palace was the highest official in the state: his name comes first in the list of 2 K 18:18; he alone appears with the king in 1 K 18:3; and Yotham bears this title when he acts as regent of the kingdom (2 K 15:5), as the vizier did in the absence of the Pharaoh.[85g]

If the reader recollects that Matthew opened his gospel with a genealogy which established Jesus as a true descendent of King David (1:1-25) and went on in ch 8–9 to demonstrate that Jesus had performed the messianic miracles predicted by Isaiah, he will readily understand the connection between Peter's profession of Jesus' messiahship in the words: " Thou art the Christ (Messiah)" and the words of Jesus, speaking as the Messiah, i.e., the Davidic King of Israel: "Thou art Peter . . . I give to you *the keys of the kingdom. . . .*"

Matthew, in short, could not have found a better way to express his belief in the primacy of Peter and his successors as the vicars of Christ than by having Jesus use the words used by a King of Judah to appoint a new vicar or viceroy or, more properly, master of the palace. It should be noted that in 28:18-20 Matthew in a similar manner utilized the context and text of Dn 7:13-14 to express Jesus' full authority as Son of Man. It is probably against the background of this Daniel text that Jesus' other words to Peter are to be interpreted: "And on this rock I will build my church, and the gates of hell will not prevail against it."

[85g] Cf. R. de Vaux, *Ancient Israel*, 130.

In Dn 2:35, 45, the "stone hewn from the mountain without a hand being put to it" destroys all the kingdoms of the world and becomes a great mountain which fills the whole earth. In Dn 7:13-15, the Son of Man who represents the kingdom of God is given an everlasting dominion "that shall not be taken away, his kingship shall not be destroyed." Equivalently, the words "and the gates of hell shall not prevail against it" (the Church, that is, the kingdom of God on earth) say the same thing as Dn 7:15 about the indestructibility of Jesus' Church founded on the rock which is Peter.

Emphasis on Peter's primacy

We presuppose Matthew has gone out of his way to emphasize the primacy of Peter because of the manner in which he composed the narrative in ch 13:53–17:27. The emphasis on Peter is unmistakable. It is also intentional.

First, Peter's name is mentioned a disproportionate number of times.[86] Second, Peter is regularly mentioned as the spokesman for the Apostles as a group as in the parallel material in Mark, but in one place where Mark does not have Peter as spokesman, Matthew changes the Markan text to make Peter the spokesman (Mt 15:15). Third, Matthew adds three Petrine pericopes, which are not only not found in Mark but are not found anywhere else in the New Testament (Mt 14:28-32; 16:17-19; 17:24-27). Fourthly, each of these unique episodes is placed strategically at the end of a section of the narrative in such a way that the episode of Peter on the waters terminates Part I of the narrative (13:53–14:33), the episode of Peter receiving the primacy promise terminates Part II (14:34–16:20),[87] and the episode of Peter paying the tax for Jesus and himself terminates Part III (16:21–17:27).[88] Fifthly, in keeping with Matthew's careful choice of his transition pericopes at the end of his narrative sections, the choice of a pericope that deals with Peter paying the tax for Jesus and himself takes on a special significance (17:24-27). Sixthly, the question with which the discourse in ch 18 opens, "Who is the greatest in the kingdom of heaven?", gives every appearance of being the kind of question the disciples would ask after such a disproportionate emphasis on one Apostle. Seventhly, if the discourse in ch 18 is truly directed to the Apostles, i.e., the leaders of the community, as we have tried to show,[89] then the fact that Peter, who has received the promise of the primacy, is made the one to ask the question about forgiveness in 18:21 takes on considerably greater significance.

Matthew's reasons

Finally, in view of Matthew's emphasis on Peter, we presuppose our greatest problem is to explain on theological grounds why Matthew, at

[86] Cf. 14:28,29; 15:15; 16:16,18,22; 17:1,4,24,25.

[87] That the summary in 14:34-36 introduces a new section running from 14:34 to 16:20 can be shown from Matthew's use of his favorite connective *tote* in 15:1 (cf. Bornkamm, Barth, Held,

op. cit., 47).

[88] Part III of the narrative complex begins at 16:21 as can be seen from the content and the parallel in Mk 8:31.

[89] See pp. 69-72.

least twenty years after the death of Peter in Rome,[90] has gone to such redactional lengths to highlight not only the pre-eminence but also the primacy of Peter in the church.

Why Matthew should have done so is a question which has nothing to do with the question of whether Jesus actually made a primacy promise to Peter, i.e., whether the words of Mt 16:17-19 are the actual historical words of Jesus. This question is important but belongs properly to the study known as the "Quest for the Historical Jesus." Neither does it have anything to do with the question about whether the saying was formulated by the early Church or Matthew himself. That is a question which belongs properly to the study of form criticism.

Why Matthew should have emphasized the primacy of Peter is a question that deals with the mind of Matthew and asks what he held theologically concerning the primacy of Peter when he wrote his gospel in the last quarter of the first century. Whatever the source of the primacy saying, whether it came directly from Jesus or was formulated either by Matthew or by the early Palestinian Church, the proper question for the redaction or composition critic is: why did Matthew choose to include in his gospel a saying which provides such massive testimony to the special position of Peter in relation to the Church as a whole?

One answer to the question would be that in Matthew's time and circumstances a situation existed which made it necessary, because of either internal or external opposition or both, to make clear to all that Christ had established in the church a teaching authority similar to but dependent on his own teaching authority. When Mark wrote his gospel in the late sixties, no such situation seems to have existed. The same can be said for Luke writing in the eighties, even though Luke gives a large place to Peter in Acts 1–15 and includes in his gospel a promise to Peter (Lk 22:31-32) which is at least implicitly primatial.

Some have suggested that it was internal opposition that elicited Matthew's teaching on the primacy. Such a situation may be reflected in the apparent references to antinomians within the community in 5:17ff, 7:15ff, 24:11ff. Antinomians, however, would be the last to be impressed by a primatial claim of authority. At most, the existence of antinomians can help to explain Matthew's insistence that the law remains and must be observed (cf. 5:17ff) and that the true disciple is one who "does" and "does all" that Jesus commanded (cf. 28:19). It hardly accounts for Matthew's pronounced emphasis on the authority of Peter and the Apostles.

It is far more likely that some form of external opposition provided the catalyst for Matthew's emphasis on Peter's teaching and disciplinary authority. It is noteworthy in this regard that the two gospels most vehemently anti-Jewish— Matthew and John — are at the same time the most insistent

---

[90] Cf. O. Cullmann, *op. cit.*, 70-152; D. W. O'Connor, *Peter in Rome.*

on the authority of Peter. For John, Peter is the vicar of Jesus the good shepherd (cf. Jn 21:15-17). For Matthew, Peter is the vicar of Jesus the Davidic king of the Jews (cf. Mt 16:17-19).

In both gospels the common enemy is the Jews, not just the Jews in general but the leaders among the Jews who contested both the authority and the existence of the Christian church. Whether the Jamnian Jews in particular constituted the spearhead of this opposition or not, it is clear that both Matthew (cf. Mt 23:1ff and passim) and John (cf. Jn 5–12) reacted vigorously.

In Matthew's gospel all the elements concerned with a conflict of authorities are present. Matthew claims that Jesus is "greater than" Moses — the teaching authority of the Jews; that Jesus' Torah is the completion and fulfillment of the Mosaic Torah — the Torah claimed by the Jews as authoritative; and that the teaching authority once held by the scribes and Pharisees (23:3) has now passed to the Apostles and the leaders of the Christian church (cf. 10:1-5, 40; 18:18; 28:18-20).

The authority claimed for Peter by Matthew in 16:17-18 would appear to be both a teaching and a disciplinary authority.[90a] In rabbinic literature the power of "binding" and "loosing" (Mt 16:19) generally implies the power of imposing or removing an obligation by one who has authority to give a doctrinal decision. Less frequently it refers to imposing or lifting an excommunication from the synagogue. If there existed in the Jamnian synod or in Judaism taken as a whole the equivalent of a 'supreme rabbi' with authority in doctrinal and disciplinary matters, then Matthew is saying not only that the Torah of Jesus is the ultimate Torah but that the vicar of Jesus is the ultimate teacher, the 'supreme rabbi' of the Christian church.

Taking into account that Matthew opposes "their synagogues" (passim) to "my church" (16:17); that he presents the Apostles as the new leaders of the true Israel (cf. 10:1-2, 40; 28:18-20); that he proclaims Jesus' Torah greater than Moses' Torah; and that he insists that Jesus is the one authoritative teacher (cf. 5:20-48; 17:5; 23:10; 28:18-19) even though he is no longer physically with his church — it seems not unlikely that Matthew goes out of his way to explicitate the authority conferred on Peter and his successors by Jesus in order to show that in the Church there are not only authoritative Apostles and bishops but one Apostle in particular who, as vicar of the "one teacher" (23:10), speaks with his authority in settling matters requiring authoritative decisions.[90b]

[90a] Cf. *Peter in the New Testament*, 95-101.

[90b] The question of the nature of, and the continuation of, the Petrine authority in the Church, i.e., whether it is both disciplinary and doctrinal or only disciplinary, and whether or not his authority continues to be enjoyed by his successors is a question beyond the scope of this study. The following studies should be consulted: G.Bornkamm, "The Authority to 'Bind' and 'Loose' in the Church in Matthew's Gospel," *Jesus and Man's Hope*, vol. I, 37-50; J. A. Emerton, "Binding and Loosing — Forgiving and Retaining," *JTS* 13 (1962) 325-331; R. Schnackenburg, "The Petrine Office: Peter's Relationship to the Other Apostles," *TD* 20 (Summer 1972) 148-152; B. Tierney, *Origins of Papal Infallibility 1150–1350*; O. Cullmann, *Peter: Disciple, Apostle,, Martyr*, 213-238; W. Pannenburg, *Theology and the Kingdom of God*, 99-100; H. Küng., *Infallibility: an Enquiry?*; R. Brown *et al.*, *Peter*

THE APOSTLES' WORK IN THE WORLD

The primary work of the Apostles is to "disciplize all nations" (*mathē-teusate panta ta ethnē*) — to make all men disciples of Jesus. They are to accomplish the work by performing two activities, each integral to the making of disciples: baptizing and teaching. By baptizing, they call upon individuals to commit themselves publicly to follow Jesus. By teaching men to observe all Jesus has commanded, they teach men to follow Jesus in doing perfectly the will of the Father. When men do God's will "on earth as it is in heaven," as Jesus had done it, God's reign is established and God's Kingdom has come. Essentially, the work is the work of establishing the reign of God in the world. It is the completion, therefore, and fulfillment of that for which the Law and the prophets were given. It is the work of achieving the goal of Salvation History.

As formulated by Matthew the work of the Apostles seems clear. But two questions intrude violently. First, in a formulation of such critical importance, why does Matthew say nothing about the preaching of the kerygma and the acceptance of Jesus by faith? Second, why does he put baptizing before rather than after teaching? In Acts 8:26-39 Philip's procedure appears normative. He first instructs the eunuch of Queen Candace. The eunuch then professes his belief in Jesus. Finally, the eunuch is baptized.

Matthew's departure from the normative missionary procedure can be explained only on the presupposition that he takes for granted the preaching of the kerygma and the subsequent act of faith in Jesus which is the *sine qua non* of discipleship. His concern in the formulation, therefore, is not with the preliminaries of discipleship which he takes for granted but with the perfection or essence of discipleship.

The gospel is written for those who are already Christians and for catechumens who are on the way to becoming Christians. For those already Christians, the kerygma, faith in Jesus, and baptism can be presupposed. For the catechumens, the kerygma and faith in Jesus can be presupposed, and baptism anticipated. For both classes, what remains is the living of the Christian life, the individual actualization of true discipleship.[91] If Matthew had been concerned about the totality of the missionary enterprise, he would have had to follow the order: kerygmatic preaching, act of faith in Jesus, baptism,[92] didache. For his audience in the eighties, it was proper to presume the first two, begin with baptism, and concentrate on the didache of true discipleship.

---

in the New Testament; J. Blank, "The Person and Office of Peter in the New Testament," *Truth and Certainty* (*Concilium* 83) 42-55.

[91] Cf. G. Barth in Bornkamm, Barth, Held, *op. cit.*, 105-125.

[92] Matthew takes for granted his audience's understanding of baptism. It is implicit in his description of the Baptist's baptism, which was supplanted by Christian baptism. It is also implicit in Mt 20:20-23 when the pericope about the two brothers is taken in its original context in Mk 10:35-40. G. Barth (*op. cit.*, 116-118) explains the Matthaean concept of conversion.

The mission to "teach"

As the prophets of the New Covenant, the Apostles' mission to teach is more akin to the mission of Moses in Dt 5:30-33 than to the mission of the later Old Testament prophets. Moses' primary function was to promulgate and teach the law. The later prophets presumed Israel's knowledge of the law. Their primary function was to serve as Yahweh's messengers to deliver to Israel Yahweh's judgment on her lack of response as a covenanted people to her suzerain Yahweh. It is this difference in function that may explain Matthew's terminology in 28:19.

It is impossible to prove that Matthew modeled his mission mandate to the Apostles in 28:19-20 on the mission mandate to Moses in Dt 5:30-33. The resemblances, however, are provocative, especially the words: "go," "teach," "that they may observe," and "all the commandments." The text bears quoting:

> *Go,* tell them to return to their tents. Then *you wait here near me* and I will give you *all the commandments,* the statutes, and decrees you must *teach them* that they may *observe* them in the land which I am giving them to possess. Be careful, therefore, *to do* as the Lord, your God, has commanded you, not turning aside to the right or to the left, but *following exactly* the way prescribed for you by the Lord, your God, that you may live and prosper, and may have long life in the land which you are to occupy (Dt 5:30-33).

It would be pressing an analogy beyond bounds to suggest Matthew is likening the Apostles as individuals to Moses. Nevertheless, the following resemblances between the Apostles in Matthew's gospel and Moses in Dt 5:30-33 suggest some such analogy might have been in Matthew's mind. First, in each case the authoritative commission is given "on a mountain." Second, Moses' commission is in relation to the Old Covenant, the Apostles' in relation to the New Covenant. Third, in each case the primary work is a work of "teaching." Fourth, in each case what is to be taught is the law — "all that has been commanded" — which for Moses is the Old Law and for the Apostles the messianic Torah of Jesus. Fifth, in each case it is specified that the recipients of the law are to "observe" it and that they are to observe "all" that has been commanded. Sixth, the law given to Moses to teach is the law he received from Yahweh on Mount Sinai; the law given to the Apostles to teach is the messianic Torah the Apostles received on the Mount of the Beatitudes in the Sermon on the Mount. Seventh, in each case the great commandment is central. In Deuteronomy, the great commandment in 6:4-9 follows immediately upon the commission of Moses in 5:30-33. In Matthew's gospel, the understanding of the "great commandment" is pivotal for an appreciation of Matthew's understanding and interpretation of the law. If Matthew wanted to underline the teaching authority of the Apostles, he could hardly have found a more persuasive analogy.

The similarities between Moses' and the Apostles' mandates are striking. The differences, however, are even more striking. Moses is sent to one nation; the Apostles are sent to "all nations." Moses is to teach all Yahweh has commanded; the Apostles, all Jesus has commanded. The difference is the difference between the period of inauguration and the period of fulfillment of the messianic promises. It is best enunciated in nuanced terms in the words of Jesus: "Do not think that I have come to abolish the law and the prophets. I have come, not to abolish them but to fulfill them" (Mt 5:17). The mission of the Apostles is to teach the messianic Torah of Jesus — the full, radical, paradise will of God. Where the radical will of God is done, there is found true discipleship. Where the radical will of God is done "on earth as it is in heaven," there is found the Kingdom of God.

As usual Matthew prepares the way in the body of the gospel for an understanding of each term in his mission mandate. He foreshadows the actual mission in the promise of Jesus: "Follow me and *I will make you fishers of men*" (4:19). He foreshadows the universal scope of the work in (1) the coming of the Magi; (2) the metaphorical names given to the Apostles: "You are the light of the world" [93] and "you are the salt of the earth"; (3) the parable of the leaven in ch 13; (4) the parable of the last judgment in ch 25:31-45.

He even succeeds in bringing out the special schooling of the Apostles for their teaching apostolate. He has Jesus say in equivalent terms to the Apostles what Yahweh at Mount Sinai said to Moses: "You wait here *near me* and I will give you all the commandments, statutes and decrees you must teach them" (Dt 5:30). Matthew shows the Apostles constantly "near" Jesus. They follow him "along the way." They are with him "inside the house." They go with him to "a desert place away from the crowds." To a large degree the five great discourses of Jesus are directed to the Apostles rather than to the crowds. In addition, Matthew goes out of his way to make it clear that the Apostles, who will later teach what they have learned from Jesus, have "understood" what Jesus taught them.[94] They have, in short, been prepared for their future teaching apostolate.

True discipleship

What all men are to "do" if they are to be true disciples of Jesus constitutes the content of the apostolic didache. In Matthew's carefully chosen words, the Apostles are to teach men "to observe all that I have commanded you (*tērein panta hosa eneteilamēn hymin*)."

---

[93] The "light" metaphor probably derives from the second Servant canticle of Isaiah in as much as the Apostles carry out the mission of the Servant, of whom Yahweh says: "I will make you a light to the nations that my salvation may reach to the ends of the earth" (Is 49:6).

[94] G. Barth in Bornkamm, Barth, Held, *op. cit.*, 105-112, analyzes the theme "understanding" in relation to the Apostles in Matthew and Mark and proves indisputably that Matthew took great pains to exhibit the Apostles as "understanding" Jesus' teaching in contradistinction to Mark who represents them as consistently failing to understand Jesus. That this was in view of their future function as authoritative teachers of the messianic Torah seems equally indisputable.

The critical terms are "observe," "all," and "commanded," and it will be necessary to explain each of them in some depth. But even the personal pronouns are important in Matthew's well articulated formulation. He could have said: "teaching them to observe all that has been commanded." By saying "all that *I* have commanded," he reasserts the sovereign authority of Jesus as formulated in 28:18 and re-echoes the theme of Jesus as one "greater than Moses" which runs throughout the gospel. By saying "all I have commanded *you*," he repeats his contention that the Pharisees are no longer the leaders of the true Israel but have been replaced by the Apostles to whom has been given now the custody of the messianic Torah of Jesus.

The critical terms dealing with the essence of true discipleship are the words: "Observe all I have commanded." For Matthew a true disciple is not just one who has professed his faith in Jesus [95] and been baptized; he is one who (1) observes, i.e., does what Jesus has commanded; (2) does "all" that Jesus has commanded, i.e., governs his life and actions by the "radical will" of God; (3) does all in the light of the great commandment of love of God and love of neighbor.

Matthew presumes those who have read his gospel understand what he means by these three characteristics of a true disciple. He presumes such an understanding because he has studiously elaborated the meaning of the three throughout his gospel. Since he has done it by means of contrast with the Pharisees and by means of his concentric-circle presentations, it is upon these we shall have to concentrate if we are to understand him.

The true disciple "does"

Throughout the gospel Matthew emphasizes the necessity of "doing" or "observing" God's law as opposed to simply knowing and talking about it but not doing it. His positive example is Jesus himself who does the will of the Father perfectly. His primary negative example is the caricatured "typical" Pharisee. His secondary negative example, and some would say his "target," is the Christian of whom Jesus says: "You can tell a tree by its fruit. None of those who cry out, 'Lord, Lord,' will enter the kingdom of God but only the one who does the will of my Father in heaven" (7:20-21). It is this same type of Christian who will say to Jesus after Jesus has condemned him: "Lord, when did we see you hungry or thirsty or away from home or naked, or ill or in prison and not attend you in your needs?" (25:44). False disciples are "non-doers."

The first words of Jesus, recorded in Matthew's gospel, characterize him as a "doer" of God's will. "Give in for now," Jesus says when John tries to dissuade him from being baptized, "we must do this if we would fulfill all

---

[95] For Matthew, the intellectual aspect of the concept of faith is transferred to the concept of "understanding" Jesus. Those in his gospel who understand, also believe. When Matthew speaks of faith, it is almost always in the sense of "trust" in the fatherly goodness of God or in the sovereign power (*exousia*) of Jesus. Cf. G. Barth, Bornkamm, Barth, Held, *op. cit.*, 112-116.

of God's demands" (3:15). It is the same throughout the gospel. It is especially so in the way Jesus voluntarily undergoes the ordeal of the passion as an act of obedience.[96] His most characteristic words in relation to the passion are the words of the agony: "My Father, if this cannot pass me by without my drinking it, your will be done" (26:42). And when he teaches his disciples to pray, he teaches them to say: "Your will be done on earth as it is in heaven" (6:10).

For Matthew, Jesus is not only a teacher but a doer as well. The summaries of Jesus' activities recorded by Matthew regularly testify to both preaching and doing. His first summary is typical: "Jesus toured all of Galilee. He taught in their synagogues, proclaimed the good news of the kingdom, and cured the people of every disease and illness" (4:23).[97]

Matthew's caricature of the Pharisees, as examples of what a true disciple is not, should be recognized for what it is — a caricature.[98] There were certainly many good and holy Pharisees. Nicodemus, Joseph of Arimathea, Gamaliel, Paul who was certainly a Pharisee before his conversion, and Matthew himself who was probably a Pharisee before his conversion, are a few of the names that come immediately to mind. Whatever the actual practice of individual Pharisees, however, there must have been enough of them more concerned about "talking" good deeds than doing them to warrant Matthew's use of the epithet "hypocrites" and to justify his caricature of them as examples of what a true disciple should not be.[99]

The caricature begins in the short discourse of the Baptist (3:8-12) and runs throughout the gospel but it is particularly noticeable in the two balanced long discourses — the Sermon on the Mount (ch 5–7) and the final great discourse which begins with the "woes" against the Pharisees (ch 23–25).

The Baptist's words, "You brood of vipers! Every tree that is not fruitful will be cut down and thrown into the fire" (3:8-10), set the stage for the presentation of the Pharisees as those who do not produce fruit, i.e., do not "do." In the Sermon on the Mount, the disciples are told: "Unless your holiness (*dikaiōsunē*) surpasses that of the scribes and Pharisees you shall not enter the kingdom of God" (5:20).

In 5:16 Jesus tells the disciples: "Your light must shine before men so that they may see goodness in your acts and give praise to your heavenly Father." Matthew's purpose here in stressing the right intention in the doing of good deeds is to prepare the way for Jesus' denunciation of the Pharisees as hypocrites in 6:2,5,16. Even when the Pharisees do good deeds, they do

---

[96] Cf. G. Barth in Bornkamm, Barth, Held, *op. cit.*, 143-147.
[97] Cf. 9:35-36; 11:2-5; 14:34-36; 19:1-2; 20:25-28.
[98] Cf. W. D. Davies, *An Introduction to Pharisaeism*, 21-28.
[99] While Matthew's caricature of the Pharisees is based upon Jesus' condemnation of their legal-

ism and pomposity, it must be remembered that in Matthew's time in the eighties there existed the equivalent of a "hot war" between the Christian Church and the Jews who paid allegiance to the Pharisees of Jamnia. The caricature of the Canaanites throughout much of the Old Testament was due to a similar situation.

them for the wrong reason, i.e., they are "looking for applause" (6:2). They do them for themselves rather than to "give praise to your heavenly Father" (5:16).

Jesus repeats the charge of hypocrisy in 15:7-9 by quoting against the Pharisees the words of Isaiah: "This people pays me lip service but their heart is far from me" (Is 29:13). The charge reaches an unparalleled crescendo in ch 23, beginning with the stern admonition, "The scribes and the Pharisees occupy the chair of Moses. You must therefore do what they tell you and listen to what they say; but do not be guided by what they do, *since they do not practice what they preach*" (23:2-3), and ending with the scorching seven "woes" which characterize the Pharisees as hypocrites, blind guides, legalists, and self-satisfied non-doers (23:13-32).

Matthew's caricature of the Pharisees is so broad, devastating,and memorable that it is often forgotten he was almost equally condemnatory of "non-doing" Christians. It is to non-doing Christians that Jesus says: "Unless your holiness surpasses that of the scribes and Pharisees you shall not enter the kingdom of God" (5:20).

The "prophets" of 7:15ff are Christians who are likened to decayed trees because they do not bear good fruit. They are told in no uncertain terms that "none of those who cry out, 'Lord, Lord,' will enter the kingdom of God but only the one who does the will of my Father in heaven" (7:21). It will profit them nothing that they prophesied in the name of Jesus or exorcised demons by Jesus' power or performed miracles in his name. If they have not done the will of the Father, Jesus will say to them: "I never knew you. Out of my sight, you evildoers!" (7:22-23).

The conclusion of the Sermon on the Mount is significant in view of the fact that Matthew regularly uses final pericopes to sum up the central message of his discourses. The ending pericope of the Sermon on the Mount likens the man who "does" to a house built on a rock; the man who "does not" to a house built on sand (7:24-27).

In the remainder of the gospel, Matthew makes it abundantly clear to Christians, as Bornkamm says,[100] that the Church is "not a collection of the elect and eternally secure but a mixed body which has to face the separation between the good and evil at the final judgment." The distinction between good and bad Christians is clear in Jesus' explanation of the parables of the darnel (13:37-43) and the net (13:47-50).

That this distinction is based on "doing" and "non-doing" is the point of a number of Matthew's later parables. In the parable of the wedding banquet (ch 22:1-14), the point is made in the pericope about the guest at the wedding banquet who was "not properly dressed for a wedding feast" (22:11). It is the point of the parable of the owner of the house who is to be ready for

[100] G. Bornkamm in Bornkamm, Barth, Held, *op. cit.*, 19.

the coming of the Son of Man by being found "at work" (24:46). The same point seems to be made in the parable of the ten virgins (25:1-13) and is certainly made in the parable of the talents (25:14-30).

The ending pericope of the last great discourse is particularly significant (25:31-46). It is balanced with the ending pericope of the Sermon on the Mount not only in its language (note the repetition of the appeal "Lord, Lord . . ." (7:21 and 25:44) but in its central point. In the final judgment the distinction between the good and the wicked will be based on one criterion — the criterion of doing or not doing. Those who "do" will be "blessed"; those who "do not" will be condemned.

Matthew's insistence on "doing" as the primary characteristic of true discipleship has sometimes been obscured by the claim that his emphasis on "doing" is primarily a polemic against anti-nomians.[101] It may, of course, be true that in Matthew's time some claimed the law no longer bound Christians and that Matthew felt obliged to refute them. Such a contention would explain his programmatic statement in 5:17, "Do not think that I have come to abolish the law and the prophets. I have come, not to abolish them, but to fulfill them." It would also explain his emphasis on doing "all" the law[102] and his references to the fulfillment of the "law and the prophets."[103]

It may be there were anti-nomians and libertine enthusiasts in Matthew's community and it may be he was giving them "the back of his hand" in statements such as those cited above.[104] Nevertheless, the main thrust of his emphasis on "doing" is upon "doing" as the primary characteristic of true discipleship. The convergence of his positive and negative examples proves this. It is aimed more at a description of the true disciple than at a peripheral group denying the validity of law. The use of the Pharisees as examples of what true disciples should not be is particularly cogent. No one would accuse the Pharisees of anti-nomianism.

In addition, Matthew's emphasis on "doing" is not so new that it should be considered aimed at a dissident group. As M. Jack Suggs has shown,[105] there is a strong wisdom background to Matthew's thought. And few literatures emphasize "doing" more than the Wisdom literature. Finally, if we have been correct in supposing Matthew's formulation of the apostolic mandate in 28:19 to be patterned upon the mandate to Moses in Dt 5:30-33, it would follow that Matthew's emphasis on "observing all the law" is nothing more than a Christian updating of the Deuteronomic insistence on doing the law as proof of love for God and as proof of true covenant response.[106]

---

[101] Cf. Bornkamm, Barth, Held, *op. cit.*, 75ff; 159ff.

[102] Cf. 3:15; 5:18; 23:3; 28:20.

[103] Cf. 5:17; 7:12; 22:40.

[104] R. Dillon, "Ministry: Stewardship of Tradition" TD 20 [Summer 1972], 112, interprets Matthew in these texts to be condemning charismatic enthusiasm as libertine excess.

[105] Cf. *Wisdom, Christology and Law in Matthew's Gospel*, 99-127.

[106] Cf. E. W. Nicholson, *Deuteronomy and Tradition*; D. Hillers, *Covenant: The History of a Biblical Idea*; G. von Rad, *Deuteronomy*.

The true disciple does "all"

The mandate to teach men to "do" what Jesus commanded contains nothing revolutionary. To do "all" is something else. It involves doing all Jesus commanded in the Sermon on the Mount (ch 5–7), the divorce legislation (19:1-12), the call to "sell what you own and give the money to the poor" (19:16-22), the call to serve rather than be served (20:24-28), and the call to take up the cross and follow Jesus (16:24-26). The difficulty of doing "all" raises three questions. First, is Matthew serious? Second, is the call to do "all" an obligation or an invitation? Third, if it is an obligation, is it possible to do "all"?

With regard to the first question, authors agree Matthew is entirely serious.[107] They point to (1) his habitual precision in the choice and use of terms; (2) the redaction, by expansion of his sources, to emphasize "all"; (3) the contention in his polemic against the Pharisees that the Torah of Jesus represents the radical, paradise will of God and that it is as a consequence the fulfillment of and superior to the imperfect Torah of Moses.

Matthew's habitual precision in his choice of terminology makes it unlikely he would include accidentally so critical a word as "all" in the missionary mandate without good reason. He could have said: "Teach them to observe what has been commanded." We have seen why he specified the teaching of what Jesus rather than Moses commanded and the teaching of what Jesus had taught to the Apostles.[108] Teaching men to observe "all" is a further specification which contrasts the content of the teaching of Jesus with the imperfect content of the Old Law. The "all" in other words specifies the "more" which renders the Torah of Jesus superior to the Torah of Moses taught by the Pharisees.

Matthew's redaction of his sources bears out this contention. In contrast to Mark (Mk 1:9) and Luke (Lk 3:21-22), Matthew goes out of his way to explain that Jesus allows himself to be baptized because, as Jesus says, "It is fitting that we should, in this way, do *all* (*pasan*) that righteousness (*dikaiōsunēn*) demands" (3:15).[109]

Redaction critics have noticed, in addition, that in his account of Jesus' temptation in the desert (4:1ff), Matthew not only shows Jesus doing the will of God perfectly, but also expands the Q source's words, "Man does not live by bread alone," by adding to them the comment, "but on every word (*panti hremati*) that comes from the mouth of God" (4:4). The words are not found in Luke's version of the Q saying (cf. Lk 4:4).

If it is true, as some have suggested,[110] that Matthew is using here a literary form or device, known from the Targums, according to which a great man

---

[107] Cf. Bornkamm, Barth, Held, *op. cit.*, 24-32; 62-75; 95-105; N. Perrin, *Rediscovering the Teaching of Jesus*, 76-78; 206; W. D. Davies, *The Setting of the Sermon on the Mount*, 418-435; J. Jeremias, *The Sermon on the Mount*; M. Jack Suggs, *Wisdom, Christology and Law*, 109-120.

[108] See pp. 137-138.

[109] The Greek is even more emphatic since it expresses the thought of fullness with the Matthaean verb *plerosai*: "to fulfill all righteousness" (*plerosai pasan dikaiosunen*).

[110] Cf. *NTA* 17 (Winter, 1973) nn. 528-529.

at the beginning of his career is shown in a vision the significance of his whole life, then the narratives of the baptism and the temptation are meant by Matthew to present Jesus' whole life as an example of the perfect doing of God's will. Since this is what constitutes perfect discipleship in relationship to Jesus and the Father (cf. 28:19), and since the theme of perfect discipleship is so central to the Sermon on the Mount which follows, it is not unlikely that Matthew has composed these two narratives in this way in order to prepare his audience for his fuller teaching on perfect discipleship in ch 5–7. Luke's accounts of Paul's vision on the road to Damascus (Acts 9; 22; 26), especially the account in Acts 26:12-18, would seem to belong to the same literary form and to serve the same purpose.[111]

That the "all" refers to the "more" contained in Jesus' messianic Torah is particularly evident in the Sermon on the Mount. Jesus' first words about the law deal with his intention to bring it to completion: "Do not think that I have come to abolish the law and the prophets. I have come, not to abolish them but to fulfill them" (5:17). It is agreed by commentators that the verb fulfill (*plērōsai*) has a special place in Matthew's terminology and theology.[112] Here, as the context of the antitheses (5:21-48) shows, the meaning of the verb is not only to establish the authority of the law and the prophets (5:17-19) but to complete the teaching of the law by going beyond the Sinai law to the ultimate paradise will of God. When Jesus says, "You have learnt how it was said to our ancestors," and then goes on to add, "but I say to you" (5:21-22,27-28,31-34,38-39), he is not abrogating what was said in the Mosaic Torah, he is going beyond it to a promulgation of the ultimate, radical will of God.

The "all" that Jesus commands goes far beyond what was commanded by Moses. The "beyond" element is expressed not only in the antitheses but in the demand with which the antitheses end: "You must therefore be perfect (*teleios*) just as your heavenly Father is perfect (*teleios*)" (5:48). How much more this calls for is expressed in the Matthaean version of the Lord's Prayer, where Jesus teaches his disciples to pray to the Father that his will "be done on earth as it is in heaven." The implication of Matthew's version is that God's will is done perfectly in heaven and that it is his will that it be done just as perfectly on earth. A comparison with the Lukan version of the Lord's Prayer (Lk 11:2-4), where the words, "Thy will be done on earth as it is in heaven," are noticeably absent, indicates the additional words are either an *ad hoc* Matthaean expansion of that formulation or Matthew's selection of the version of the prayer used in his church in the eighties.[113] In either case, the additional words express perfectly Matthew's conception of the "more" and the "beyond" in the messianic Torah of Jesus.

Speaking about the "massive elevation of the teaching of Jesus in the

[111] Cf. E. Haenchen, *The Acts of the Apostles*, 328.
[112] Cf. Bornkamm, Barth, Held, *op. cit.*, 62-75;
W. F. Albright, *Matthew*, 57-59.
[113] Cf. J. Jeremias, *The Prayers of Jesus*, 58-95.

Sermon on the Mount," W. D. Davies contends that "apart from the internal demands of the Christian community, it was the necessity to provide a Christian counterpart to 'Jamnia' that best illustrates this."[114] The "massive elevation of the teaching of Jesus in the Sermon on the Mount" is Matthew's method of demonstrating not only that Jesus is one "greater than" Moses but that Jesus' Torah is "greater than" the Torah of Moses.[115]

It is greater because where Moses forbade murder, adultery, etc., Jesus went beyond the overt act to the roots of man's actions — to the angry word, the lustful gaze, etc. It is the will of God according to the teaching of Jesus that man eliminate not only the overt evil act but even those initial internal acts which lead to overt actions. Thus, the Torah of Jesus goes beyond the Torah of Moses because it goes to the radical, or, as it is sometimes called, the paradise will of God.[116]

How far the paradise will goes beyond the Torah of Moses is expressed adequately in the antitheses (5:21-48). It is expressed especially clearly, however, and in "paradise will" terminology, in Jesus' dispute with the Pharisees concerning the question of divorce (19:3-12). In his reply to the Pharisees, Jesus repudiates divorce absolutely. He declares categorically, citing as his authority the paradise will of God expressed in the Adam and Eve story (Gn 2:24), that it has been God's will from the very beginning, i.e., from the time of paradise, that there should be no divorce for anyone under any circumstances (19:4-6).

When the Pharisees object that Moses permitted divorce, Jesus absolves Moses of blame because, as he says, "it was because you were so unteachable (hardhearted)," but at the same time he clearly shows that his own teaching goes beyond the teaching of Moses precisely because it promulgates the radical paradise will of God. Particularly *significant for Matthew's understanding of the radical will of God as the* content of Jesus' messianic Torah is the fact that Matthew includes the divorce legislation of 19:3-9 in the list of Jesus' antitheses in 5:21-48 (cf. 5:32).

Is it necessary to do all?

Granting Matthew is entirely serious in calling upon men to do "all" Jesus commanded, a second question arises. Does Matthew understand the command to do "all" as an obligation binding under pain of damnation or as simply an urgent invitation to do "all"? The question admits no easy answer.[117]

The antitheses as a group (5:21-48) imply serious obligation. Matthew certainly considered the Old Law obligatory (cf. 23:3,23). There is no reason to believe he looked upon the commands of Jesus as any less obligatory. The

[114] *The Setting of the Sermon on the Mount,* 315.
[115] Cf. R. N. Longenecker, *The Christology of Early Jewish Christianity,* 32-38.
[116] Cf. N. Perrin, *The Kingdom of God in the Teaching of Jesus,* 76-78; W. D. Davies, *Torah in the Messianic Age and/or The Age to Come.*
[117] Cf. P. S. Minear, *Commands of Christ.*

statement of Jesus introducing the antitheses implies as much: "I tell you, unless your holiness surpasses that of the scribes and Pharisees you shall not enter the kingdom of God" (5:20). The statement with which Jesus concludes the antitheses is equally indicative of serious obligation: "You must be perfect as your heavenly Father is perfect" (5:48).

On the other hand, the Church down the centuries has never *obliged* men to do the "all" the "more" expressed in the antitheses of the Sermon on the Mount (Mt 5:21-48). Nor does Matthew, if we understand correctly his teaching in the discussion of Jesus with the rich young man on the question of what has to be done "to enter into life" (19:16-26).

In the discussion there is a clear distinction between what is necessary "to enter into life," namely, the keeping of the commandments, and the "more" called for by Christ in order to be "perfect" (*teleios*), namely, "sell all you possess and give it to the poor." When the rich young man refuses to do the "more," Jesus makes the declaration that "it is easier for a camel to pass through the eye of a needle than for a rich man to enter the kingdom of heaven" (19:24). To this the Apostles object: "Who then can be saved?" And Jesus makes the concession: "For men this is impossible; for God everything is possible" (19:25-26).

Undoubtedly, the primary function of the pericope is to urge the observance of the "more" called for by Jesus. Neverthless, the objection of the Apostles and the subsequent concession on the part of Jesus suggests the possibility that Matthew faced the same problem we face concerning the difficulty of doing the "all" and the "more" demanded by Jesus and concluded that the obligation was not so serious that it involved the loss of eternal life for those who were not up to it.

It seems, in conclusion, that for Matthew the command to do "all' meant more than a simple "take it or leave it" invitation. Whether we call it an obligation or a very urgent invitation remains a matter of debate. What is important, however, is that Matthew looked upon the will to do all that Jesus commanded as a characteristic of the true disciple.

Is it possible to do all?

Even when we conclude that Matthew is serious in his emphasis on doing "all" and that his command to do "all" is more than a simple "take it or leave it" invitation, we are still left with the far more elemental question: Is it possible for any man, much less "all nations," to do all that Jesus commanded?

The difficulty of answering the question affirmatively has led to a number of evasive explanations. J. Jeremias considers three — the theory of the perfectionist ethic, the theory of the impossible ideal, and the theory of the interim-ethic — and rejects them in turn.[117a]

[117a] *The Sermon on the Mount.*

The theory of the perfectionist ethic understands Jesus to have taught that the perfect observance of God's law as law is the means by which man achieves his salvation. It is rejected on the basis that neither Jesus nor Matthew ever expected that man by himself could possibly achieve a perfect observance of the law of God.

The theory of the impossible ideal understands Jesus to have realized it was impossible for man to do the paradise will of God on his own but to have purposely commanded the impossible in order thereby to force man to realize his hopeless condition and have him throw himself entirely upon the mercy of God. The theory is rejected on the basis that Matthew is serious not only in his command to do "all" but in his expectation that it is in some way truly possible for man to do all that Jesus commanded.

The theory of the interim-ethic understands Jesus to have been mistaken in thinking the world would shortly come to an end and to have as a consequence been convinced that men could reasonably be expected to achieve at least for the brief period before the end the heroic conduct called for in the Sermon on the Mount. The theory is rejected on the basis that (1) the tone of Matthew's gospel is not that of an interim-ethic; (2) the date of the gospel — forty to fifty years after the resurrection — rules out any thought of a brief period of heroic conduct; (3) the Matthaean community is already settled down to living the Christian life in the world in a normal day-to-day manner; (4) the Matthaean Church envisions a task of disciplizing all nations and a period of time adequate for the task which would be far longer than that presupposed for a brief period of heroic interim-ethical conduct.

The question however remains. Is it possible for man to do the "all" and the "more" called for in the Sermon on the Mount? Jeremias' explanation is that the Sermon on the Mount presupposes forgiveness, conversion, and the experience of a new life in Christ. The "more" therefore is not expected of all men but only from those who have already experienced the influence of Jesus in their lives. It is on the basis of Christ living in them that they can be called to forgive as Christ forgave and to love as Christ loved.

Jeremias' explanation goes a long way toward the solution of the difficulty. Ultimately however, it runs into a wall. The facts of life and the chronicle of Christian experience appear to belie the possibility of even Christians living a life based on the conduct called for in the Sermon on the Mount. It is from the saints that we expect heroic conduct. And the saints are few.

If there is an adequate explanation of the problem, it probably lies in the direction indicated by N. Perrin.[117b] Perrin accepts the realized eschatological premise of Jeremias that "the gift of God clearly precedes the demands

[117b] Cf. *The Kingdom of God in the Teaching of Jesus*, 202-206.

of God." He concludes, however, that one must distinguish between partial and complete, beginning and completion of realized eschatological life:

> In the case of the forgiveness of sins, for example, men must respond in terms of forgiveness to others as they move from the first experience of forgiveness towards the perfect sacral relationship with God in the "temple not made with hands." Or in the case of the law of love, men must respond in terms of loving one another, including their enemies, as they move from the initial impact of the love of God in their experience towards the perfect fellowship of love "sitting at table with Abraham, Isaac and Jacob in the Kingdom of God." In both of these cases, and in all others that could be mentioned, the initial impulse derives from the impact of what God is doing in human experience and the response to this is the dynamic by means of which men move from the beginning towards the consummation. So the eschatology does not stand at the beginning only . . . Rather eschatology stands both at the beginning and the end.[117c]

Perrin's solution is attractive but it does not explain what the dynamic is "by means of which men move from the beginning towards the consummation." It is here perhaps that Matthew's understanding of faith as trust in Jesus' power (*exousia*) may help to explain what the dynamic is and at the same time suggest a solution to the impasse of the apparent impossibility of doing all that Jesus commanded.

For Matthew the ability to do God's will perfectly seems to depend on man's faith-trust in Jesus. The greater the faith, the greater man's ability to do the difficult or almost impossible. Peter walking on the water is a parade example of doing the impossible (14:29). Peter sinking is a parade example of inability to do the impossible without faith in Jesus (14:30). Jesus' rebuke, "Man of little faith, why did you doubt?" (14:31), may well be indicative of Matthew's understanding of the relationship between faith and doing, between the impact of the eschatological life force and the response of realized eschatological living or doing.

It has been observed that Matthew distinguishes between those who accept and those who reject Jesus as well as between those who accept Jesus and have faith and those who accept Jesus and have little or no faith. Those who cry "Lord, Lord" at the end of the Sermon on the Mount (7:22) and in the parable of the last judgment (25:44) are typical of those who have accepted Jesus but have little or no faith. Matthew distinguishes between what we would call intellectual faith, i.e., understanding and accepting Jesus, and faith as trust in Jesus' power.[118] The distinction runs throughout the gospel [119] but it is particularly indicated in Matthew's redaction of the miracle accounts in ch 8–9.

In 10:22 Jesus tells his Apostles: "The man who stands firm to the end

---

[117c] *Op. cit.*, 203-204.
[118] The difference in the Markan presentation of the disciples as those who "do not understand" and the Matthaean presentation of the disciples as those who understand but have little faith is analyzed by G. Barth (Bornkamm, Barth, Held, *op. cit.*, 114-116).
[119] Cf. 10:22; 14:29-31; 17:14-20; 21:21-22.

will be saved." In 14:29-31 he shows that standing firm means having faith by showing Peter not standing firm on the waters because, as Jesus says, he is a man of "little faith." In 17:14-20, when the disciples ask Jesus, "Why were we unable to cast it (a devil) out?", Jesus answers: "Because you have little faith. I tell you solemnly, if your faith were the size of a mustard seed you could say to this mountain, 'Move from here to there,' and it would move; nothing would be impossible for you." The same understanding of faith and the impossible is expressed in 21:21-22,

> I tell you solemnly, if you have faith and do not doubt at all, not only will you do what I have done to the fig tree, but even if you say to this mountain, "Get up and throw yourself into the sea," it will be done.

In ch 8–9, the instruction on the necessity of faith for true discipleship is imparted, almost subliminally, by the redactional technique of re-editing the miracle accounts in such a way that what is emphasized is not the miracle but the need for faith in Jesus. In short, Matthew uses his miracle accounts not only to demonstrate Jesus' authority "in deed" but also to catechize his readers on the necessity of faith for true discipleship. The technique has been admirably analyzed by H. J. Held.[120]

Whatever the emphasis in the telling of the miracle stories in tradition (and it was probably on the miracle itself as in Mark generally), Held has shown that in Matthew's telling of the events the emphasis is not on the wonders but on the faith of those for whom the wonders were worked.

Four characteristics of Matthew in the telling of the miracle events are noted. First, Matthew generally abbreviates the accounts, eliminating descriptive details and secondary characters; e.g., compare Matthew's version (Mt 8:28-34) with Mark's version (Mk 5:1-20) of the Gadarene demoniac and Matthew's version (Mt 9:20-22) with Mark's version (Mk 5:25-34) of the woman with the hemorrhage.

Second, Matthew generally characterizes as suppliants the people who come to Jesus seeking help; e.g., compare Matthew's version (Mt 8:23-27) with Mark's version (Mk 4:35-41) of the storm at sea.

Third, Matthew tends to turn miracle accounts into didactic conversations which emphasize faith; e.g., Mt 9:27-31; 17:14-20; 21:18-22.

Fourth, Matthew frequently turns miracle accounts into pronouncement narratives so that the presentations tend to emphasize more what Christ says than what he does; e.g., Matthew's version of the cure of the blind men (Mt 9:27-31) and the woman with a hemorrhage (Mt 9:18-22).[121]

These characteristics coincide with Matthew's own predilection for teach-

[120] Cf. Bornkamm, Barth, Held, op. cit., 165-210.

[121] H. J. Held (op. cit., 242) concludes: "The observation that the emphasis in these healing stories actually lies on this saying of Jesus about faith confirms that the point is to be found in it and not in the healing itself."

ing and with his presentation of Jesus as the messianic teacher. More important they help the reader come to a better understanding of Matthew's mind on the nature and importance of faith.

The importance of faith for discipleship is taught by Matthew in two ways. First, and most important, Matthew uses the adjective "of little faith" (*oligopistos*) of those who do not measure up as disciples because their faith is weak.[122]

In addition to using the expression "of little faith," Matthew redacts his miracle accounts, as indicated above, in such a way that faith or trust in Jesus is made paradigmatic for discipleship. The two ways of showing the importance of faith for discipleship are combined in Matthew's redaction of the story of Jesus walking on the water (14:22-33) where the miracle of walking on the water is subordinated to the teaching about faith implicit in the accusation made to Peter: "Man of little faith, why did you doubt?" (14:31).

Perhaps equally significant for Matthew's attitude toward faith and discipleship is the difference in the way Mark and Matthew speak about the disciples understanding Jesus. Where Mark regularly has Jesus berate the Apostles for their lack of understanding, Matthew does not contest their understanding but their failure to trust Jesus. Matthew as a consequence regularly distinguishes between those who can be called disciples in as much as they understand and acknowledge Christ and those disciples who are poor disciples because their works do not correspond to their profession of faith, or, more properly, because actually they have little or no faith.

It is for this reason that Matthew ends the Sermon on the Mount, which is addressed to believers, with the words of Jesus: "Not everyone who says to me 'Lord, Lord' will enter into the kingdom of heaven" (7:21). They have understood but they have not acted on their faith and therefore have not been true disciples.

It is the same understanding of true discipleship that distinguishes between the darnel and the wheat (13:30), the good fish and the bad fish (13:48-50), and the sheep and the goats (25:31-46).

To understand is not enough. The true disciple must trust and act. How far this trust can go is made clear in Mt 21:21-22, "If you have faith . . . even if you say to this mountain, 'Get up and throw yourself into the sea,' it will be done."

In addition to this use of the term "of little faith," Matthew also uses the formula, "As you have believed, so let it be done to you"[123] to emphasize the importance of faith.

The true disciple for Matthew, therefore, not only understands and accepts Jesus' teaching. He believes Jesus, trusts Jesus, relies on Jesus, and

---

[122] Cf. 6:30; 8:26; 14:31; 16:8; 17:20; and implicitly in 21:21-22.

[123] Cf. 8:13; 9:29; 15:28; and, implicitly, 9:22; 9:2.

commits himself to the love of Jesus. In addition, he not only accepts Jesus' teaching, but in and through faith does what Jesus asks of him with generosity and confidence. Faith is the dynamic that makes all things possible.

In summary, it would seem the didactic purpose of the miracle accounts in ch 8–9 was directed to the instruction of those Christians of Matthew's time who had little or no faith in the sense of a faith which trusted in the power and love of Jesus under *all* circumstances and particularly in time of persecution.

If we have been correct in our interpretation of Matthew's understanding of faith as the dynamic by means of which men move toward a greater and more perfect response to God's impact on their lives, it may well be that in Matthew's mind it is by means of ever firmer faith that man finds it possible to do *all* that Jesus has commanded. The "greatest in the kingdom of heaven" is, by Jesus' definition, the one who is like a little child (Mt 18:1-4), i.e., one who is utterly and totally dependent on God and trusts God as a child trusts its mother.

The most radical law

For Matthew the most radical law is the law of love.[124] "This evangelist," as V. P. Furnish says, "regards the love command as the hermeneutical key to the law, the essence of 'the law and the prophets,' and that which most distinguishes Jesus' teaching from the Pharisaic tradition."[125] The man who loves God and neighbor does all that God wills him to do.

The love command is so pivotal in Matthew's theology that without understanding it, it is impossible to adequately appreciate his mind and message. It conditions everything he says about law. It separates him from the Pharisees of Jamnia in the interpretation of the law. And it brings him into substantial agreement with Saint John and Saint Paul in relationship to the place of law in the Christian's day-to-day living.[126]

In dealing with Matthew's understanding of the law of love, we shall have to remember he reveals his mind by concentric-circle presentation of his subject. It will be necessary, therefore, to consider each concentric presentation by itself and then synthesize what is common to each. It will be necessary as well to advert to the fact that in almost every place in which Matthew treats the law of love, he does so in a context of polemic with the Pharisees and contrast between the Torah of Moses and the Torah of Jesus.

We shall treat first Matthew's four concentric presentations of the love command[127] and then briefly a number of other texts and pericopes relevant to the Matthaean interpretation of the love commandment.[128]

[124] Cf. V. P. Furnish, *The Love Command in the New Testament*, 30-34; 45-54; 74-84; 194-218; W. D. Davies, *The Setting of the Sermon on the Mount*, 264-315; N. Perrin, *The Kingdom of God in the Teaching of Jesus*, 201-207; C. Spicq, *Agape in the New Testament*.
[125] *Op. cit.*, 74.
[126] See below concerning the reconciliation of Paul and Matthew's apparently conflicting viewpoints on the law, pp. 154-157.
[127] Cf. 5:21-48; 6:1-7,12; 11:28–12:14.
[128] Cf. 5:23-24; 9:13; 12:7; 18:23-35; 24:12-13; 25:31-46.

The first two presentations occur in the Sermon on the Mount and derive their special impact from their position in the Sermon as a whole and from their context of polemic with the Pharisees. If one considers the structure of the Sermon to follow an outline of introduction (5:2-19), body in two parts (5:20-48 and 6:1–7:12), conclusion (7:13-27), it becomes clear that anything Jesus has to say about the law of love in 5:20-48 and 6:1–7:12 becomes critically important for an understanding of Matthew's mind on the subject.

It should be observed first that both panels are prefaced by the statement: "I tell you, if your virtue (*dikaiōsunē*) goes no deeper than that of the scribes and Pharisees, you will never get into the kingdom of heaven" (5:20). What follows in the two presentations is set immediately in a context of polemic with the Pharisees. In the first presentation (5:21-48), the law of Jesus is contrasted with the imperfect law of Moses followed by the Pharisees. In the second presentation (6:1–7:12), the virtue, or justice, or righteousness (*dikaiōsunē*), i.e., the way of acting, of Jesus' disciples, is contrasted with the virtue of the Pharisees (cf. 5:20) and shown to be more perfect primarily because it is manifested by deeds and not just by talking but also because it is governed overall by the golden rule (7:12) which is only another way of saying: "You shall love your neighbor as yourself."

Two aspects of Matthew's presentation are particularly significant. First, he is out to contrast "the more" of Jesus' messianic Torah with "the less" of Moses' imperfect Torah. Second, he is out to contrast the response of true disciples to the law of Jesus with the response of the Pharisees to the law of Moses. What is important in each presentation is that the law of love takes the climactic position (cf. 5:43-48; 7:12).

In the first panel (5:21-48), Matthew draws attention to the love command by the very fact that he lists it among the commandments of the decalogue to which it does not properly belong (note that he does the same in 19:18-19). He indicates its importance by placing it last (the climactic position in Matthew), by likening those who love their enemies to God the Father, and by concluding with the command: "You must therefore be perfect just as your heavenly Father is perfect" (5:48).[129] The messianic Torah of Jesus goes beyond the Torah of Moses precisely in that it calls for love for all men, even enemies.[130]

In the second panel (6:1–7:12), the contrast is not between the Torah of Moses and the Torah of Jesus but between the way in which the Pharisees worship God and the way in which Christians are to worship God. The emphasis is on motivation and doing. Christians are not to imitate the "hypocrites" (6:2,5,16). Again, as in the first panel, the climactic position is given

[129] Cf V. P. Furnish, *op. cit.*, 53; Bornkamm, Barth, Held, *op. cit.*, 97-105.
[130] The same emphasis on the more demanded of Christians is found in 19:16-22, where the more called for in being "perfect" is not, as in 5:43-48, the loving of enemies but the selling of all one owns to give it to the poor.

to the love command. Christians are commanded: "So always treat others as you would like them to treat you; that is the meaning of the law and the prophets" (7:12). As Barth says: "All the preceding directions of the Sermon on the Mount, which are concluded by 7:12, are thereby subordinated to the love commandment. This is the ground and secret goal of all the commandments."[131] By saying, "That is the meaning of the law and the prophets," Matthew implies what he will make clear in 22:34-40. Everything in the law and the prophets is not only summed up in the love command, but is subordinate to and subject to the love command for its interpretation.

In 11:28–12:14 Matthew shows that he knows well how to draw the consequences that flow from making the love command the goal of all the commandments and the ultimate criterion in the light of which all that is contained in the law and the prophets is to be interpreted.

The context of polemic with the Pharisees is evident throughout. The section begins with Jesus' declaration: "Shoulder *my* yoke (a common rabbinical term for the law), for *my* yoke is easy and *my* burden light" (11:29-30). The contrast is between the law as interpreted by the Pharisees and the law as understood by Jesus.[131a]

In the two cases — the case of the disciples picking corn on the Sabbath (12:1-8) and the case of curing on the Sabbath (12:9-14) — Jesus' interpretation, as opposed to the interpretation of the Pharisees, is shown to be dominated by the love commandment. It is not said that the Sabbath law does not bind. What it said is that the law of love — feeding the hungry and curing the sick — supersedes the Sabbath law.

What has been implied in the Sermon on the Mount from the climactic position given to the love commandment at the end of the antitheses (5:43-48) and at the end of the section on Christian as opposed to Pharisaic observance (7:12) and what has been demonstrated in Jesus' benign interpretation of the Sabbath law in 12:1-14 is formulated in 22:34-40.

Unlike Mark (12:28-34), whose questioner is a friendly scribe approved and praised by Jesus as "not far from the kingdom of God" (Mk 12:34), Matthew presents the question of the "greatest commandment" in a context of polemic. The Pharisees get together to trap Jesus (Mt 22:34). Behind their apparently innocent question lies the intention and the hope that Jesus will say something that can be used against him. The trap cannot consist in getting Jesus to agree with them. On this score, two elements of Jesus' answer can be ruled out. The Pharisees would agree with Jesus on Dt 6:5 as the greatest commandment of the law. They would also agree with him that the second, "You must love your neighbor as yourself" (Lv 19:18), is like to the first commandment. The trap and the disagreement must therefore be

---

[131] Bornkamm, Barth, Held, *op. cit.*, 80.
[131a] If the contrast were between the content of Jesus' and Moses' Torah (cf. 5:21-48), Jesus could not have said, "my yoke is light," since the Torah of Jesus calls for doing more than the Torah of Moses.

found in Jesus' additional comment: "On these two commandments hang the whole law and the prophets also" (22:40).[132]

Since Matthew is no more out to show Jesus agreeing with the Pharisees here than he was in the Sermon on the Mount or in the two test cases concerning the Sabbath in 12:1-14, we can eliminate immediately the interpretation of Jesus' words which would agree with the teaching of the Pharisees, namely, that the declaration means that everything in the law and the prophets can be deduced from these two commandments. We are left then with the meaning of the declaration with which the Pharisees would not agree, namely, that the love commandment is above all other commandments in importance and that all other commandments as a result must give way when there is conflict with the love commandment. What Jesus declares and what the Pharisees deny is the interpretation of the love commandment which Jesus had applied in the two test cases of 12:1-14. Where love of neighbor is in conflict with any other law, even the law of the Sabbath as in 12:1-14, the law of love takes precedence.

That this is Jesus' understanding of the law is borne out not only in 12:1-14 but in 5:23-24; 9:13; 12:7. In 5:23-24 Christians are told that Jesus' Torah demands that they be reconciled to a brother Christian before making an offering at the altar. Love of neighbor, manifested by forgiveness, precedes in importance the offering of sacrifice to God.[133]

The paramount importance of the love command is brought out in two other texts (Mt 9:13; 12:7). In 9:13 and 12:7 Matthew quotes Hosea: "What I want is mercy, not sacrifice" (Hos 6:6). Since the quote is not found in Matthew's source (cf. Mk 2:15-17, 23-28), it should be considered a Matthaean addition. What Matthew intends to say by adding these words is that as far as God is concerned, mercy or loving-kindness (the better translation of Hosea's Hebrew term *hesed*) is far more important than sacrifice. The thought is entirely consistent with 5:23-24, the necessity of being reconciled with one's brother before offering sacrifice, and with 22:34-40, the necessity of placing the love commandment above all other commandments in importance and precedence.

The clearest evidence for the importance of the love commandment according to the mind of Matthew is found in the parable of the last judgment in 25:31-46. When men stand before God in judgment to account for their observance of all that Jesus has commanded, they will be judged according to their observance or non-observance of only one commandment — the law of love. Beyond the obvious emphasis on the law of love, two other aspects of the parable should be noted. First, nothing whatever is said about any other commandment. Second, the parable as it is situated in Matthew's gospel constitutes the last thing Jesus says in his teaching discourses. The

---

[132] Cf. V. P. Furnish, *op. cit.*, 30-34.

[133] Cf. 6:14-15; 18:21-35 for the importance of forgiveness in Matthew's theology.

usual ending formula which follows differs from the preceding ending formulas by the addition of one word, "Jesus had now finished *all* he wanted to say . . ." (26:1). If we have been correct in stating that Matthew uses his end pericopes in the discourses to sum up his message, then surely it is significant that the last thing Jesus says is that in the final judgment the only thing that will count is the observance of the law of love.[134]

Matthew and Paul

The reader who turns from Matthew's gospel to Paul's Philippians, Galatians, and Romans senses immediately markedly different attitudes toward the Law.[135] In Matthew's gospel Jesus declares: "Do not imagine I have come to abolish the Law or the Prophets. I have come not to abolish but to complete them" (Mt 5:17). Paul says: "But now the Law has come to an end with Christ, and everyone who has faith may be justified" (Rom 10:4). In Matthew's gospel Jesus says: "Alas for you, scribes and Pharisees, you hypocrites! You who pay your tithe of mint and dill and cummin and have neglected the weightier matters of Law — justice, mercy, good faith! These you should have practiced without neglecting the others" (Mt 23:23). The apparently contradictory quotations could be multiplied. But it is not necessary. No one can read Paul after Matthew without wondering how the two can possibly be reconciled in their attitudes toward the Law. Where Paul, especially in Galatians and Romans, seems positively hostile to the Law, Matthew throughout his Gospel insists that the Law not only has been brought to perfection by Jesus but must be observed as a whole by Christians.

The solution to the problem will not be found through the matching of texts where Paul and Matthew apparently agree (e.g., Mt 22:34-40 and Rom 13:8-10). Nor will it be found by saying that Matthew and Paul were speaking about a different Law. In each case they are speaking about the same Law but from a different viewpoint and under drastically different circumstances.

When Paul spoke with such apparent hostility to the Law, he was speaking at a time and in a context of warring theological opinions. In Galatians especially, but also to some extent in Philippians and Romans, when Paul attacks those who put their trust in the keeping of the Law, he is attacking them precisely because they say, or appear to say, that simply by keeping the Law a man can be saved. Paul's gospel is that man is saved through faith in Jesus not by the observance of the Law. As he says in Galatians: ". . .

---

[134] Cf. J. A. T. Robinson, "The Parable of the Sheep and the Goats" *NTS* II (1955–56) 231-239; R. Maddox, "Who are the 'Sheep' and the Goats' "? ABR (1965) 18-28; V. P. Furnish, *op. cit.*, 79-84.

[135] See J. L. Houlden, *Ethics and the New Testament*; P. Furnish, *The Love Command in the New Testament*; C. D. Moule, "Obligation in the Ethic of Paul," *Christian History and Interpretation* (1967); P. Minear, *Commands of Christ*; G. McCauley, *The Truce of God*; J. M.

Gustafson, "The Place of Scripture in Christian Ethics," *Interpretation* 24 (1970) 430-444; W. D. Davies, *The Setting of the Sermon on the Mount*, 365-366; S. Lyonnet, "St. Paul: Liberty and Law" in L. Salm's, *Readings in Biblical Morality*; Bornkamm, Barth, Held, *Tradition and Interpretation in Matthew* (passim): J. Jeremias, *The Sermon on the Mount*; R. Dillon, "Ministry: Stewardship of Tradition" *TD* 20 (Summer 1972) 108-115.

we hold that faith in Christ rather than fidelity to the Law is what justifies us, and that none can be justified by keeping the Law" (Gal 2:7). Paul is not just against the Mosaic law, he is against any law, even the new law of Christ, if a man thinks that he can find salvation in the keeping of such law. As S. Lyonnet says: "To the extent that the New Law of Christ is a code of written law, to the extent that it contains the teachings of faith and moral precepts that govern human attitudes and acts, the New Law does not justify any more than did the Old Law since its nature is not different; it remains a norm of conduct, not a principal of activity." [136]

When Matthew wrote toward the end of the first century, some thirty years after Paul wrote Romans, there was no longer any overt debate about the question of faith versus law. For Matthew as for Paul, faith was elemental — the DNA of the spiritual life. [137] For Matthew, as for both Christians and Jews in general, the Law represented God's gift to man. The Law was the explicitation of what a good God wanted from his creatures *for their good*. The keeping of the Law was man's way of doing God's will "on earth as it is in heaven." It was man's way of showing that he accepted the reign of God in his life. It was man's way of acknowledging through his actions that he belonged to the Kingdom of God. In short, Matthew's attitude toward the Law was the same as that of the Wisdom writers of the Old Testament for whom the Law was a gift from God and for whom "the beginning of wisdom [was] the fear of the Lord" (i.e., observance of the commandments). [138]

Paul and Matthew certainly agree on the centrality of the law of love (cp. Mt 22:34-40 and Rom 13:8-10). Prescinding from the theological debate with the Judaizers who claimed that man was saved by keeping the Law, Paul would also agree with Matthew that the Law is a gift of God. It would seem equally true that Paul was emotionally more on the side of liberty than was Matthew, but we shall never know exactly how Matthew felt about liberty since he had no occasion, as Paul did, to express himself on the subject.

In summary, for Paul any written, outside law, whether of the Old Testament or the New Testament, would seem to be at best a necessary evil. But a necessary evil even for Paul is a good of sorts. Matthew, on the other hand, sees the Law as a means of knowing the will of God and as a help toward doing it in as much as it is governed by the overall law of love. For Matthew, the law is not a necessary evil but a positive good. Matthew's radicalization of the Law in the antitheses demonstrates that his aim is the perfect doing of the will of God, not just the keeping of the Law for the sake of the Law. In this, Paul and Matthew would be in full agreement however different their approaches. [139]

[136] S. Lyonnet, *art. cit.*, 75.
[137] pp. 147-150.
[138] Cf. M. Jack Suggs, *Wisdom, Christology, and Law in Matthew's Gospel*, 99-127.

[139] See W. D. Davies, *The Setting of the Sermon on the Mount*, who says that for Paul the Sermon on the Mount would "not be an alien importation into the faith" (p. 366).

Appendix A

THE HISTORICITY OF THE GOSPELS

Christians down the centuries have subscribed to the historicity of the Gospels as a matter of tradition, faith, and reasoned conviction. The tradition and the faith remain constant. The conviction, however, in recent years has tended to erode under the impact of critical historical studies. In what sense the erosion is justified and in what sense it is not, constitutes the problem. Since the problem admits neither an easy nor a brief solution, it seems best to have recourse for a solution to two excellent guidelines on the subject issued by the Church. The first is par. 19 of Vatican II's *Dogmatic Constitution on Divine Revelation*:

> Holy Mother Church has firmly held, and continues to hold, that the four Gospels just named, whose *historical character* the Church unhesitatingly asserts, *faithfully hand on* what Jesus Christ, while living among men, really did and taught for their eternal salvation until the day He was taken up into heaven (Acts 1:1). Indeed, after the Ascension of the Lord the Apostles handed on to their hearers what He had said and done. This they did with that *clearer understanding* which they enjoyed *after* they had been instructed by the glorious events of Christ's life and taught by the light of the Spirit of truth. The sacred authors wrote the four Gospels, *selecting* some things from the many which had been handed on by word of mouth or in writing, *reducing* some of them to a *synthesis, explaining* some things in view of the situation of their churches, and preserving the form of proclamation but always in such fashion that they told us the *honest truth* about Jesus. For their intention in writing was that either from their own memory and recollections, or from the witness of those who 'themselves from the beginning were eye-witnesses and ministers of the Word' we might know 'the truth' concerning those matters about which we have been instructed' (Lk 1:2-4; italics added.)

The second is the earlier and longer Instruction "Concerning the Historical Truth of the Gospels" issued by the Pontifical Biblical Commission on April 21, 1964.[1] The Instruction runs to approximately 3000 words in 18 paragraphs and attempts an answer to the questions and difficulties raised repeatedly in the last few decades against the historical character of the Gospels. It is a guideline on the subject from the highest competent authority.[2] In addition, it provides both the background and the explanation of the more concise statement on the subject in par. 19 of the *Dogmatic Constitution on Divine Revelation*. We will deal with it, therefore, more at length.

[1] Cf. *AAS* 56, 1964.
[2] For the full text of the Instruction and an excellent commentary, see J. A. Fitzmyer, *Theological Studies* 25 (1964) 386-408.

156

The central concern of the Instruction is expressed in the third paragraph: "Today the labors of exegetes are all the more called for by reason of the fact that in many publications circulated far and wide the truth of the events and sayings recorded in the Gospels is being challenged." The Instruction then continues with a number of exhortations to exegetes before getting to the heart of the matter in par. 5-10.

Par. 5 gives a greenlight for the use of the form-critical method but with a warning to the exegetes to be wary of the "scarcely admissible philosophical and theological principles . . . mixed with this method, which not infrequently vitiate both the method itself and the conclusions arrived at regarding literary questions." There follows a catalogue of the well-known heresies of the 19th century rationalists condemned by the last five Popes.

What is significant is not the condemnation of these heretical old chestnuts but the implicit approval of the form-critical method when its reasonable elements are divorced from the false philosophical and theological principles that frequently accompany them.

What some of these elements are is indicated in the following four paragraphs which constitute the heart of the Instruction. The first paragraph is especially important:

> In order to determine correctly the trustworthiness of what is transmitted in the Gospels, the interpreter must take careful note of the three stages of transmission by which the teaching and the life of Jesus have come down to us.

The three stages of transmission cover three periods of time and three periods of development of the Gospel material from its beginning in the words and events of our Lord's life to its definitive form in the Gospels.

The Commission's reference to the three stages of transmission is an explicit approval of the principal discoveries of the Form-crtical and Redaction-critical schools. The importance of this can hardly be overestimated.

The three stages of transmission referred to have been spoken of in different ways over the last forty years. In Europe and especially in Germany they have been commonly spoken of as the *Sitz im Leben Christi*, the *Sitz im Leben Kirche*, and the *Sitz im (Leben) Euangelium*. In American circles they have been spoken of as the three levels of Gospel transmission.

What are the three levels of the Gospels?

The *Sitz im Leben Christi* or first level describes the Gospel material in its most primitive form; namely, the actual events of our Lord's life and the words preached by him during his three year ministry in Palestine. One may speak here of the original sayings and actual events of the life of Christ. Obviously when one speaks of this stage or level one speaks of the historical and theological bedrock of the Gospel materials.

The *Sitz im Leben Kirche* or second level describes these same events and sayings of Christ's life as they came to be preached by the Apostles and others and adapted to the moral, dogmatic, and catechetical needs of the early Apostolic Church.

In this stage it is important to note that the sayings of our Lord and the events of his life are not distorted nor destroyed. But they are *adapted* to the needs of new audiences who have never seen or heard our Lord in person. They are adapted also to new situations and new problems which did not exist during the ministry of Christ.

This stage, during which the original words and deeds of Christ were being preached throughout the major part of the Roman Empire, lasted approximately sixty years, i.e., from Pentecost when the Apostles began to preach down to the writing of the last Gospel at the end of the first century.

The third stage or level, the *Sitz im Euangelium*, describes the Gospel material in its ultimate stage, as it exists now in the four Gospels. In this stage the words of Christ, which were originally preached by him to a limited Jewish audience and were later preached by the Apostles to a wider but still limited audience throughout the Roman Empire, are now synthesized and organized into written documents which bear the personal impress of their authors, the four inspired evangelists.

The history of the material on these three levels may be visualized by comparing it with the construction of a pyramid. The quarry from which the stones for the pyramid are taken is the life of Christ. The multitude of individual stones from which the pyramid will be constructed are shaped and polished gradually over the course of several decades. Finally a master architect comes along — the evangelist — and builds the shaped stones into a Gospel-pyramid — an edifice which has structural design, organic unity, and literary beauty.

What is true of a pyramid is true of each Gospel. No individual Gospel would exist if Christ had not provided the quarry, allowed for the gradual shaping of the stones, and finally inspired an individual evangelist to construct one of those literary monuments we commonly call a Gospel. We may say of each Gospel what St. Paul in another context said of the rock in the desert: "The Rock is Christ" (1 Cor. 10:4).

In the Instruction the three stages or levels of the Gospel material are treated in successive paragraphs; and to emphasize the distinction between the three levels the original document has the words *"Christ Our Lord"* printed in italics at the beginning of the paragraph dealing with the *first level*, the words *"The Apostles"* in italics at the beginning of the paragraph dealing with the *second level*, and the words *"Sacred Authors"* in italics at the beginning of the paragraph dealing with the *third level*.

When the Biblical Commission speaks about each of these levels, it is important to remember that the Commission is basically concerned with the historical *truth* of the Gospels. At the same time, it should be noted that it does not concentrate on the word *"historical"* but on the word *"truth."*

The Instruction keeps two elements of Gospel truth in tension but not in discord; namely, the *reliability* of the basic historical content of the Gospels and the *literary manner* in which this content was communicated.

The emphasis, therefore, is not upon the word "historical" in the strict scientific sense of the word but on the word historical in the wide sense. What the Biblical Commission emphasizes is that the free literary presentation of the words and deeds of Christ in the Gospels is not incompatible with history in the *wide sense of the word*; namely, as testimony to events which really happened. This is indicated in a key sentence in the tenth paragraph of the Instruction which reads as follows:

> From the results of the new investigations it is apparent that the doctrine and the life of Jesus were not simply reported for the sole purpose of being remembered, but were "preached" so as to offer the Church a basis of faith and of morals.

The tension mentioned above is caused precisely by the difficulties many have in distinguishing between the simple reporting of events and words to be remembered and the preaching of those same events and words not just to be remembered but to serve as a basis for the teaching of faith and morals. The Instruction is written for those who would deny that the Gospels are historical *unless* we admit that they are a simple report of things to be remembered. The Instruction wishes to explain that the Gospels are *not* such a simple report of things to be remembered; they are preached versions of the events of our Lord's life, but they are nevertheless *historical in a true sense of the word.*

A simple reporting of things to be remembered would require that chronological order be followed and that words be quoted literally. *A preached version* of the same would allow the author the liberty of sometimes changing the chronological order and quoting freely as long as he preserved the sense of the words or the content of the doctrine. Such liberties which certainly were taken by the evangelists do not destroy the fundamental historicity of the Gospels. Simple examples would be the Sermon on the Mount in Matthew where many sayings of our Lord are included but not in their true chronological context; John's placing of the driving of the money-changers from the Temple at the beginning of our Lord's public life instead of at the end where it is in the Synoptic Gospels; and the formula for the institution of the Eucharist which is expressed in a different way every place it is given.

The problem of historicity

In paragraph three, the Instruction states that "many writings are being spread abroad in which the truth of the deeds and words contained in the

Gospels is questioned." Why is the truth of the deeds and words contained in the Gospels questioned? It is questioned because any dispassionate reader of the Gospels can see that the evangelists took great liberties with the chronological and topological order of events in our Lord's life and even greater liberties with our Lord's words.

Do these liberties destroy the historical truth of the Gospels? Fundamentalists will not admit that such liberties are verified. They do not have to face the problem. The Instruction, however, admits the liberties. It must, as a consequence, explain how in the light of such liberties one can still claim that the Gospels contain true history.

The Biblical Commission's answer is not a black versus white solution. It has admitted the Gospels are not simple reporting but a preached version of the events and words of Christ, preached in such a way that they will "offer the Church a basis of faith and morals." Having admitted so much, it must explain how a preached version can nevertheless contain valid testimony to the historicity of these events and words.

The Commission's answer lies in its explanation of the three levels through which the Gospel materials passed. In passing through the second and third levels the basic historical content of what Jesus said and did was subjected to adaptations and reorientations; but, it was neither destroyed nor distorted to any appreciable degree. The adaptions and reorientations were necessary because of the circumstances of the different audiences to whom the material was directed.

Justification for the adaptations is found in the purpose proposed to themselves by the apostolic preachers and the later evangelists. Their purpose was to lay a theological foundation for the faith and morals of the Christians to whom they preached or for whom they wrote. Such a foundation was based upon an interpretation of what Christ had said and done.

Interpretation presumed something to be interpreted. For the evangelists this something was the teaching of Christ as contained in his words and illustrated by his acts. One may validly distinguish between interpretation and the thing interpreted but disagreement with the interpretation does not justify one in denying the fact upon which the interpretation is based. It is on this basis that the Gospels can be said to give valid witness to the words and deeds of Christ.

Commentary on the instruction

What has been said above summarizes the essential answer of the Biblical Commission concerning the historical truth of the Gospels. What follows is meant as a brief commentary on the salient paragraphs of the Instruction. The text is given, then the commentary.

> To judge properly concerning the trustworthiness of what is transmitted in the Gospels, the interpreter should pay diligent attention to the three

stages of tradition by which the doctrine and the life of Jesus have come down to us.

The key words are: "To judge properly" and "trustworthiness." It should be noted that the Biblical Commission does not say "strict historicity" but "trustworthiness," because the question at issue is not strict historicity but historicity in the wide sense.

> Christ our Lord joined to himself chosen disciples, who followed him from the beginning, saw his deeds, heard his words, and in this way were equipped to be witnesses of his life and doctrine.

The key words here are "equipped to be witnesses." Eyewitness testimony is conceded by all to have an authority not shared by any other testimony, and the material in the second and third stages of the Gospel development was based upon this eyewitness testimony.

> When the Lord was orally explaining his doctrine, he followed the modes of reasoning and of exposition which were in vogue at the time. He accommodated himself to the mentality of his listeners and saw to it that what he taught was firmly impressed on the mind and easily remembered by the disciples.

The significant words are: "accommodated himself to the mentality of his listeners." If Jesus Himself followed the modes of reasoning and of exposition which were in vogue in his time and accommodated himself to the mentality of his listeners, a fortiori preachers of the Gospel and the evangelists could be expected to do the same in their turn.

> They (the Apostles) faithfully explained his life and words, while taking into account in their method of preaching the circumstances in which their listeners found themselves.

As Jesus had accommodated himself to the mentality of his listeners, so his apostles took into account the circumstances in which their listeners found themselves. The Biblical Commission emphasizes this point because it is the condition of the audience that determines the approach of the preacher and requires him to adapt the message to their mentality. One does not preach in the same way to children and adults, to Jews and Greeks, to those who have seen Jesus in the flesh and those who are hearing about him for the first time thirty or forty years after his resurrection.

> On the other hand, there is no reason to deny that the apostles passed on to their listeners what was really said and done by the Lord with that fuller understanding which they enjoyed, having been instructed by the glorious events of the Christ and taught by the light of the Spirit of Truth.

The significant words here are not "passed on . . . what was really said and done" but "passed on . . . with fuller understanding." If we stopped with the words "passed on . . . what was really said and done" and omitted the qualification "with fuller understanding," we would be in danger of characterizing the apostolic preaching and the Gospels based upon them as simple reports of what had happened. When in fact as the Instruction clearly says "the doctrine and the life of Jesus were not simply reported for the sole purpose of being remembered, but were 'preached' so as to offer the Church a basis of faith and of morals." It is this fuller understanding, moreover, which helps to explain chronologically premature statements in the Gospels. One may cite, as examples, the tremendous theological content of the Infancy narratives, the frequent testimony to Christ's divinity in the early parts of St. John's Gospel, and perhaps even the testimony of Peter at Caeserea to Christ's divinity.

To clarify the meaning of the words "passed on . . . with fuller understanding," the Instruction uses the example of our Lord's own words to His apostles after the resurrection:

> So, just as Jesus himself after his resurrection 'interpreted to them' the words of the Old Testament as well as his own, they too interpreted his words and deeds according to the needs of their listeners.

One thinks here immediately of the disciples on the way to Emmaus whose "hearts were burning as he interpreted the Scriptures to them." Fuller understanding did not destroy the facts as they remembered them; it bathed them in a more clear light. At the same time, however, it explains why they felt fully justified in making certain adaptations and even additions.

> Devoting themselves to the ministry of the word, they (the apostles) preached and made use of various modes of speaking which were suited to their own purpose and the mentality of their listeners . . . But these modes of speaking with which the preachers proclaimed Christ must be distinguished and (properly) assessed: catechesis, stories, testimonia, hymns, doxologies, prayers — and other literary forms of this sort which were in Sacred Scripture and were accustomed to be used by men of that time.

The significant words are "and other literary forms of this sort which were in Sacred Scripture and were accustomed to be used by men of that time." The Biblical Commission does not tell us what these other literary forms were. It leaves the question open. But most scholars would include here two popular literary forms of the first century: midrash and apocalyptic.

The most important paragraph in the Instruction (paragraph 9) deals with the third level of the Gospel materials, the *Sitz im Euangelium*. It begins:

> This primitive instruction was committed to writing by the Sacred Authors in four Gospels for the benefit of the churches, with a method suited to the peculiar purpose which each (author) set for himself.

The significant words are: "method . . . suited to . . . purpose." Although the Instruction has a great deal to say about literary forms and even mentions a number of those discovered and described by the Form-critical school, it is only here that it comes near to defining a Gospel.

Taking these words at face value, a Gospel from the literary viewpoint could be defined as: *an arrangement of the traditional preaching about Christ in such a way that doctrines considered important by the author are expressed by the pattern of the book as a whole.* The emphasis here on the "method . . . suited . . . to purpose" which each author sets for himself is in full agreement with the later key statement of the Instruction that the "doctrine and the life of Jesus were not simply reported for the sole purpose of being remembered, but were preached so as to offer the Church a basis of faith and of morals."

The importance of these combined statements is that they shift our attention (without however removing it entirely) from the all-consuming and passionate quest for the historical-historical to the theological-historical, which was in fact the purpose set for themselves by the evangelists.

The Instruction continues with what amounts to a description and an approval of redaction criticism. Both redaction criticism and form criticism have been mentioned. It may help to distinguish them at this point.

Form criticism studies individual literary units, their genesis and their development; for example, the parable, the wisdom saying, the miracle story, the midrashic story, doxologies, hymns, prayers, catechetical stories, genealogies, etc.

Redaction criticism studies how the evangelists compiled and arranged these different literary units to make up the theological-historical composition that we know as a Gospel. It explains how these individual literary elements were adapted, interpreted, and even rephrased in order to fit them into the more expansive literary pattern of the Gospel as a whole.

Matthew 13, in which we find a collection of seven parables in sermon form, will serve as an example. Form critical studies will tell us, if they are successful, what each of these parables meant when first spoken by Jesus and also what they meant or what they were used to teach in the preaching of the Apostles. Redaction criticism will attempt to explain why Matthew gathered all seven into one chapter; what each parable means *in this setting* in relation to the others; and what meaning *the chapter* as a whole has in the grand pattern of Matthew's Gospel.

Concerning redaction criticism of the Gospels, the Biblical Commission speaks as follows:

> From the many things handed down they (the evangelists) selected some things, reduced others to a synthesis, others they explicated as they kept in mind the situation of the churches. With every means they sought that their readers might become aware of the reliability of those words by which they had been instructed. Indeed, from what they had received the sacred writers above all selected the things which were suited to the various situations of the faithful and to the purpose which they had in mind, and adapted their narration of them to the same

situations and purpose. Since the meaning of a statement also depends on the sequence, the evangelists, in passing on the words and deeds of our Saviour, explained these now in one context, now in another, depending on their usefulness to the readers. Consequently, let the exegete seek out the meaning intended by the evangelist in narrating a saying or a deed in a certain way or in placing it in a certain context. For the truth of the story is not at all affected by the fact that the evangelists relate the words and deeds of the Lord in a different order, and express his sayings not literally but differently, while preserving their sense.

What is significant about this paragraph is first of all the Biblical Commission's admission that the Gospels have a redaction history and, secondly, its nuanced expression of the historicity of the Gospels. One can only say 'nuanced' because the Instruction nowhere uses the words historicity or historical. It uses instead the words 'reliability' and 'the truth of the story.' We are back again at the tension mentioned earlier — the tension between the reliability of the basic historical content of the Gospels and the literary manner in which this content is communicated.

The Biblical Commission admits the evangelists made a selection from the material at hand and made adaptations. In addition to selecting and adapting, they freely changed the sequence of events. All of these digressions from strict historical writing are justified by the Instruction on the basis of the needs of the faithful and the particular purpose of each evangelist in constructing his Gospel. Having admitted so much, the Biblical Commission nevertheless concludes: "The truth of the narrative is not at all affected by the fact that the evangelists relate the words and deeds of the Lord in a different order and express his sayings not literally but differently while preserving their sense."

The reliability and the truth of the narrative here can only mean that the Gospels are theological-historical narratives, that both the theology and the history are reliable and true in a proper sense of the words, but that the influence of the evangelists' theological purpose must be taken into account in assessing the basic historical content of the narrative. For this assessment the scholar must take into account, as the Instruction has already emphasized, the three stages of tradition through which the Gospel material passed and the sane conclusions of the form critical and redaction critical schools.

After all is said and done the question remains: by what right did the Apostles and the evangelists take such liberties with the deeds of our Lord's life and the words which he spoke? By what right did they depart from the chronological and topological order of events in his life? By what right did they quote him loosely, out of context, and sometimes even against his original context? By what right did they even put words on his lips that he never actually uttered? By what right do ordinary mortals so tamper with the words and deeds of the Son of God?

The answer lies in the attitude of the Apostles and evangelists to our Lord. He had told them; "I no longer call you servants but friends. As the Father has sent me, I also send you" (John 15:15).

As friends, loved and trusted by Jesus, the Apostles and evangelists responded with love and trust. When he sent them out into the world to preach what he had taught them, they went out and preached *him.* They did not go out as cold-fact historians, nor as secretaries consulting notes to make sure they were quoting him verbatim. They preached him whom they loved. Their love did not make them blind. It made them see as they had not seen in the beginning. It gave them security, freedom, and the enthusiastic desire to use any accepted human means to make others see and love him whom they had seen and whom they loved. They realized in themselves the meaning of our Lord's words: "The truth will make you free."

Appendix B

THE MAKING OF A GOSPEL

Scholarly insights, despite the labor involved in their discovery and the high-sounding terminology in which they are expressed, have the disconcerting effect of being so common-sensical that the intelligent reader is inclined to say: "Just what we always thought." The reader is forewarned, therefore, that when we speak about the formation of the gospels, the significance of such associated terms as gospel, kerygma, didache, form criticism and redaction criticism, and the meaning of the visual versus the conceptual approach and the vertical versus the horizontal approach, we are speaking about matters he already understands but in a different way and under different terminology.[1] When the reader sees how so much of what the scholars talk about in their terminology coincides with what he already understands from his own experience in literary and historical matters, he will have gone a long way toward understanding the gospels.

The formation of the gospels

The formation of the gospels deals with how the gospels came to be. The material in a gospel, like the contents of any book dealing with a famous person, goes through three stages, each of which the reader must take into account if he is to understand and evaluate the gospel as a literary work.

The deeds, the words, the events of a famous man's life constitute the first stage and the source from which a book ultimately draws its material. But the book is usually written after the death of the subject. And unless the author has been an eye-witness of every word and event, he will have to depend upon what others tell him, based upon their recollection, their understanding, and their appreciation of what was significant in the deeds, words, and events of the subject's life. The material, in other words, has come to be shaped by the memory, the understanding, and the views of others over the course of some years. It is no longer exactly as it was when it originated. It has been shaped, and it is from the shaped material that the author has to build his book. The material, in short, has gone through three stages: (1) the situation in life of each deed, word, and event as it was originally in the life of the subject; (2) the situation in life of those who passed on the account of what had happened; (3) the situation in life of the author who took the shaped accounts of what had happened and made them into a book addressed to the needs and understanding of his audience.

Roughly speaking, the gospels went through these three stages. What

---

[1] W. D. Davies' *An Invitation of the New Testament* is a splendid and scholarly example of presenting technical matters in non-technical and easily intelligible terms.

Jesus actually said and did between the years 27–30 A.D. constitutes the first stage of the materials out of which the gospels eventually were written.

In the second stage, the time between Pentecost and the writing of Mark's gospel, the apostles and others preached about what Jesus said and did. During this period the preachers adapted their account of the words and deeds of Jesus to the needs and understanding of their particular audiences. They shaped the material by repeating it in different terminology and in different contexts and eventually hit upon more or less stereotyped forms of expression for the events, words, and deeds they preached about.

In the third stage, sometime between 65 and 100 A.D., the evangelists came along, made a selection of the stereotyped sayings and stories in circulation as a result of the long period of preaching, and arranged the material they had selected in book form. In this literary arrangement, which we call a gospel, the individual stories and sayings acquired a meaning which they perhaps did not always have as used by the preachers nor perhaps even as used by Jesus himself.

When the scholar speaks of redaction or composition criticism, he is talking about the third stage — the work of each evangelist in selecting, arranging, and interconnecting the sayings of Jesus and the stories about Jesus into a book about Jesus.[2] When he speaks about form criticism, he is talking about the second stage — the shaping of the sayings and stories about Jesus during the forty or fifty years of oral transmission that elapsed between the events themselves and the time they were incorporated in the written gospels.[3] When he speaks about the "Quest for the Historical Jesus," he is talking about getting back through the third and second stages to the first stage.[4]

When the scholar talks about the 'gospel' as a book he means the third stage. When he speaks about the gospel as the revelation brought by Jesus and manifested in his words and deeds, he is thinking about the first stage.[5]

The word kerygma belongs properly to the second stage — the period when the preachers announced the good news of the gospel — and refers to the 'headline' content of the apostolic preaching. Kerygma implies the brevity of preaching and the brevity of formulation characteristic of announcements. But it also implies a certain completeness in brevity in the sense that it contains those elements of the good news which the preachers considered essential for their hearers' call to the faith.

Didache belongs in one sense or another to all three stages. Jesus himself not only announced the good news, he explained it. His explanation or teaching constitutes what is known as didache. The preachers did the same in the second stage. They not only announced the basic good news, they at-

---

[2] See N. Perrin, *What is Redaction Criticism?*
[3] See H. K. McArthur, *What is Form Criticism?*
[4] See G. Bornkamm, *Jesus of Nazareth*; J. M. Robinson, *A New Quest of the Historical Jesus.*
[5] See pp. 104, 157.

tempted to explain it to those who accepted the kerygma and wanted to know more about its meaning for their lives. In the third stage, the evangelists wrote their gospels precisely to give a deeper understanding of the good news. In a very real sense the gospels constitute what could be called depth didache as opposed to the less systematic didache of the preachers.

The terms gospel, kerygma, and didache require some explanation.[6] For the sake of brevity, we will treat only the nature of each as a concept, the etymology, the purpose as a form of communication, and the audience to which each is directed.

Gospel

The term signifies good news, glad tidings, with the emphasis on the 'good' and the 'glad.'[7] Luke's announcement is typical: "Behold I announce to you good news of great joy" (Lk 2:10). In the Old Testament background of the term, it is most often associated with the good news from and about God in relation to Israel and mankind (cf. Is 40:9; 52:7-9; 61:1; 1 Sam 31:9). In the New Testament, the background of the term, especially in Paul and Luke, may have some connotation of the Greek-Roman idea of the benefits brought to the citizens by the Emperor.

The term derives from the Hebrew verb *bassar*, meaning to announce tidings of joy or victory or celebration (cf. 1 Sam 31:9; Is 61:1). Thus the emphasis is on 'announcing'; the 'good news' aspect is only implicit in the verb. The herald or announcer of the good news is called the *mebasser* (a noun derivative of the verb *bassar*). Again the emphasis is on the kind of messenger or herald (cf. Is 40:9) and the message of good news is implicit (cf. Is 52:7-9).

What the 'good news' is one finds expressed in the word 'glory' (Greek: *doxa*), derived from the Hebrew *kabod*, a term used in the Old Testament to convey the sense of a manifestation or revelation of God, either in the sense of the power of God (cf. Ex 24:15-18), or the holiness of God (cf. Is 6:1-9), or the powerful, saving God (cf. Is 40:1-9; 60:1-5). "In its developed form," the term 'glory,' as Davies says, "stands for the revelation of God, his manifestation of Himself through His control of the lives of nations and men. God's glory is revealed not so much as knowledge of what he is in his essense, as in what he does; it is His revelation of Himself, particularly in certain events."[8] It is in this sense that Deutero-Isaiah saw the glory of God manifested in the return of Israel from Babylon, and the New Testament authors saw the glory of God revealed in the life, death, and resurrection of

---

[6] See W. Marksen, *Mark the Evangelist*, 117-150; W. D. Davies, *Invitation to the New Testament*, 39-49, 147-162; D. Stanley, *The Apostolic Church in the New Testament*, 195-213; W. Pannenburg (ed.) *Revelation as History*; B. Gerhardsson, *Memory and Manuscript*.

[7] In any investigation of the meaning of the term, it should be remembered, as Marksen says, that "Synoptic usage indicates considerable dif- ferences. Mark uses only the noun *euangelion*, Luke only the verb *euangelizesthai*. It is striking that Luke never uses the verb in passages where the Markan parallel uses the noun. Matthew is not consistent. He uses the verb on only one occasion and never uses the noun absolutely but always with a supplement" (*Mark the Evangelist*, 118-119).

[8] Cf. W. D. Davies, *op. cit.*, 46.

Jesus. Thus, Christ himself is, in himself, the 'good news,' the revelation of the glory of the Father (cf. Jn 3:15). This is the sense of the word in 1 Tim 1:11, ". . . the good news of the glory of the Blessed God" (cf. also 2 Cor 4:3-6 and Jn 1:14, 18).

The purpose of the good news in the New Testament is to bring about the revelation of the invisible saving God through the visible, incarnate Son, who is the image of the Father and the ultimate revelation of the Father as loving Lord and Savior. This revelation is meant to confirm earlier revelation, give the ultimate substance to faith and hope, and call all men to a response of gratitude and love which is to be manifested in a new life lived in Christ. As K. Barth says: "The Gospel is never against men, it is always for men. That is why all true preaching is good to hear, helpful and full of light — like God's smile upon men, the Yes he addresses to creatures whom he loves, the promise that one day the victory Christ won over death at Easter will be the only thing that counts, the eternal joy of all humanity finally delivered from sin and death." [9]

The audience to whom the good news of the New Testament is announced is all mankind. But as the New Testament authors insist, especially Paul and Matthew, the good news is addressed first to the Jews and then to the rest of mankind. Thus, as we shall see, the kerygma is for all, but didache is for believers, for those who have heard the kerygma, believed, and accepted Jesus.

Kerygma

The kerygma designates the lapidary or 'headline' content of the apostolic preaching, with emphasis on preaching and the brevity preaching entails in comparison with the lengthier presentation proper to a book. [10]

In the early years of Christianity the content of the preaching almost necessarily concentrated on the essentials of the Christian message — the passion, death, resurrection, and glorification of Christ (cf. the kerygmatic sermons of Peter and Paul in the Acts of the Apostles). Gradually the content came to include something about the main periods of Christ's life: the Baptist period, the public life in Galilee, and more about the last days in Judea.

The noun kerygma derives from the Greek verb *kerusso* — to herald, or announce, or preach. The purpose of the kerygmatic preaching was by announcing the ultimate eschatological good news to call all men to the kingdom of God and to the conversion of life proper to citizens of the kingdom.

In its kerygmatic form, the apostolic preaching was directed primarily to those who had not heard the good news: to pagans, who had heard nothing at all about salvation history and the ultimate good news of Christ, and to

---

[9] Cf. K. Barth, *Romans*. [10] Cf. H. Riesenfeld, *The Gospel Tradition*, 51-93.

the Jews who had heard only the preliminary Old Testament promises of salvation.

Didache

Didache, from the Greek verb *didasko*, to teach, means teaching or explanation of doctrine and represents the stage that followed upon acceptance of the kerygma. Those who accepted Christ were brought by means of didache to a deeper knowledge and understanding of the Christ event. Thus, the kerygma constitutes the substratum upon which the didache builds and expands.

The purpose of the didache was to expound the substance of the good news preached in the kerygma. As H. Riesenfeld puts it: "In distinction from the proclamation of the kerygma, the awakening and comforting message, 'the news' about the kingdom of God, the teaching, didache, aims at leading deeper into its nature and its now-revealed secret to those who have come to listen and have been won over by the message." [11]

The didache was for believers — those already converted and looking to deepen their knowledge and understanding of Christ and the new life that had to follow from conversion. The preachers and teachers regularly complemented the kerygmatic preaching by attempting to explain in some depth the sense and significance of the kerygma. To the extent that this was done on the level of the ordinary Christian, it amounted to what we would call catechesis. In the Pauline letters and the gospels, however, the didache goes far beyond ordinary catechesis and amounts to what we would call depth didache or, more properly, theology.

D. Stanley asks the question: "In what way can apostolic teaching be said to have influenced the form of our canonical gospels?" His answer explains the close relationship between the kerygma, the didache of Jesus and the apostolic preachers, and the depth didache of the four evangelists:

> What Jesus *did* (his redemptive death and resurrection, the work of the ministry) forms the basis of the apostolic kerygma. What Jesus *taught* (understood by the apostles in the light of Pentecost) forms the basis of the apostolic teaching. We have already remarked on the place of honor which all the evangelists give to Jesus' teaching and on their care to explain the more significant actions of his life. This all comes under the notion of didache. But over and above that, the very form which the Gospels take is determined, to a large extent, by the evangelists' preoccupation with teaching the believer the inner sense of the kerygma. The kerygma has provided the basic blueprint for the Gospel form in the quadripartite plan which includes the major events from the appearance of the Baptist to the resurrection of Christ. To the didache, however, must be attributed the undeniable *cachet personnel* with which each of the four Evangelists has impregnated the basic material so as to give his own characteristic version of the good news of Jesus Christ.[12]

[11] H. Riesenfeld, *op. cit.*, 64; D. Stanley, *op. cit.*, 213-214.   [12] D. Stanley, *op. cit.*, 212-213.

Of the gospels, therefore, one may say: (1) they are the literary stage of the didache; (2) they are based primarily on the didache of Christ himself and secondarily on the kerygma and didache of the apostles; (3) they present four different theological expositions of the good news which is essentially the manifestation of the glory of the invisible Father through the life and works of the visible Son; (4) they are, in literary form, theological-historical presentations, i.e., they are visual-conceptual expositions, combining narrative pictures of what was done by Christ with interpretations in speech form (Christ's authentic words and their own interpretative speeches).[13] In contrast to the evangelists' visual-conceptual literary presentation, Paul, in his exposition of the didache in the epistles, used an almost entirely conceptual form of presentation.

[13] R. M. Frye (*Jesus and Man's Hope,* Vol. II, 219) suggests the gospels be categorized as dramatic history and gives the following rule of thumb definition of the genre: "A dramatic history is a literary work which presents a basically historical story with economy and narrative effectiveness, which remains essentially faithful to the historical tradition but which may alter elements of that tradition as appears necessary in order to present *multum in parvo*, and which is designed to convey important insights and understandings (both factual and interpretative) to a wide audience."

Appendix C

THE SYNOPTIC QUESTION

The synoptic question arises from the substantial verbal agreement between Matthew, Mark, and Luke.[1] One notes that six hundred out of the six hundred and sixty-one verses in Mark appear in Matthew; and three hundred and thirty out of the six hundred and sixty-one are found in Luke. Did Matthew and Luke borrow from Mark?

Approximately two hundred and thirty verses not found in Mark at all are common to Matthew and Luke. Did Matthew and Luke borrow these two hundred and thirty verses from some other pre-existing document?

These are the most obvious questions raised by the substantial verbal agreement. But other questions can be asked. For example, is it possible, as some hold, that Mark made a Reader's Digest condensation of Matthew's Gospel?[2]

Is it possible that all three evangelists were ignorant of any written sources and worked independently, using for source material the common *oral* traditions of Jesus' words and deeds?[3] In this case, the common material in the triple tradition, i.e., the three hundred and thirty verses common to Matthew, Mark, and Luke, would stem from the same oral source concerning Jesus' *deeds*; and the common material in the double tradition, i.e., the two hundred and thirty verses common to Matthew and Luke, would stem from the same oral source concerning Jesus' *sayings*, namely, the so called "Q" source.[4]

Is it possible that all three used kindred intermediary documents, which are now recoverable only by identifying the groupings of pericopes which represent these sources?[5]

The possibilities are not endless, but they are discouraging. All solutions up to the present can be proposed only as hypotheses. There is no universally accepted solution. The two source hypothesis, i.e., the dependence of Matthew and Luke upon Mark and the "Q" source, commands the widest ap-

[1] Cf. A. Gaboury, *La Structure des Synoptiques*; H. Riesenfeld, *The Gospel Tradition*; B. Gerhardsson, *Memory and Manuscript*; D. G. Buttrick (ed.), *Jesus and Man's Hope*, Vol I, has three excellent but conflicting studies of the synoptic question: X. Leon-Dufour, "Redaktionsgeschichte of Matthew and Literary Criticism," 9-36; D. L. Dungan, "Mark — The Abridgement of Matthew and Luke," 51-98; J. Fitzmyer, "The Priority of Mark and the "Q" Source in Luke," 131-170; W. R. Farmer, *The Synoptic Problem: A Critical Analysis*; J. M. Robinson and H. Koester, *Trajectories Through Early Christianity*, 71-113; H. Kee, *Jesus in History*; V. Taylor, *New Testament Essays*, 90-118; E. P. Sanders, *The Tendencies of the Synoptic Tradition*; P. Parker, *The Gospel Before Mark*; B. C. Butler, *The Originality of St Matthew: A Critique of the Two Document Hypothesis*.

[2] Cf. D. L. Dungan, *art. cit.*; W. L. Farmer, *op. cit.*

[3] Cf. B. Gerhardsson, *op. cit*; H. Riesenfeld, *op. cit.*

[4] Cf. H. Kee, *op. cit*; V. Taylor, *op. cit*; A. M. Farrer, "On Dispensing with Q," *Studies in the Gospels: Essays in Memory of R. H. Lightfoot*, ed. D. E. Nineham, 55-88.

[5] Cf. A. Gaboury, *op. cit.*

proval in scholarly circles. But even those who opt for the two source hypothesis do so with reservations and qualifications.

Most solutions can be reduced but not restricted to either a documentary or an oral tradition solution. The documentary solution attempts to solve the problem by positing preexisting written sources, subsequently used in different ways by Matthew and Luke; e.g., the two source theory mentioned above, and the presupposition of earlier versions of each of the gospels.[6]

The oral traditions' solution attempts to solve the problem by positing different forms of the same oral tradition. The oral tradition is presumed to have developed in different localities and to have thereby acquired the elements which account for the differences between the three forms of the tradition found in the synoptic gospels. It is presupposed in this hypothesis that the basic oral tradition may have crystallized in such places as Antioch (the Markan tradition), Palestine (the Matthean tradition), Rome or Greece (the Lukan tradition).

A more extensive discussion of the synoptic question lies beyond the scope of this brief appendix and, for those interested, is available in the works cited above. What is more important is the effect studies of the synoptic question have had on the interpretation of the gospels.

Purportedly, the importance of solving the synoptic question lies in discovering the hermeneutical key it would supply to explaining the different theologies of the synoptic evangelists. The reasoning is based on the theory that differences between the gospels and their common sources will indicate the theological purposes of the evangelists.[7]

There is a good bit of truth in this contention, but it is somewhat of a half truth. It is in addition the long way around. There is a shorter way.

The truth is that the proper key to the theological purposes of any evangelist lies primarily in an analysis of his work as a whole and only secondarily in a comparison between his use of sources and that of another evangelist. The first approach is called the vertical, the second, the horizontal approach.

The vertical approach is the ordinary approach to the interpretation of any properly literary work. It consists of an analysis of the work as a whole in order to ascertain thereby the author's purpose and viewpoint.[8]

The horizontal approach is the extraordinary approach in as much as it is rarely used and used then only in the interpretation of works which are not considered properly and uniquely the literary work of one man. The horizontal approach presupposes for the most part that the works under consideration represent only the editing of preexisting documents by dif-

---

[6] Some opt for earlier versions of each gospel, e.g., a proto-Mark, a proto-Matthew, and a proto-Luke. R. T. Fortna, *The Gospel of Signs*, defends a proto-John, and with more convincing reasons than those who defend earlier versions of Matthew, Mark, and Luke. The existence of an early Aramaic Matthew continues to have its defenders.

[7] Most gospel commentaries suffer in intelligibility because they spend so much time attempting to explain these horizontal differences instead of explaining the gospels in the light of the authors' theological purposes.

[8] Cf. Q. Quesnell, *The Mind of Mark*, 53.

ferent authors and consists in a comparison of the differences in editing in order to ascertain the purposes and viewpoints of the editors.

It has been, for the most part, because the synoptic gospels were not in the past considered to be the proper literary works of individual authors that the horizontal approach to their interpretation was utilized. In the horizontal approach the pre-existing sources are considered of vastly greater importance than the minds of the men who edited them. It would be the proper and adequate approach only if the evangelists were nothing more than editors or compilers or redactors in the strictest sense of the word.[9]

Recent gospel research, however, has been almost unanimous in recognizing the synoptic evangelists as individual authors who have produced properly literary works. As a result, it has come to be recognized that the only adequate approach to an understanding of their works is the same ordinary approach as that used for the interpretation and understanding of other properly literary works i.e., the vertical approach.[10]

An example may clarify. It is because the plays about Joan-of-Arc by G. Shaw, M. Anderson, and J. Anoilh are considered properly literary works that critics, without a second thought, use the vertical approach to interpret them. The horizontal approach to the interpretation of these plays would consist in ascertaining how each author arranged and edited the historical sources dealing with the life of Joan-of-Arc. Since no-one, even for a moment, considers these playwrights to be editors, no-one ever, as a consequence, utilizes the horizontal approach to understand their plays.

The lack of intelligibility in many gospel commentaries is due in large part to a hang-over from the time when the evangelists were considered to be hardly more than inspired editors.

In as much as the synoptic evangelists evidence a much greater respect for and fidelity to the sources they used than modern authors, the horizontal approach retains some validity and provides some help in interpreting their gospels. In interpreting the mind and message of Matthew, therefore, we have not ignored the value of the horizontal approach. But we have consistently considered it secondary and subsidiary to the value of the vertical approach. Our understanding is that the true key to the interpretation of a gospel is the purpose of the author and that the author's purpose is revealed primarily by an analysis of his work as a whole rather than by comparison with other gospels utilizing the same or similar source material.

[9] Cf. X. Leon-Dufour, *art. cit*, p. 9-11, concerning redaction criticism in the strictest sense of the word.
[10] R. M. Frye in *Jesus and Man's Hope*, Vol II, 193-221, has admirably expressed the importance of interpreting literary works, and especially the gospels, by using the vertical approach.

BIBLIOGRAPHY

Albright, W. F. and Mann, *Matthew*. Anchor Bible. (New York: Doubleday, 1971).

Anderson, C. C., *The Historical Jesus: a Continuing Quest*. (Grand Rapids: Erdmans, 1972).

Barrett, C. K., *The Signs of an Apostle*. (Philadelphia: Fortress, 1972).

Baum, G. *The Jews and the Gospel*. (Westminster, Md., 1961).

Beare, F. W. *The Earliest Records of Jesus*. (Nashville: Abingdon, 1962).

————. "The Mission of the Disciples and the Missionary Charge: Mt 10 and Parallels," *JBL*, 89 (March 1970), 1-13.

Benoit, P. *The Passion and Resurrection of Jesus Christ*. (New York: Herder and Herder, 1969).

Blair, E. P. *Jesus In the Gospel of Matthew*. (New York: Abingdon, Press, 1960).

Bligh, J. *Galatians*. (London: St. Paul Publications, 1969).

————. "The Origin and Meaning of *Logos* In the Prologue of St. John," *Clergy Review*, 40 (1955), 405.

Bloch, R. *Dict. de la Bible suppl.* "Midrash." Col. 1263-1281.

Boers, H. "Where Christology Is Real," *Interpretation*, 26 (July, 1972), 300-327.

Boice, L. M., *The Sermon on the Mount: an Exposition*. (Grand Rapids: Zondervan, 1972).

Bonnard, P. *L'Evangile selon Saint Matthieu*. (Neuchatel: Delachaux et Niestlé, 1963).

Boring, M. E. "How May We Identify Oracles of Christian Prophets in the Synoptic Tradition — Mk 3:28-29 as a Test Case," *JBL*, 91 (December 1972) 501-521.

Bornkamm, G. *Jesus of Nazareth*. (London: Hodder and Stoughton, 1960).

————. "The Authority To 'Bind' and 'Loose' in the Church in St. Matthew's Gospel," *Jesus and Man's Hope*, ed. D. G. Buttrick, Vol. I, 37-50.

————. *The New Testament: A Guide to its Writings*. (Philadelphia: Fortress, 1973).

————. "The Risen Lord and the Earthly Jesus," *The Future of Our Religious Past: Essays In Honor of R. Bultmann*, ed. J. M. Robinson (New York: Harper and Row, 1971).

Bornkamm, Barth, Held. *Tradition and Interpretation in Matthew*. (Philadelphia: Westminster, 1963).

Borsch, F. H. *The Son of Man in Myth and History*. (Philadelphia: Westminster Press, 1967).

Bourke, M. "Infancy Gospel," *New Catholic Encyclopedia*.

Brandon, S. G. F., *The Fall of Jerusalem and the Christian Church*. (London: SPCK, 1957).

————. "The Literary Genre of Mt 1-2," *CBQ*, XXII (1960), 174ff.

Brown, R. *Jesus, God and Man*. (Milwaukee: Bruce, 1967).

————. *The Gospel According to John*. Vol. I, Anchor Bible. (New York: Doubleday, 1969).

Brown, R., Domfried, K. P., and Reumann, J. (eds.), *Peter in the New Testament*. (New York: Paulist Press, 1973).

Bruns, J. E. "The Magi Episode in Matthew 2," *CBQ*, XXII (1961), 51-54.

Bultmann, R. *Jesus Christ and Mythology*. (New York: Scribner, 1958).

————. *The History of the Synoptic Tradition*. (Oxford: B. Blackwell, 1963).

————. *Theology of the New Testament*. (New York: Scribner, 1955).

Butler, B. C. *The Originality of St. Matthew. A Critique of the Two-Document Hypothesis*. (Cambridge: University Press, 1951).

Buttrick, G. D. (ed.). *Jesus and Man's Hope*. 2 vols.

Clarke, F. "Tension and Tide in St. John's Gospel," *Irish Theological Quarterly*, XXIV, (1957), 154-167.

Conzellmann, H. *An Outline of the Theology of the New Testament*. (New York: Harper & Row, 1969).

———. "History and Theology in the Passion Narratives of the Synoptic Gospels," *Interpretation*, XXIV (April, 1970), 192-194.

———. *Jesus*. (Philadelphia: Fortress, 1973).

Cope, L., *Matthew: A Scribe Trained for the Kingdom*. (Th.D. Dissertation, Union Theological Seminary, 1970).

Coutts, J. "The Authority of Jesus and of the Twelve," *JTS*, VIII (1957), 111-118.

Cullmann, O. *The Christology of the New Testament*. (London: SCM Press, 1959).

———. *Peter: Disciple, Apostle, Martyr*. 2nd ed. (Philadelphia: Westminster Press, 1962).

Davies, W. D. *Introduction to Pharisaeism*. (Philadelphia: Fortress Press, 1967).

———. *Invitation to the New Testament*. (Garden City, N.Y.: Doubleday, 1969).

———. *The Sermon on the Mount*. (Cambridge: University Press, 1966).

———. *The Setting of the Sermon on the Mount*. (Cambridge: University Press, 1964).

———. *Torah in the Messianic Age and/or the Age to Come*. (Philadelphia: Society of Biblical Literature, 1952).

Davis, C. T. "Tradition and Redaction in Mt 1:18–2:23," *JBL*, 90 (December, 1971), 404-421.

deVaux, R. *Ancient Israel*. (New York: McGraw-Hill, 1961).

Dodd, C. H. *According to the Scriptures*. (London: Nisbet, 1957).

———. *The Interpretation of the Fourth Gospel*. (Cambridge: University Press, 1955).

———. *The Parables of the Kingdom*. (London: Nisbet, 1958).

Dungam, D. L. *The Sayings of Jesus in the Churches of Paul*. (Philadelphia: Fortress Press, 1971).

Dupont, J. *Les Beatitudes*. (Bruges: Abbaye de Saint-André, 1958).

Ehrhardt, A. *The Apostolic Succession*. (London: Lutterworth, 1953).

Elliott, J. H. "Ministry and Church Order in the New Testament: A Tradition Historical Analysis (1 Pt. 5:1-5 and Parallels)," *CBQ*, 32 (July 1970), 367-391.

Ellis, Peter F. *The Men and the Message of the Old Testament*. (Collegeville: The Liturgical Press, 1963).

Fannon, P. "Matthew Revisited," *Scripture*, 17 (October, 1965), 97-103.

Farrer, A. "On Dispensing With 'Q,'" *Studies in the Gospels*, ed. D. E. Nineham. (Oxford: B. Blackwell, 1955), 55-108.

Feine P. and Behm, J. *Introduction to the New Testament*, Rev. W. G. Kümmel. (Nashville: Abingdon Press, 1965).

Fenton, J. C. *The Gospel of St. Matthew*. Pelican Gospel Commentaries. (Baltimore: Penguin books, 1963).

Feuillet, A., "La Synthese eschatologique de saint Matthieu (XXIV–XXV), *RB*, 56 (1949), 340–364, 57 (1950), 62–91, 180–211.

Filson, F. V. "Broken Patterns in the Gospel of Matthew," *JBL*, 75, (1956), 227ff.

Fitzmyer, J. A. "The Priority of Mark and the 'Q' Source in Luke," *Jesus and Man's Hope*, ed. G. D. Buttrick, Vol. I. 51-98.

Frye, R. M. "A Literary Perspective for the Criticism of the Gospels," *Jesus and Man's Hope*, ed. D. G. Miller and D. Y. Hadidian. Vol. II, 193-221.

Fuller, R. H. *Foundations of New Testament Christology*. (New York: Scribner, 1965).

———. *The Formation of the Resurrection Narratives*. (New York: MacMillan, 1971).

———. "The 'Thou Art Peter' Pericope and the Easter Appearances," *McCormick Quarterly*, 20 (1967), 309-315.

Funk, R. W. "Beyond Criticism in Quest of Literacy: The Parable of the Leaven," *Interpretation*, 25, (April, 1971), 149-170.

Furnish, V. P. *The Love Command in the New Testament*. (Nashville: Abingdon Press, 1972).

Gerhardsson, B. *Memory and Manuscript*. (Uppsala, 1961).

Glasson, T. F., *Moses in the Fourth Gospel*. (Illinois: Alec Allenson, Inc., 1963).

Grindel, J. "Matthew XII 18-21" *CBQ*, 29 (January, 1967), 110-115.

Gundry, R. H. *The Uses of the Old Testament in Matthew's Gospel.* (Leiden: E. J. Brill, 1967).

Gutierrez, G., *Theology of Liberation.* (Maryknoll: Orbis, 1973).

Hahn, F. *Mission in the New Testament.* (Naperville: A. R. Allenson, Inc., 1965).

Hare, D. R. *The Theme of the Jewish Persecution of Christians in the Gospel According to St. Matthew.* (Cambridge: University Press, 1960).

Harkman, L. *Prophecy Interpreted.* (Lund, Sweden: CWK Gleerup, 1966).

Higgins, A. J. B. *Jesus and the Son of Man.* (Philadelphia: Fortress Press, 1964).

Hillers, D. *Covenant: the History of a Biblical Idea.*

Iglesia, S. Munos. "Literary Genre of the Infancy Gospel in St. Matthew," *Theology Digest,* IX (Winter, 1961), 15-20.

Ingelaeres, Jean-Claude, "La 'parabole' du Judgement Dernier (Matthieu 25:31-46)", *Revue d'Histoire et de Philosophique Religieuses,* 50 (1970), 23-60.

Jeremias, J. *Jerusalem in the Time of Jesus.* (Philadelphia: Fortress Press, 1969).

———. *Jesus' Promise to the Nations.* (Naperville, Ill.: A. R. Allenson, 1958).

———. *New Testament Theology.* (New York: Scribner, 1971).

———. *The Central Message of the New Testament.* (New York: Scribner, 1965).

———. *The Parables of Jesus.* (New York: Scribner, 1963).

———. *The Prayers of Jesus.* (Naperville, Ill.: A. R. Allenson Inc., 1967).

———. *The Problem of the Historical Jesus.* (Philadelphia: Fortress Press, 1964).

———. *The Sermon on the Mount.* (Philadelphia: Fortress Press, 1963).

Jerome Biblical Commentary. eds. J. Fitzmyer, R. Brown, R. Murphy. (Englewood Cliffs: Prentice Hall, 1968).

Keck, L. E., "The Sermon on the Mount", *Jesus and Man's Hope.* (Pittsburgh Theological Seminary, 1971), Vol. II, 311-322.

Kee, H. C. *Jesus in History.* (New York: Harcourt, Brace & World, 1970).

Kilpatrick, G. D. *The Origins of the Gospel According to St. Matthew.* (London: Oxford University Press, 1950).

Kingsbury, J. D. *The Parables of Jesus in Matthew 13.* (Richmond: John Knox Press, 1971).

Küng, H. *The Church.* (New York: Sheed and Ward, 1967).

———. *Infallible? An Inquiry.* (Garden City, N.Y.: Doubleday, 1971).

Lambrecht, L., "The Parousia Discourse: Composition and Content in Mt. XXIV–XXV", *L'Evangile selon Matthieu: redaction et theologie,* ed. M. Didier; Gembloux; Duclot (1972), 309-342.

Lindars, B. *New Testament Apologetic.* (Philadelphia: Westminster Press, 1961).

Lohr, C. H. "Oral Techniques In the Gospel of Matthew," *Catholic Biblical Quarterly,* XXIII (October, 1961), 404ff.

Lund, W. W. *Chiasmus in the New Testament: A Study in Formgeschichte.*

Maddox, R. "Who Are the 'Sheep' and the 'Goats'?," *ABR,* (1965), 18-28.

Malina, B. J. "The Literary Structure and Form of Mt XXVIII 16-20" *NTS,* (1970), 87-103.

Maly, E. H. *The Priest and Sacred Scripture.* (Washington: Publications Office, U.S. Catholic Conference, 1972).

Manson, T. W. *Studies in the Gospels and Epistles.* ed. Matthew Black. (Manchester: University Press, 1962).

———. *The Sayings of Jesus.* (London: SCM Press, 1964).

Marksen, W. *Mark The Evangelist.* (New York: Abingdon, 1969).

Marshall, I. H. "The Synoptic Son of Man Sayings in Recent Study," *New Testament Studies,* 12, (1965–66), 327-351.

Martin, R. P. "St. Matthew's Gospel in Recent Study," *Expository Times,* 80 (May, 1969), 132-136.

Martyn, J. L. *History and Theology in the Fourth Gospel.* (New York: Harper & Row, 1968).

McArthur, H. K. "From the Historical Jesus to Christology," *Interpretation,* 23, (1969), 190-206.

————. *In Search of the Historical Jesus.* (New York: Charles Scribner's Sons, 1969).

McBrien, R. *Do We Need the Church?* (New York: Harper & Row, 1969).

McConnell, R. S. *Law and Prophecy in Matthew's Gospel. The Authority and Use of the Old Testament in the Gospel of Matthew.* (Basel: F. Reinhardt, 1969).

McEleney, N. J. "Authenticating Criteria and Mk 7:1-23," *CBQ,* 34 (October, 1972), 431-460.

McIntyre, J. *The Shape of Christology.* (Philadelphia: Westminster Press, 1966).

McKenzie, J. L. *Authority in the Church.* (New York: Sheed and Ward, 1966).

————. *Dictionary of the Bible.* (Milwaukee: Bruce, 1965).

McKnight, E. V. *What Is Form Criticism?* (Philadelphia: Fortress Press, 1969).

Metz, J. *Theology of the World.* (New York: Herder & Herder, 1969).

Meye, R. P. *Jesus and the Twelve.* (Grand Rapids Michigan: Eerdmans, 1968).

Michaels, J. Ramsey, "Apostolic Hardships and Righteous Gentiles. A Study of Matthew 25:31-48", *JBL,* 84 (Mar. 1965), 27-37.

Minear, P. *Commands of Christ.* (Nashville: Abingdon, 1972).

Montefiore, C. G. *The Synoptic Gospels.* (New York: Ktav Publishing House, 1927, rev. ed. 1968).

Mowinckel, S. *He That Cometh.* (Oxford: Blackwell, 1959).

Neusner, J., *The Rabbinic Traditions about the Pharisees before 70 A.D.* (Leiden: Brill, 1971).

Nicholson, E. W. *Deuteronomy and Tradition.* (Oxford: Blackwell, 1967).

Nineham, D. E. *Saint Mark.* Pelican Gospel Commentaries. (Baltimore: Penguin Books, 1964).

Nineham, D. E. (ed.). *Studies in the Gospels.* (Oxford: B. Blackwell, 1955).

O'Conner, D. W. *Peter in Rome.* (New York: Columbia University, 1969).

Outga, G., Agape: *An Ethical Analysis.* (New Haven: Yale University Press, 1972).

Pannenburg, W. *Jesus God and Man.* (Philadelphia: Westminster Press, 1968).

————. *Theology and the Kingdom of God.* Philadelphia: Westminster Press, 1969).

Perrin, N. *The Kingdom of God in the Teaching of Jesus.* 1967.

————. *Rediscovering the Teaching of Jesus.* (New York: Harper & Row, 1967).

————. *What Is Redaction Criticism?* (Philadelphia: Fortress Press, 1969).

————. "The Evangelist as Author: Reflections on Method in the Study and Interpretation of the Synoptic Gospels and Acts", *BR,* 17 (1972), 5-18.

Quesnell, Q. *The Mind of Mark.* (Rome: Pontifical Biblical Institute, 1969).

Radermakers, J., *Au fil de l'evangile selon Saint Matthieu,* 2 vols., (Heverlee: Institut d'Etudes Theologiques), 1972.

Rahner, K. *The Episcopate and the Primacy.* (New York: Herder & Herder, 1962).

Richards, H., *The First Christmas: What Really Happened?* (London: Fortana, 1974).

Riesenfeld, H. *The Gospel Tradition and Its Beginnings.* (Philadelphia: Fortress Press, 1970).

Robinson, J. M. *A New Quest of the Historical Jesus.* (London: SCM, 1959).

————. *The Problem of History in Mark.* (London: SCM, 1957).

————. "The Recent Debate on the New Quest," *JBR,* 30 (1962), 198-208.

Robinson, J. M. and Koester, H. *Trajectories Through Early Christianity.*

Robinson, J. A. T. "The Parable of the Sheep and the Goats," *NTS,* II, (1955-56), 231-239.

Rohde, J. *Rediscovering the Teaching of the Evangelists.* (Philadelphia: Westminster Press, 1968).

Schnackenburg, R. "The Petrine Office: Peter's Relationship to the Other Apostles," *TD,* 20 (Summer, 1972), 148-152.

Schweizer, E. "Law Observance and Charisma in Matthew," *New Testament Studies,* 16 (1970), 213-230.

————. *Jesus.* (Richmond: Knox, 1971).

Sloyan, G. S., *Jesus on Trial.* (Fortress, 1973).

Smith, M., "Mixed State of Church in Matthew", *JBL,* 82 (June 1963), 149-168.

Stendahl, K. *The School of St. Matthew,* 2nd ed. (Philadelphia: Fortress Press, 1968).

Steward, P. C. "The Authorship of the Gospel According to Matthew: A Reconsideration of the External Evidence," *New Testament Studies*, 14 (1967–68), 15-33.

Strack, H. L. *Introduction to the Talmud and Midrash*. (New York: Scribner, 1963).

Suggs, M. Jack. *Wisdom, Christology, and Law in Matthew's Gospel.*

——. "The Passion and Resurrection Narratives", *Jesus and Man's Hope*, Vol. II Pittsburgh Theological Seminary, (1971), 323–338.

Taylor, V. *The Gospel According to St. Mark*. (London: MacMillan, 1959).

——. "The Life and Ministry of Jesus," *Interpreter's Bible*, Vol. VII.

Teeple, H. "The Origin of the Son of Man Christology," *JBL*, 84 (1965), 213-260.

——. *The Mosaic Eschatological Prophet*. (Pennsylvania: Society of Biblical Literature, 1957).

Tierney, B. *Origins of Papal Infallibility 1150–1350*. (Leiden: Brill, 1972).

Trilling, D. W. *The Gospel According to St. Matthew*. In Series, "The New Testament for Spiritual Reading," ed. J. L. McKenzie, (London: Burns & Oates, 1969).

Vanhoye, A. *Structure and Theology of the Accounts of the Passion in the Synoptic Gospels*. (Collegeville, Minn. The Liturgical Press, 1967).

Van Tilborg, S. *The Jewish Leaders in Matthew*. (Leiden: Brill, 1972).

Wright, A. G. *Midrash*. (New York: Alba House, 1967).

Wuellner, W. H. *The Meaning of "Fishers of Men"*. The New Test. Lib. (Philadelphia: Westminster Press, 1967).

OLD TESTAMENT READING GUIDE

A series of 30 booklets covering the whole Old Testament. Each booklet contains the text of the book treated; an introduction discussing author, time and place of composition, purpose, content, etc., of book under consideration; a full commentary on the text verse by verse; review aids and discussion topics. Quantity discounts. Single copy, $.45

Set of 30 booklets: $12.00

THE LITURGICAL PRESS   **Collegeville, Minn. 56321**

NEW TESTAMENT READING GUIDE

A series of 14 booklets covering the whole New Testament. Each booklet contains the complete text of the book treated; an introduction discussing author, time and place of composition, purpose, content, etc., of book under consideration; a full commentary on the text verse by verse; review aids and discussion topics. Quantity discounts.   Single copy, $.45

GENERAL INTRODUCTION TO SACRED SCRIPTURE
Reverend William G. Heidt, O.S.B., M.A., S.T.D.

1   INTRODUCTION TO THE NEW TESTAMENT
Reverend Roderick A. F. MacKenzie, S.J., M.A., S.S.L.

2   GOSPEL OF SAINT MARK
Reverend Gerard S. Sloyan, S.T.L., Ph.D.

3   GOSPEL OF SAINT LUKE
Reverend Carroll Stuhlmueller, C.P., S.T.L., S.S.L.

4   GOSPEL OF SAINT MATTHEW
Reverend David Michael Stanley, S.J., S.S.D.

5   ACTS OF THE APOSTLES
Reverend Neal M. Flanagan, O.S.M., S.T.D., S.S.L.

6   INTRODUCTION TO THE PAULINE EPISTLES, 1—2 THESS.
Reverend Bruce Vawter, C.M., S.T.L., S.S.D.

7   EPISTLES TO THE GALATIANS, ROMANS
Reverend Barnabas M. Ahern, C.P., S.T.L., S.S.D.

8   FIRST AND SECOND CORINTHIANS
Reverend Claude J. Peifer, O.S.B., S.T.L., S.S.L.

9   PHILIPPIANS, EPHESIANS, COLOSSIANS, PHILEMON
Mother Kathryn Sullivan, R.S.C.J., Ph.D.

10 SAINT PAUL'S PASTORAL EPISTLES
Reverend Robert T. Siebeneck, C.PP.S., S.T.L., S.S.L.

11 EPISTLE TO THE HEBREWS
Reverend John F. McConnell, M.M., S.T.L., S.S.L.

12 EPISTLES OF SAINT JAMES, JUDE, PETER
Reverend Eugene H. Maly, S.T.D., S.S.D.

13 GOSPEL OF SAINT JOHN AND THE JOHANNINE EPISTLES
Reverend Raymond E. Brown, S.S., S.T.D., Ph.D., S.S.D.

14 THE BOOK OF THE APOCALYPSE
Reverend William G Heidt, O.S.B., M.A., S.T.D.

Set of 15 booklets: $6.00

THE LITURGICAL PRESS   Collegeville, Minn. 56321